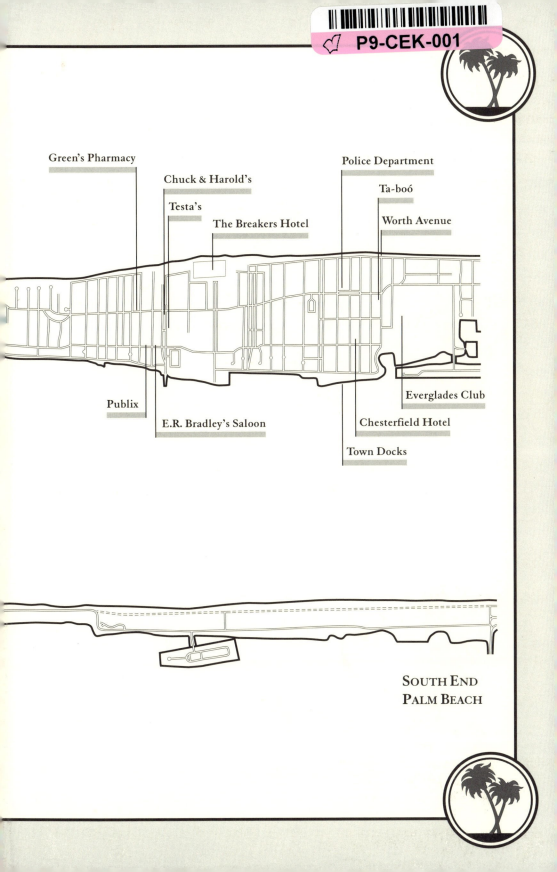

Green's Pharmacy

Chuck & Harold's

Testa's

The Breakers Hotel

Police Department

Ta-boó

Worth Avenue

Publix

E.R. Bradley's Saloon

Everglades Club

Chesterfield Hotel

Town Docks

SOUTH END
PALM BEACH

The Season

The Season

INSIDE PALM BEACH
and
AMERICA'S RICHEST SOCIETY

Ronald Kessler

HarperCollins*Publishers*

HarperCollins books may be purchased for educational, business, or sales promotional use. For information please write: Special Markets Department, HarperCollins Publishers Inc., 10 East 53rd Street, New York, NY 10022.

FIRST EDITION

Designed by William Ruoto

Library of Congress Cataloging-in-Publication Data

Kessler, Ronald, 1943–
    The season : inside Palm Beach and America's
richest society / Ronald Kessler. — 1st ed.
       p.   cm.
      ISBN 0-06-019391-3
      1. Palm Beach (Fla.)—Social life and customs.
2. Palm Beach (Fla.)—Biography. 3. Rich people—Florida
—Palm Beach—Social life and customs. 4. Rich people
—Florida—Palm Beach—Biography. I. Title
F319.P2K47 1999
975.9'32—dc21   99-16918

99 00 01 02 03 ❖/RRD 10 9 8 7 6 5 4 3 2 1

FOR PAM, GREG, AND RACHEL KESSLER

CONTENTS

PROLOGUE

During World War II, Frank Lahainer, an Italian count and real-estate tycoon from Trieste, saved the lives of sixty Jews by hiding them from the Nazis in apartments he rented. In 1957 Lahainer married his voluptuous, redheaded seventeen-year-old secretary, Gianna. In 1980 they moved to New York, where they bought an entire floor of the Trump Tower. They held on to their twenty-room estate in Trieste, complete with discotheque and swimming pool, and their one-hundred-foot yacht, along with the Italian chef.

Gianna (pronounced "JAN-na") loved fine things, and Frank indulged her every whim. He bought her a twenty-five-carat engagement ring from Harry Winston, a white Rolls-Royce Corniche, a thirty-two-carat sapphire, and a twenty-six-carat emerald.

In 1982 they bought a three-thousand-square-foot apartment in the opulent Biltmore in Palm Beach. The apartment overlooks both the Atlantic Ocean and the inland waterway surrounding the 3.75-square-mile island—a sliver of land known throughout the world as the most wealthy, glamorous, opulent, decadent, extravagant, self-indulgent, sinful spot on earth.

Frank and Gianna traveled around the world five times, buying for their homes museum-quality eighteenth-century furniture with price tags of as much as $300,000. For their New York apartment, they bought a $1 million Picasso.

In time, Frank contracted leukemia, and he died in Palm Beach on March 9, 1995, at the age of ninety. His fortune was estimated at $300 million. Frank left everything to Gianna, who was then fifty-seven.

It was poor timing. Frank died in the middle of the social season. Gianna decided to postpone the funeral so she wouldn't miss any of the glittering parties, balls, and receptions that give Palm Beach residents their reason to exist. Instead of having him buried, she had her husband embalmed and stored at the Quattlebaum-Holleman Burse Funeral Home for forty days, until the season was over.

Part of the delay was necessary because Gianna wanted to bury her husband in Trieste, just east of Venice across the Gulf of Venice, and the paperwork would take up to two weeks. During that time, she had some dental work finished and attended to her income tax return. The rest of the delay was so that she could enjoy the season. After all, Gianna explained, she had already bought tickets for the top social events.

"I wanted to go to the parties," Gianna said. "He was ninety. I am sixty. So why should I wait? I did everything for my husband. I did his injections. I was faithful." She said, "I went to a party at the Breakers, I went to a party on a yacht with Ivana Trump, I went to a party at Mar-a-Lago," Donald Trump's 140-room club in Palm Beach, built by cereal heir Marjorie Merriweather Post and her second husband, E. F. Hutton. In fact, three days after Frank's death, Gianna threw a party at the Biltmore, complete with beluga caviar and Dom Pérignon champagne.

"My new life was going on," she said. "Why should I wait? I would miss the season."

SUMMER / FALL

prelude

1. PRETENDERS

In early June, just as Barton Gubelmann, the grand first lady of Palm Beach's Old Guard, was explaining how Palm Beach society works, the phone rang.

"Oh, shit. Let the maid take it," the eighty-year-old scion said in a gravelly voice. Behind her, beyond the lily ponds and the burgeoning sea-grape trees, the Atlantic glistened.

An invitation to one of Gubelmann's gala dinner parties is coveted more than acceptance by the Everglades Club or the Bath & Tennis Club, the two WASP clubs that dominate Palm Beach social life and conversation. For her last party of the season, on May 9, Gubelmann dressed as a milkmaid. The invitation billed the party "Operation Deep Freeze" and explained: "Barton Is Cleaning Out the Freezer and Wants the Cupboard Bare." Dress called for "Flip Flops and Aprons."

The seventy-eight guests, who dined on pheasant pie, ham, and cold beef tenderloin, included Palm Beach mayor Paul R. Ilyinsky and his wife, Angelica; Lesly Smith, the town council president whose late husband, Earl, was ambassador to Cuba; Durie Appleton, a girlfriend of John F. Kennedy who was erroneously said to have been married to him; Prince Michel de

Yougoslavie, ousted Yugoslav royalty; Chris Kellogg, an heir to the Wanamaker department-store fortune; Angela Koch (pronounced 'coke'), wife of near-billionaire William Koch; Princess Maria Pia of Italy; Jane Smith, from Standard Oil Company of New Jersey money; and Cynthia Rupp, an heir to the Chrysler fortune.

Unlike many other Palm Beach socialites, Gubelmann has no publicity agent and no bio to hand out. Why should she? She *is* Palm Beach society. After social queens Mary Sanford and Sue Whitmore both died in 1993 (Whitmore having succeeded Sanford as queen), the *Palm Beach Daily News* handicapped Gubelmann eight to one to rule over Palm Beach society. She said she didn't want the job.

Self-deprecating, irreverent, and publicity-shy, Gubelmann is a contrast to Palm Beach's plastic strivers. She is the widow of Walter Gubelmann, an America's Cup financier whose father, William, invented handy gadgets like the bicycle coaster brake and the basic mechanisms used in adding machines, typewriters, and early calculators. If she wasn't already rich, Gubelmann would make a good CEO. Shrewd and smart, she exercises her authority deftly and like a good boss rarely reveals her true powers.

Like other Palm Beach socialites, she shuttles back and forth among her homes. During the season, she lives in Palm Beach, where she has what she calls her "very small house" on South Ocean Boulevard, just two houses north of the home John Lennon and Yoko Ono owned. Assessed at $2.9 million, Barton's house is a gray-shingled contemporary with a pagodalike roof. At the entrance is a lily pond with a fountain, and in back is the requisite pool, rarely used. Inside, on an upholstered chair, sits a green pillow embroidered with the words IT AIN'T EASY BEING QUEEN. Outside, the vanity plate on her Mercedes reads GLAMMA.

Now, in off-season, Gubelmann was preparing to make her annual pilgrimage to her palatial home in Newport, Rhode Island. Gubelmann would fly there with one of her maids, her dog, and her cat, having bought tickets for each of the animals. Her assistant, Arthur "Skip" Kelter, a graying man with a perpetually bemused expression, would drive up in her Mercedes. A Chevy van with another driver would haul a twelve-foot trailer containing her clothes and Skip's computer.

J. Paul Getty said, "If you can actually count your money, then you are not really a rich man." Asked how much she is worth, Gubelmann responded in kind: "I don't know," she said. "I don't sit home and count it. I have no idea. Someone must have it on some piece of paper. We have lawyers and accountants and bookkeepers." But Gubelmann is said to be worth close to $100 million. When asked about that, she said, "Is that what it is? I'm glad to know it. I'll spend some money today."

Palm Beachers hold Gubelmann in awe, and many doubted she would ever meet with me, much less be candid. I first came to Palm Beach four years earlier to conduct research on Joseph P. Kennedy for my book *The Sins of the Father*. Residents like Dennis E. Spear, the caretaker of the Kennedy estate, and Cynthia Stone Ray, one of Rose Kennedy's former secretaries, filled me in—not only on the Kennedys, but on the secrets, lore, and rituals of Palm Beach. Spear took me to Au Bar, where Senator Edward M. Kennedy had been on the night that his nephew William Kennedy Smith picked up the woman who would later accuse him of raping her—a charge that a jury found to be without basis. Cynthia gave me a tour of Palm Beach's mansions.

I was drawn to this bizarre town. Like most people, I hadn't realized that Palm Beach is located on a fifteen-mile-long subtropical barrier island, of which twelve miles is Palm Beach. On the rest, the southern tip, are the towns of Manalapan and South Palm Beach. The island's width varies at different points from five hundred feet to three quarters of a mile. Lake Worth, a coastal lagoon that is part of the Intracoastal Waterway, separates the island from the mainland about a half mile away. In 1870 settlers cut a ditch between the northern end of Lake Worth and the Atlantic. The inlet was later enlarged, and another was cut at the southern tip of the barrier strip, turning it into an island.

With only 9,800 residents, Palm Beach is inherently a very small town—only a few times larger than Gilmanton Iron Works, the New Hampshire village where Grace Metalious's *Peyton Place* was set. Here, on $5 billion worth of real estate, live some of the richest people in the world. For many tycoons, Palm Beach is a reward, a realization of life's pleasures in a self-contained paradise. For the heirs of old wealth, Palm Beach offers a synthetic society that reveres lineage and breeding rather than accomplishment. The celebrities who gravitate to Palm Beach ratify the residents' sense of their own importance.

It was Edmund Burke who said, "It is, generally, in the season of prosperity that men discover their real temper, principles, and designs." When an unimaginable concentration of wealth combines with unlimited leisure time on an island not quite three times the size of New York's Central Park, human foibles and desires, lust and greed, passion and avarice become magnified, intensified. Like laboratory rats fed growth hormones, every resident becomes an oversized actor in an exaggerated drama.

With vigilant police, ubiquitous personal security staffs, and screens of tall ficus encircling every mansion, Palm Beachers protect their impossibly rich society from outside scrutiny. Behind the hedges, the games that Palm Beachers play—their affairs, scams, murders, snubs, intrigues, jealousies, pretenses, bigotry, and occasional generosity—make *Dynasty* and *Dallas* look like nursery tales. From the steamy divorce of Roxanne Pulitzer to the rape trial of William Kennedy Smith, the beautiful island is celebrated for its scandals. Glitzy as it is, Palm Beach is a town lost in time.

The climax of the rituals that draw characters like Barton Gubelmann to Palm Beach is the season, a frenetic rush of glittering social events. Everyone has his own definition of the season, but most say it begins after Thanksgiving and extends until the end of April. High season—when the most prestigious social events take place—runs from January through March. During these balmy months, when most of the country is suffering through the winter, the black-tie society balls that are Palm

Beachers' raison d'être take place. Tourists descend on the island, and the population swells to more than 25,000. The season is the lens through which everything else is viewed, the standard that measures the rest of the year and, by extension, life itself.

After my research for the Kennedy book, I returned to Palm Beach for a vacation with my wife, Pamela Kessler. Nearly every year after that, we have come back. During the most recent visit, we went to Testa's, one of Palm Beach's best restaurants. Having consumed a bottle of Chardonnay during dinner, we walked around the block. I said to Pam, "Wouldn't it be great to do a book on Palm Beach?"

"That's the only book I would collaborate with you on," she said.

As a former *Washington Post* reporter and author of *Undercover Washington*, about the spy sites of the capital, Pam brought a professional perspective. Suddenly, the subject of idle chitchat became a serious concept.

Having penetrated the CIA, the FBI, and White House detail of the Secret Service for some of my previous books, I didn't think unraveling the story of Palm Beach would be too difficult. I wasn't prepared for some of the unique impediments I would later encounter.

In contrast, Barton Gubelmann turned out to be more than forthcoming. Before we sat down in her living room, she looked me in the eye and asked, "So what is this all about?" I returned her gaze and said I was interested in the wild stories, the colorful tales, the bizarre characters, and how things work.

In a town of pretense, directness is prized. It establishes trust and encourages candor. She responded in kind. When I asked about Palm Beach parties with nude men or women as centerpieces, Gubelmann allowed as how she hadn't been to one but said, "You got an address?" When asked about gigolos, she said, "How do you define *gigolo*? I mean, I think every single man around here is a gigolo." When asked what members of society do, Gubelmann replied, "Most of the people that are my age don't do a damn thing but play cards, go to art classes, have dinner parties." As for hidden honeys, she had this to say: "Mistresses have their own houses, or they're at the Breakers Hotel or have a chic apartment." In any case, they're of no interest to her. "Either the men are sleeping with somebody else's wife or they aren't," she said. Gubelmann previously lived next to the Kennedy estate. "Jack was my next-door neighbor," she said. "I was having a baby, and he was having back trouble, so we did not have a romance, okay?"*

Her shih tzu, Gertie, sauntered past, then came back and turned belly-up to be petted by Pam, who was with me. "You can take him," Gubelmann said, her enormous blue eyes never blinking.

Gubelmann belongs to both the Everglades Club, which has an eighteen-hole par 71 golf course, and the Bath & Tennis Club, which is on the beach and has a freshwater and a saltwater pool. "They were looking for members," she said. "They were desperate." Until a year ago, neither club allowed members to bring Jews even as guests, according to Gubelmann. Now, she said, Jews are allowed in as guests but not as members.

"The one club nobody can get into is the Palm Beach Country Club," she said, referring to the Jewish club. "I don't think they have a dozen Christian members. The only person I haven't seen [at the clubs] is a black person."

The way to be accepted socially is to organize fund-raisers, Barton explained. "There are two or three new charities each year. New diseases. We have ball tickets and parties to raise money. That seems to be the stepping stone into what they call Palm Beach society. You get tired of running balls. I'm afraid I have run some. The Heart, Hospital, Four Arts balls. I ran one for that unfortunate social disease. What's it called? AIDS. A good way to start is to give a lot of money to the Preservation Society of Palm Beach. This is the way these girls work it, you see. I know how they do it. I put them on the board."

The younger women are on the prowl, maneuvering to be accepted by the older ones. Someone is "always on the make. There are pretenders to the throne," Gubelmann remarked. One

---

*Occasionally, quotes from one event or interview have been shifted to another.

example is Celia Lipton Farris, who is worth several hundred million and has chaired key Palm Beach charity events. "Celia Farris is not Old Guard," said Gubelmann. "She is an amusing lady. But Celia Farris has never had what I would call social standing. But who am I to say?"

Going to the study of her cypress-ceilinged mansion, Gubelmann brought out a black book called *The Social Index-Directory* and handed it to me. Under each family listing are addresses for as many as five additional homes, in places like Monte Carlo, Paris, London, New York, and Newport, along with the names of their planes and yachts.

"What does it mean to be in the social index?" Gubelmann said. "Not a goddamn thing. It's just a phone book."

Having learned from other sources that the directory, known as "the black book," is now owned by the family of Robert Gordon, who is Jewish, I asked Gubelmann if she knew who owns the publication.

"I'll be damned if I do know who owns it now," she said. "Would you like to meet him? I don't think that would be any trouble at all. I can pick up the phone and call him."

"Skip," she called to her assistant. "Let's see who runs this thing."

A few minutes later Skip reported back.

"Robert Gordon owns the index," he said.

"Oh, my friend Arlette's husband?" Gubelmann said. "Well, bless his little cotton heart. I'll be damned. That's why it's gotten bigger." She was referring to the fact that dozens of Jews have been added. Gordon, who has an advisory board that helps make selections, was already in the black book with gold lettering. But now the Old Guard refers to it as "the Sears catalogue."

Gubelmann gave me a twelve-by-sixteen-inch card listing some three hundred names. The Fanjuls, a prominent Palm Beach family of sugar growers, send the card out each year as a Christmas greeting. "The hell with the index," Gubelmann said. "This is what everyone wants to make. This is the enviable list. The new people want to be on that card. It's perfectly ridiculous, you know."

2. THE GOOD HUSTLER

A few days after my meeting with Barton Gubelmann, on a bank of Lake Worth, an egret poised languidly on one leg, watching a school of fish coast by. It was too hot to fly, and it was too hot to fish. And for people in Palm Beach, it was too hot to swim—and anyway, the sand fleas were biting. Some days in June it's even too hot to go outside—a sweltering, tropical miasma, without a breeze. But June is peak blooming time for Florida's indigenous plants. The stunning poinciana tree, aflame with scarlet flower clusters, is a sight the seasonal visitor never sees. Instead, the plants that bloom in winter in Palm Beach are exotics—such as oleander, imported from the Mediterranean.

In his home on the water four miles north of Gubelmann's, Kirby Kooluris poured me a praiseworthy Chardonnay as he described his life as a "walker." Unlike a gigolo—a young man who has sex with older, wealthy women—walkers are often homosexual. In return for free meals and entertainment, they escort wealthy women to society balls and other events. Often the men have adopted phony titles. Sometimes they're paid.

Kooluris knows fine wines and enough French to impress. He

has expressive brown eyes and silver hair. He is enveloping, engaging, and deferential, smiling into his listener's eyes.

Many people "think that what I'm doing is glamorous," Kooluris told me. Every night something goes on. He ticked off some of the events he has attended—a ball at Mar-a-Lago, dinner under the stars at the Everglades Club, a reception at Ivana Trump's, a dinner party at the home of Douglas Fairbanks, Jr. "I went to a birthday party at the home of Betty Swope," a grande dame of Palm Beach society. "The crunchy driveway, the wonderful old home. A wonderful dinner followed by a musicale. We have dukes, earls. It's American royalty."

Kooluris lives in two different worlds. In the rich set of Palm Beach society, he knows practically everyone, along with their pertinent lineage, source of wealth, previous spouses, and lovers.

"Everyone here has a game," said Kooluris. "Many women play the game of being society hostess. There is a game to look like you're interested in golf or croquet or horses. Some people want you to believe their stories. It's part of the camouflage, of not having anything in your life that's disturbing." In Palm Beach "there are the charity-ball people and then many club people who are so arrogant and snobbish they wouldn't give a nickel to a guy on the street," Kirby said. "They haven't made the fortunes themselves. They sit in clubs all day and tell themselves how marvelous they are. Privately, they'll agree that they aren't."

If a wealthy woman buys him a ticket to a charity ball, it's "what justifies the games that people play to be seen," he said. It's a victimless crime. "They lead a very indulgent lifestyle when most of the world is in big trouble." Meanwhile, Kooluris gets to go to all the right parties and meet the right people. Palm Beach is his stage.

Being gay, Kooluris has another set of friends. Lately, the fifty-four-year-old Kooluris has been trying to get help for Bill, a thirty-five-year-old lover who is a former private pilot. At 2:00 A.M., police arrested Bill riding a bicycle on the Lake Trail, which winds for five miles along the western edge of Palm Beach. The police said Bill was drunk and resisted arrest. Moreover, the bike had been stolen. But Kooluris told the judge at the arraignment that he had purchased the bike at a church sale. He couldn't understand why his word was not enough to get the charges dropped.

"He did resist arrest, but I said to the judge, 'Wouldn't you be angry if someone accused you of stealing something?'" Kirby said.

A graduate of the University of Virginia, Kooluris married a woman worth $60 million. They lived in a Palm Beach home designed by Belford Shoumate. Under the divorce settlement, the home—on the north end of the island—is his. The white poured-cement house is Art Deco with nautical allusions. From the outside, it looks just like a beached boat, all its edges rounded off for smooth sailing. From inside, the unrivaled centerpiece of the house is the large porthole over a sofa in the great room. The circular window frames a magnificent magenta bougainvillea sprawling over a fence, like a living painting by Gauguin.

Designated a historic landmark by the town, Kirby's house won the House of the Future Award at the 1939 New York World's Fair. It was home to pianist and Polish prime minister Ignace Paderewski when he was exiled by the Nazis. With round windows, gleaming ribbons of woodwork, private terraces, and caramel-colored burl-wood parquet floors overlooking a pool and Lake Worth, it's now worth $3 million.

Howard Simons, the late managing editor of the *Washington Post*, used to compare my reporting to peeling an onion, ring by ring. One thing led to another, and eventually I penetrated the center. Finding Kirby wasn't quite that difficult. Cynthia Stone Ray, Rose Kennedy's former secretary, introduced me to David Miller, an art appraiser who is a friend of Kirby. Miller, in turn, introduced me to Kirby. James Hunt Barker, another escort whom I called out of the blue, introduced me to Barton.

At first, Kirby was hesitant. He spoke vaguely of being a walker. When I asked if he is gay, he said, "I've been around, put it that way." Eventually, he came to enjoy our meetings and opened up. I would learn about the events in his life as they were happening.

As he poured more Chardonnay into my glass, Kooluris explained that the wine was a gift from the former personal secretary to Princess Grace, who is married to the manager of the Flagler Club, which charges guests an extra $100 a night for special coddling on the top two floors of the Breakers Hotel at 1 South County Road.

Kooluris said the wine came from Russia. But examination of the bottle revealed it was a 1996 Sonoma-Cutrer Estate Bottled Russian River Ranches Chardonnay from Windsor, California. Kooluris later explained: "You might call it fictionalizing to make life more exciting. It's like glamorizing a story, like telling a story to a child."

Everyone in Palm Beach does it. The ocean lapping at the beach washes away all traces. In the same way, facts are fungible, stories embellished, everything sugarcoated. The seriously rich live for the moment—for the next wave. Beyond the grand social events that are planned a year in advance, Palm Beachers hate to be tied down. "Call me when you get in" or "call me the night before" they say, always leaving an opening in their schedules for a better invitation. Even mailing a letter requires too much commitment. They would rather drop off material when driving by a home or hotel than make a statement by addressing an envelope. When everything on the island is five or ten minutes away, that makes a certain amount of sense. But there's also an element of snobbery: If the recipient doesn't live in Palm Beach, he's not worth the effort required to mail a letter.

Kooluris's challenge has been to live the Palm Beach life without working. Even if it has a "negative" sound, being a walker has allowed him to do just that. "Some people think a walker means you need a meal, or are a fag or an opportunist," Kirby said. "That could be true for most. But I do this because I am invited, and I like the people I go out with. They're not saying, 'Here's two hundred fifty dollars to come with me for the evening.'

They're inviting me for the evening. If it's five hundred dollars to go to this ball, that's what it is, and I don't hear about it. My responsibility is to be there and make sure they have a lively time, as I would with any friend."

There are good hustlers and bad hustlers, he told me. "The bad hustler says, 'What I can get from this?' The good hustler says, 'What can I give these people so they'll want me around for the rest of their lives?' I consider myself a very lazy man. I haven't cooked a dinner for a dinner party for ten years. But I'm invited to many of them." Still, he said, "people don't think I'm a taker. If they have troubles, I'm happy to hear their story. If they want to go to Savannah to visit their family, I'm game. If I were making three hundred dollars like a lot of these guys who charge, I would be a different person. I wouldn't be able to move in the echelons I do."

If Kirby escorts a married woman, he makes sure he is friends with her husband. He's not about to make enemies with powerful people who are worth hundreds of millions. "If I'm going to get laid, it's going to be with people whom I've known for many years," he said.

"I have a sensitivity to making other people feel good about themselves. I love that. As a favor, I'm not opposed to pressure-cleaning the roof or washing the car. I can change into black tie the next hour. I try to make it interesting for the person who has invited me and to connect others to that person," he said. "I've been trying to figure this out, because I've been doing this forever. I don't know what it is. It's more than being a walker. It's less than being a walker. Maybe it's being an ambassador for happiness. It might be a little of something I saw in a 1968 movie called *Boom!* with Elizabeth Taylor and Richard Burton. It's about a rich, ill-tempered woman who's dying on an island. Burton brings a little pleasure to her at the end of her life."

After an evening out, Kooluris always phones his hostess the next day to thank her. But for all his polish, he occasionally makes a gaffe. At a black-tie bash at the Henry Morrison Flagler Museum, a wealthy single woman toppled into a fountain, and her teased hair became wet.

"God, you look prettier this way," Kooluris said.

The woman burst into tears and has not spoken to him since.

"She had Texas teased hair," Kooluris said with a shrug. "All of a sudden you saw a pretty face beneath all that cotton."

James Hunt Barker, the former owner of an art gallery, used to squire Marylou Whitney, the widow of Cornelius Vanderbilt Whitney, to clubs and balls. Whitney, around seventy-five, just married John Hendrickson, thirty-two. The owner of thirteen King Charles spaniels, Barker is a good dancer and conversationalist, but he told me he can't afford to join a club. Besides, he doesn't need to.

"When each club has four hundred widows, how do you get those girls to go to dinner at the clubs?" Barker said. "They won't go unless they have a guest, and they prefer a male. I can't pay a lump sum just to join a club. If women get to town without a husband, they can't get in a club unless they are very powerful financially. The clubs will let in men anytime, as long as they can pay that bill and are polite."

This is the way of Palm Beach, where going to parties substitutes for going to work. Walkers are "at every party," Barton had told me earlier. "We need extra men. They are attractive men, they play cards, they dance well, they are entertaining. Some are straight and some aren't. I couldn't care less. There are a lot of gay men in town. They take the ladies out, they're charming. I have two or three that I go out with."

By definition, sex doesn't enter into the deal. In contrast to walkers, gigolos—who also operate in Palm Beach—are not polished enough to accompany women to social events. They service wealthy women sexually and are paid either in cash or through bank accounts set up for them. Kooluris has all the social graces and would never accept money.

"The people I know are not interested in sex," Kooluris said. "They have wonderful memories of their husbands. They are very respectful. 'Would you care to go to this lovely cocktail party?' They're not saying, 'Be here.' It would be different if you are paid."

In any case, Kooluris's orientation, which he still has not con-fided to his family, is gay. "I'm sure my family suspects," he said. "But they're still trying to marry me off. So if I have someone like Bill in my life, it's on the QT. I can move from one world to the next like a chameleon. Maybe that's why he was aggressive [with the police], because he was treated as a back-door person. He could have felt hurt."

At Kirby's house, the phone rings every ten minutes. One call was from Ben Johnson, a handsome former model who married Johanna "Ancky" Revson, a model who had been married to Charles Revson of Revlon fame. Johnson met Ancky at Palm Beach's Colony Hotel. He had twenty dollars in his pocket. She was fifty; he was twenty-nine. Soon they were married.

"To marry rich, you dine where the rich dine, you drink where the rich drink, and you sleep where the rich sleep," Johnson later explained.

During the marriage, Johnson continued to carry on with a variety of men and women. One night after the couple had sepa-rated, the police were called to Johnson's home. They found him moaning in pain, sitting naked on the steps with his hands hand-cuffed behind him. Inside his house, officers found a quantity of cocaine, a whip, and leather wristbands. Paul Elrod, who was also in the house, said Johnson had picked him up at a bar, promising him cocaine. Once they got home, Johnson stripped naked and paraded around wearing nothing but a blond wig and metal clips on his nipples.

During divorce proceedings, Ancky testified that Ben depleted her fortune with his "horrible" gambling habits, diminishing her bank balance from $7 million to between $3 and $4 million. Only one of the cars Ben bought her during their marriage was a Rolls-Royce, she complained. After they were married, Johnson told her he was impotent, and they had no sex after that, she said. But when Ancky became ill after yet another disastrous marriage, Johnson took care of her.

Kooluris said it was Johnson who urged him to marry Joan, from whom he is now divorced. "He invited me to lunch and said, 'There'll be no girl who loves you and will love you as much as Joan loves you. You'd better marry her.' I was too stupid to be married to someone of that quality. She was first-class."

But isn't he homosexual? I asked him.

"I'm not even sexual," Kirby said. "I can't find any takers. I'm too finicky. I'm not a bar person—gay or otherwise. When I was younger, I could play around fast, make quick kills. Success in that game is youth. I'm not interested in being a sugar daddy to someone. This Bill thing happened by accident. He's not really interested in guys. He just happened to wind up hanging around me. So once in a while, he'll be reading porno stuff, and he gets worked up and will start on me. I can't have a relationship with someone, because no one with a brain would understand the way I live. Any well-adjusted human being wouldn't go for this resort life the way I lead it."

In any case, "Joan knew from before we got married that I had other sexual interests," Kirby said. "I told her that from time to time I have this little fantasy. She said, 'Oh my.' I said if you want to cancel all these things in our lives, I'm sure the people who are coming to honor us will understand. She said, 'I have no choice because I'm in love with you.' So no one was betrayed."

During the season, Kooluris rents out his house for just over $20,000 a month and stays with friends or house-sits. If things really get tight, he sells a painting from his impressive collection of his great-uncle Nathan Dolinsky's work. Renting out his house and getting free sumptuous meals, Kirby lives the life of a prince. Whether attending Adnan Khashoggi's birthday party or going to the finest French restaurants with J. Paul Getty's family, Kirby secures all the privileges of living in Palm Beach without the huge expense. "They are more accepting here of people who are floating," Kooluris said, referring to himself.

Kirby tries to derive a sense of self-worth from his home and art collection. He seems to hope that his appreciation of them might somehow substitute for his own lack of achievement. While he is a talented photographer, he has never had the drive to become successful at it. Lovingly, he showed me the main staircase of his home, a treble-clef shape with lighted nooks displaying knickknacks. In one bedroom, Kirby said, the architect wanted to achieve a certain color for the leather on the chairs— the dull translucent green that you see when an ocean wave drops over your head. To get the color, the architect sent the material to a car manufacturer.

Kirby may give others happiness, but his family, from Short Hills, New Jersey, doesn't understand. Once when his mother, Hortense, a former dancer trained by protegés of Isadora Duncan, visited, Kooluris asked a favor of his friend Lucien Capehart, one of the island's three society photographers: Would he mind letting him sit behind a desk at Capehart's studio on South County Road to create the impression he had a job?

Capehart has lived his own charmed life. He once dated Princess Sybil de Bourbon-Parme, whose lineage goes back to Louis XVI, and Donna Long, daughter of Ann Light, J. Paul Getty's fourth wife.

Capehart obliged. To promote Kirby's story, he had a sign made up with Kirby's name on it. He placed the sign on a desk in his studio. When Kirby's uncle, a retired surgeon, visited with Kirby's aunt, Kirby and Capehart orchestrated the same ruse.

"Pretending is a way of life here," Kirby told me. "We call Palm Beach Fantasy Island. Where I run into trouble is people sometimes feel they own you. At a function, I'll bump into the family or friends of one of the women I escort. We'll chat, and the woman who invited me might come up to them and say, 'He's mine.' A guy is very valuable in this town."

3. BOOBS "R" US

That night, Kevin O'Dea, the night manager of Ta-boó, Palm Beach's trendiest and most successful restaurant and bar, put his arms around the heir to one of America's great fortunes. Slim women turned their blond heads as O'Dea led the woman and her younger boyfriend past the inviting bar and the sixty-gallon goldfish tank to the dining room with the fireplace, the most desirable location. Here, along Worth Avenue, Palm Beach's answer to Rodeo Drive, lucky diners can watch whoever comes in the door—everyone from Celine Dion and Aretha Franklin to Ivana Trump, Roxanne Pulitzer, and Rod Stewart.

"I hug and I kiss everybody in town," O'Dea told me. "I'm just that way." And while embracing the women who enter the bar, O'Dea can't help but notice that half the women have breast implants. "You can tell fake boobs," he said. "Sometimes I think there's a place around here called Boobs 'R' Us. This is plastic surgery central. I know women who can't close their eyes at night. One girl I know who is very attractive came in with a collagen job on her lips. She looked like Howdy Doody. It doesn't make you look younger. It makes you look weirder. A forty-year-old woman has football-size boobs. Within three minutes of meeting me, she told me her boobs cost five thousand dollars. She shows as much as she can of them all the time."

O'Dea greets patrons with exuberance. Even when he doesn't really know their names, they assume he does.

Despite having done scheduling for the Grateful Dead, despite his former years of drinking and drugging, Kevin looks about ten years younger than his professed age of fifty. He is attractive, with a narrow face, a good tan, and a ready smile. With his commanding voice, he announces to new acquaintances that he is a "sober alcoholic," a member of Alcoholics Anonymous.

For O'Dea, Palm Beach has been his redemption, a place where he has stayed away from drink for eight years, ever since he became night manager of Ta-boó at 221 Worth Avenue. He guides people to their tables, listening to their confessions, advising them on their love lives, trying to make them happy. "The restaurant business is show business," O'Dea said. "It's entertainment. I'm out there, and I have a starring role."

Palm Beachers trust O'Dea. Women ask his advice on prospective dates. Male patrons confide the names of the women they are currently bedding.

"I see if they have a wife and are screwing around a lot," O'Dea told me. "They will call and say, 'I'm coming in tonight with my wife.' These are top people in town. I just don't say anything about their girlfriend. They have beautiful young mistresses. They're blatant about bringing them out." Sometimes O'Dea thinks an older man has brought in his daughter, so he seats them across from each other, and it turns out that the young woman is the man's girlfriend or wife. O'Dea has to apologize and offer to move her to a seat on a banquette next to the man.

I was introduced to Kevin by a fellow AA member, a Palm Beacher whom I met at the Chesterfield Hotel, where I stayed. Kevin would later say my credentials as a journalist convinced him to talk with me. He compared me with Andy Warhol, an observer within the ranks of the glitterati. Kevin's reading of people turned out to be uncannily accurate. He would recommend others to talk to, letting me use his name. After spending the equivalent of days with them, I would find that they were exactly as Kevin had characterized them.

Not everyone solicits his opinion. An attractive professional woman came in a lot. "She wanted to get married, but she was blind to the facts," Kevin said. "This character who looked like Orson Welles came in. They had a romance. They were making wedding plans. She moved in with him."

The next thing Kevin knew, the wedding was off. "He was a total con," Kevin told me. "He had conned her out of all her money. She posted what happened on the internet with his picture." The man kept returning. "The last time I saw him, he was in with a new blond wife."

If Kevin knows everyone's love life, he also sees how the richest people in the world indulge themselves. One evening, a couple from the international set called for reservations from their Lear jet. "They had beluga caviar. The check was eleven hundred dollars, and they tipped six hundred," O'Dea said. Another Palm Beach couple never eats in the restaurant but sends the manservant to Ta-boó five nights a week to pick up dinner. A lone diner orders four ounces of beluga—at $50 an ounce—with each of his meals. One mogul confided to O'Dea, "My wife spends thirty thousand dollars a year on her hair, and it doesn't look any better than anybody else's."

"We get Arab royalty," Kevin said. "First you get the bodyguards, then royal family, and then the servants. The bodyguards order. The royal family is fed first, then the rest. We've had sultans give hundred-dollar bills to everybody who works in the restaurant."

A man called to make a reservation. "I want to propose at the table," he told O'Dea. "Before dessert, I'm going to lean over and pop the question. Then, do you think you could come out with flowers?"

The man brought his entire family. As they sat around the table, the customer proposed. O'Dea had a server take a photo. Fortunately, the woman said yes.

One night at six-thirty a waiter came rushing to the front of the restaurant with an urgent request. "I have to have some Twinkies," he said. "This guy at table four is going to pay me five hundred dollars if I can get him Twinkies in half an hour."

"Cut me in, and I'll send for the Twinkies," O'Dea said.

When they arrived, the pastry chef put the Twinkies on a large plate and surrounded them with raspberry sauce and whipped cream.

"He not only paid five hundred for the Twinkies, he tipped a hundred seventy-five dollars on a six-hundred-dollar check," O'Dea said. "I made fifty dollars."

Ta-boó offers something for everyone. With dark green ceilings and peach accents, it serves everything from cheeseburgers, club sandwiches, and pizza to beluga caviar, whole Dover sole, lobster, rack of lamb, osso bucco, and roast prime rib of beef—all mouthwatering. For lunch, megamillionaires' wives dine on cold fresh poached salmon or warm steak salad with strips of grilled marinated filet mignon. For dessert, a chocolate walnut brownie drenched in hot fudge sauce, all made from scratch in the kitchen, is enough to make a chocolate lover break down in tears. At night, the sixteen-seat black-granite bar attracts handsome men and alluring women looking to connect over Taittinger champagne, $12 a glass. On Friday and Saturday nights after ten, patrons dance to disco music.

Customers range from trust-fund babies who live on inherited wealth and the newest of the nouveau riche to mainstays like Mildred "Brownie" McLean, a grande dame of Palm Beach society.

"It's funny what happens to people who live on inherited money," O'Dea told me. One Saturday night, twelve trust-fund babies came in. "They ordered food and drinks. Then it came time to pay the check. About half of them wandered out before check time." The bill came to $600, and the poor guy who tried to organize everybody to pay got stuck with $470 of it.

O'Dea hears anti-Semitic remarks. "I have a friend who is Jewish and a tennis player," O'Dea said. "She was invited to play tennis at the Everglades Club. She was told to leave because she is Jewish. This was five or six years ago. I know Jewish girls who were raised here, and they were at a birthday party for one of their school friends at the Bath & Tennis Club. They had to call their mother to take them home because Jews weren't allowed."

During the season, the wait for a table can be fifteen to twenty minutes, but patrons used to getting their way still insist on being seated in particular rooms or at their usual tables.

As on the rest of the island, games of wealth and privilege are played out at Ta-boó. "Everyone in Palm Beach wants recognition," O'Dea said. "That's the big thing. I don't care whether it's Joe Blow or Mrs. Firestone. They say, 'I am me, and I deserve that.'"

"There's a pecking order to the rooms and tables near the fireplace," O'Dea said. "I state as a policy that I can't guarantee particular tables. It's impossible for me to do. I'm doing four hundred meals a night. You don't know who's a billionaire, sometimes, and who is the latest guy in town with a tux looking for a rich wife, and he's got nothing. My policy is to treat everyone democratically, like human beings. I try to meet the demands. If I let their whims set the agenda, everyone else feels slighted. It's like a chess game. You're constantly trying to juggle things to make people happy."

Wealthy customers make a game of returning orders, posturing and seeing how much power they can exert.

"I go along except when they're blatantly trying to rip me off," O'Dea said. "They'll order six stone crabs, eat five, and say they are bad and want more. Or they see someone else's order and return what they have, claiming the sauce is not up to par."

On occasion, "I lose it," said O'Dea, who nearly chain-smokes Camel filters. When he runs out, he substitutes Winston Lights. "We pour six-ounce glasses of wine, a quarter bottle of wine. We have a large glass so you get the nose of the wine. Somebody called me over and said, 'This glass isn't full.' I said, 'It's six ounces. If that's not enough for you, I can't make you happy.' I knew I was offending him. But I get tired of getting got all the time. I eventually went back to him and took him a glass of wine."

O'Dea sees an endless variety of rituals surrounding drinking.

"One woman who orders a martini requires five glasses," O'Dea said. "One for ice, one for vodka, one for vermouth, one for gin, and one for olives and onions. We know her, and that's what we do for her."

In Palm Beach, desperate women want to get married and find financial security, and the men mainly want to have sex. "There is a whole crew of my regular girls who have been married at least once and are very attractive," O'Dea said. "They may have money in their own right, but they want more. They may be worth five million. They want to find a guy worth fifty-five million."

For many of them, he says, "beauty is their only stock-in-trade, and there's nothing inside. I see a lot of women who have all the physical attributes, but there's nothing else there. Beauty really comes from inside."

Late at night O'Dea has seen "women disappear under tables, and gentlemen with very happy smiles. When you mix men, women, and alcohol, almost anything can happen. I've seen the flirtation and drinking and intoxication and people leaving together. Then the next day, I've heard rape. Sometimes they get drunk and change their minds and say it was rape. William Kennedy Smith was a great example."

In that case, there was no corroboration of twenty-nine-year-old Patricia Bowman's claim that Smith raped her—and several signs that she consented to sex but then became enraged when Smith called her Kathy instead of Patricia while they were having sex. She testified, for example, that she removed her panty hose prior to the sex act. She also claimed that she screamed, yet despite the still night, no one heard her. Smith was acquitted. "It's easy for women to be victimized," Kevin said, "and it's also easy for them to victimize a man."

On the island, "there are gold diggers you wouldn't believe," O'Dea said. He came to work one day and a very attractive blonde was sitting at the bar at 5:00 P.M. A friend introduced her to Kevin. She showed Kevin some of the beautiful short dresses she had just bought on Worth Avenue. The next night she came in again, showing lots of cleavage. "I have a job for you," she said. "I'm going to come to this restaurant, and you're going to find me a husband. I'll take care of you, Kevin."

"Okay. What are you looking for?"

"Oh, fifty to sixty years old, lots of money."

A few months later, a pretty Danish woman came in with a woman O'Dea used to date. The Danish woman said, "Kevin, do you know anybody for me? I think it's about time I found someone."

"What are your qualifications?" Kevin asked.

"Someone who is fifty or sixty and rich," she said.

"Golly," Kevin said. "You want something no one else wants."

Kevin hooked her up with a movie producer, but she wasn't satisfied. He had to be richer. Before they went out on a date, Kevin told the producer not to bother.

It works both ways. The town is full of rich women who find the help attractive. One young woman, heir to a retailing fortune, picks up bartenders. She lets "every guy in the bar paw her" through her $5,000 dresses.

"A very wealthy French divorcée came in," O'Dea recalled. "She would order Louis Roederer Cristal from France, a hundred-and-ninety-five-dollar bottle of champagne, and tip a hundred dollars. She hit it off with a bartender, and they dated. Then they spent a weekend in Miami together. The bartender quit. The next time I saw them was at Au Bar," infamous as the place where William Kennedy Smith picked up Patricia Bowman. "The former bartender and the divorcée were just stopping in town. They had spent the summer in the South of France and were on their way to Southeast Asia."

Another bartender rode his bicycle to work and lived in a studio apartment. He began going out with the heir to a vast fortune. "Two months later, he was driving a Ferrari," O'Dea said. "They never moved in together. They were just great pals and lovers. She took care of him. Now he's retired at fifty with a trust. He has income for the rest of his life."

The call girls who show up at the bar are stunning and fresh-faced.

"One gal is gorgeous and sophisticated," O'Dea said. "She has big breasts. Her price is up to a thousand dollars a night. If you asked her what she does, she would say she is an investor. She's smart with her money."

Even the help is rich. "I get hostesses who work for me for eight dollars an hour and drive sixty-thousand-dollar cars," O'Dea said. "You get a lot of rich people who are divorced and want something to do. The father of one waitress was a billionaire. She would fly home on weekends on her father's private jet."

Until he died in August 1995, Neil Cargile, a cross-dresser, regularly came in wearing a minidress, stockings, and five-inch heels. An accomplished pilot who owned a single-engine Mooney airplane, Cargile grew up in Nashville and designed and operated dredges used for deepening rivers and harbors and for recovering diamonds and gold. He was the subject of a 1995 *New Yorker* profile by John Berendt, author of *Midnight in the Garden of Good and Evil*.

Cargile declared simply that dressing as a woman was "fun." He made no attempt to hide his masculine voice or gait. Dorothy Koss, his pretty blond girlfriend, helped him with his makeup. When in drag, Cargile called himself SheNeil. A month before Cargile died at sixty-seven after a bout with malaria, Palm Beach police arrested him for drunk driving after he left Ta-boó. He insisted he had been singled out because he was wearing a red sequined minidress.

"We had a deal," O'Dea told me. "He couldn't come in drag until after ten P.M."

Another eccentric, a longtime resident of the Colony Hotel, will be "on his tenth martini by three P.M.," O'Dea said. "Charming fellow with this stentorian voice. He was an escort who married a wealthy woman. No sex was involved. But he took care of her through her illness. She passed away and left everything to him."

Until she died at age ninety-four in December 1996, Carolyn M. Skelly regularly hobbled into Ta-boó. Her father, William Grover Skelly, was a mule skinner before striking it rich in the Oklahoma oil boom. In 1917 he founded Midland Refining Company. He acquired other oil-related businesses and created Skelly Oil, one of the country's biggest independent oil companies.

Late in life, Carolyn Skelly was extremely frail, and this attracted trouble. In 1982, robbers at La Guardia Airport took $1 million in jewelry that Skelly was carrying. Two years later, two women, including one of her former maids, stole more than $2 million in jewels from her thirty-six-room château in Newport, which was across the street from Barton Gubelmann's home. Then in December 1996 Skelly awoke in the middle of the night to find a burglar armed with a knife in her bedroom. He escaped with jewelry valued at more than $1 million.

During the season, Skelly lived at the Colony Hotel, just up the street from Ta-boó. A male walker always accompanied her to the restaurant. As soon as Skelly died, her family began fighting over her estate, estimated at $47 million.

The will she had signed in December 1969 left Skelly Oil stock to a son, a daughter, and five grandchildren. The bulk of her estate went to two additional grandchildren who had lived with her for several years before her death. But at her death, Skelly owned no Skelly Oil stock, and this gave her heirs a basis for contesting the will. Eventually, they agreed on a settlement. In the end, her assets were valued at only $15.1 million.

Ta-boó has seen a few brawls. "This guy was at the bar, a young, hip guy," Kevin said. "He probably had some powder in his nose. He was ordering champagne for everybody and being very loud and boisterous." He began bothering a man sitting at a table, and someone said, "Please calm this guy."

"Who's that son of a bitch?" the loud man said. In a second, tables were flying. Kevin called the police.

One evening a woman confronted another woman at the bar.

"I was just in Hong Kong with your husband," she said. "He tells me you're just a money-grubbing bitch."

The wife threw her drink in the mistress's face. After the bartender called for help, O'Dea walked over to the women and asked what was going on.

"I'm sleeping with her husband, and I know what she did to him," the mistress explained. "I just went up to her and told her. Then she threw a drink at me." The mistress seemed dumbfounded at the woman's reaction.

The next day the husband came in, and O'Dea mentioned the encounter to him. He was shocked but then started laughing. It turned out the mistress had mistakenly accosted someone else's wife.

4. BELUGA CAVIAR

"I've lived here twenty years, and already I have seen such changes in this town," said Barbara Pearson Johnson, whose husband was president of a defense contractor, with a sigh. "Everyone was very gay and beautifully coiffed," Johnson said to murmurs of agreement. "We would pick up clothes at Lilly Pulitzer's and go to Petite Marmite for lunch. Life started at eleven P.M. People would be coming from parties at the Everglades or the Beach Club or Breakers Hotel. They would dance their feet off. A great deal of the old money has moved away. It's a whole new group of faces."

Kay Rybovich, whose late husband, John, made the acclaimed Rybovich fishing boat, and her guests placed their orders for Bloody Marys or fresh lemonade, grilled dolphin or shrimp salad, at the Sailfish Club four miles north of Ta-boó. Among the clubs on the island, the Sailfish has some of the best food. The club is unpretentious, with a long pine-paneled dining room and trophy fish on the walls. On this Sunday afternoon, our table overlooked the club's dock, where attendants riding golf carts transferred prime beef filets and Cristal champagne from white Rolls-Royce Corniches and red Ferrari convertibles onto white megayachts gleaming in the brilliant mid-June sunshine. Television mogul Alex Dreyfoos, Jr.'s yacht the *Lady Caroline*, sugar baron Alfonso "Alfie" Fanjul's *Crili*, and developer Llwyd Ecclestone's *The Reel Estate* all tie up here.

As the drinks arrived, Johnson said, "A lot of people who chair these [charity] parties have just come into town and want to make friends and become known. They kind of come and go. We don't have the old standbys like Sue Whitmore and Brownie McLean and Mary Sanford. They're not old families. A lot of people do this [chair balls] to get onto the A-list. That doesn't work. The only way to get on the A-list is by knowing these people all your life."

Rybovich is a gracious, pretty lady with blue eyes, a gentle face, and cheeks like fresh peaches. A founder of the International Women's Fishing Association, she is on the boards of local organizations like the Palm Beach Historical Society and the Palm Beach Round Table, which brings in speakers ranging from Donald Trump to Gerald Ford. Rybovich said she came to Palm Beach as a young girl in 1924.

In those days, during off-season, the town turned off the traffic lights. "There was a genteelness in the old days," Rybovich said, expressing a view commonly held by the Old Guard. "Palm Beach was almost royalty. The people here had lovely homes with up to thirty servants. They had a head servant, a head guard man. Today it's different. It's not the same quality. Look at the difference between the people living here then and now. They didn't show their wealth. Now they display it openly. It's new money versus old money."

Still, Palm Beachers—eighty-seven percent of whom are millionaires—get by.

By design, no signs along Interstate Route 95 point to Palm Beach, sixty-five miles north of Miami. Even after crossing one of the three bridges from West Palm Beach, the island's poor cousin on the mainland, drivers can't be sure they have arrived in Palm Beach. No signs welcome them to the island paradise. If they have to ask where Palm Beach is, they shouldn't be there.

The contrast with West Palm, a city of 68,703 with strip malls, is palpable. Royal palms, the most stately and noble of all, line the resort's streets, along with coconut palms, a more humble tree that produces coconuts. The coconut palms must be trimmed twice a year lest a ripe coconut crash through the roof of a Lamborghini Countach or a Rolls-Royce Corniche convertible. Like mountain climbers, with crampons on their shoes, trimmers hired by the town scale the palm trees to castrate them with serrated machetes. The coconuts pop into the street and bounce away, chased by a workman from the cleanup crew that follows the climbers around. As the men sweep through the town square on South County Road at Australian Avenue, kitchen workers, hotel employees, and store clerks slip out and pick up the ripest, fattest, yellowest coconuts from the street, then return to work, looking sheepish but self-satisfied.

The coconut palms are the legacy of a drunken party held after a Spanish ship called the *Providencia* ran aground on January 9, 1878. Bound for Barcelona from Havana, the ship carried a cargo of hides, coconuts, and wine. The crew and local settlers consumed the wine, and the captain gave the Americans twenty thousand coconuts. The palms that grew from the coconuts are still on the island, and the party is still going on.

In 1892 the palms entranced Henry Morrison Flagler, a partner with John D. Rockefeller in the Standard Oil Company and a leading figure in American industry. Flagler decided to turn Palm Beach into America's Riviera—a playground for the rich and famous. Over Flagler Memorial Bridge at the north end of the island, he extended his Florida East Coast Railway to Palm Beach and built the 1,150-room Royal Poinciana Hotel, then the world's largest hotel, as a draw. It was in the Royal Poinciana that Joseph P. Kennedy, whose winter home was on the island, later would begin his three-year affair with movie star Gloria Swanson. Because the Poinciana was on Lake Worth, Flagler added an offshoot, the Palm Beach Inn, on the ocean in 1895. Renamed the Breakers Hotel in 1901, it was destroyed by fire and rebuilt in 1903.

The hotel's cottages were the winter homes of John D. Rockefeller, John Jacob Astor, Andrew Carnegie, and J. P. Morgan. They traveled down in their own railroad cars. As a wedding present to his third wife, Mary Lily Kenan, Flagler also built Whitehall, a 55,000-square-foot marble Beaux Arts palace that is now the Henry Morrison Flagler Museum. Assessed at $51.6 million, the Breakers is now run by descendants of Mary Lily.

If the palms are Palm Beach's signature ornament, the lush hedges allowed to grow as high as sixty feet have a more prosaic function. Money buys privacy, and the precisely manicured hedges shield from the public such structures as Abraham D. Gosman's $12.1 million, 81,000-square-foot home at 513 North County Road and Nelson Peltz's $18 million, 46,700-square-foot home at 548 North County Road. Lesser homes with 20,000 square feet have fifteen bedrooms, twelve bathrooms, several libraries, media rooms, saunas, gymnasiums, pizza parlors, and formal or great rooms, along with the usual parlors, dens, recreation rooms, and living rooms. Bedroom closets run to 1,000 square feet. By comparison, a spacious four-bedroom house in the suburbs with living room and family room has about 2,500 square feet.

Among the megaresidents who have homes of Babylonian splendor on Palm Beach are John Kluge (worth $10.5 billion from Metromedia); Ronald O. Perelman ($4.2 billion from Revlon and other investments); Si Newhouse, Jr. ($4.5 billion from publishing); Estée Lauder's sons, Ronald ($4.4 billion from cosmetics), and Leonard ($4.4 billion from the same company); David Koch ($3 billion from oil), and William Koch ($650 million from Oxbow Corporation, an energy conglomerate); Edgar Bronfman, Sr. ($4.3 billion from Seagram); Diana Strawbridge Wister ($900 million from a Campbell's Soup inheritance); Nelson Peltz ($840 million from leveraged buyouts, Royal Crown Cola, and Snapple); and Sidney Kimmel ($825 million from Jones New York, Evan Picone, and Saville apparel).

Billionaire Donald Trump drops in at Mar-a-Lago at 1100 South Ocean Boulevard, a 125,000-square-foot home that he bought for

$10 million in 1985 and turned into a club in 1995. Jimmy Buffett, Buffalo Bills owner Ralph Wilson, Rush Limbaugh, and Rod Stewart also own homes on the island.

A recent addition is La Follia, a $27 million, 37,000-square-foot beachfront mansion built by financier Irwin Kramer and his wife, Terry Allen Kramer, a Broadway producer. The coquina-clad manse comes with walk-in refrigerators and freezers as well as a walk-in wine cellar. The master suite alone is 4,500 square feet, twice the size of a normal home.

Sydell L. Miller, worth $1.3 billion from her hair-care company, Matrix Essentials, just built a 37,268-square-foot home with forty-two rooms and a basement garage for seventeen cars. She paid $11.25 million for an adjoining 16,200-square-foot estate with marble columns and two wine-tasting rooms (one for red, one for white). Then she tore it down.

Most of the owners of the larger homes occupy them for only a few months during the season. In the meantime, electric bills are $4,000 to $5,000 a month, and property taxes can exceed $500,000 a year. The bill for landscape maintenance for a five-acre estate is $140,000 a year, not to mention the cost of maintaining year-round staffs of chefs, butlers, maids, chauffeurs, and gardeners.

Residents re-create their homes as often as they do their faces.

According to Michael Rosenow, a Palm Beach interior decorator who resells furniture, "it's very common for people in Palm Beach to spend thirty or forty thousand dollars on home furnishings, and two months later they change their minds and say, 'Take it out.' Some of the furniture gets more use from the movers than from being in people's homes. They have these fabulous homes, and the sofas have never been sat on. If you have a twenty- or thirty-thousand-square-foot home, how much can you sit, unless you have parties all the time?"

At the western end of Australian, Brazilian, and Peruvian avenues, the docks on Lake Worth are lined with yachts. Some call their yachts home, and understandably. Edward Germaine, an eighty-four-year-old real-estate tycoon from Buffalo, lives on an eighty-six-foot yacht. It's staffed by an all-female crew, headed by forty-seven-year-old Hope Fiene. Germaine ventures onto land only at night.

"He keeps the hours of a vampire," said Karen Lane, the municipal dockmaster of Palm Beach. "The crew looks after him, feeds him, gives him a haircut, cuts his toenails. At night he comes out. He looks like Howard Hughes in his latter days."

The mayor of Palm Beach, Paul R. Ilyinsky, keeps his yacht, *Angelique,* tied up at the municipal docks as well. A member of the Romanov family, which ruled Russia from 1613 until the Russian Revolution of 1917, Ilyinsky gives a "State of Palm Beach" address each April before the civic association. Like the rest of Palm Beach's elected officials, he serves without pay.

Beautiful people are everywhere—blondes wearing white tank tops and microminiskirts and long-haired, blue-eyed brunettes with bodies that make men's heads spin. The men are handsome, tan, and very fit. Beauty is the coin of the realm, a lesson in evolution. People who do not consider themselves very attractive or very successful do not show up on the island. Those who do are assumed to be wealthy, part of the club. "If you're here at all, that says something," said Kirby Kooluris.

Daily, celebrities pop in—Claudia Schiffer, Elizabeth Taylor, Sylvester Stallone, Tom Cruise, the Rolling Stones, Christie Brinkley, Burt Reynolds, Matt Lauer, Kim Basinger, Harrison Ford, Ann-Margret, Marla Maples, Pamela Anderson Lee, Madonna, Whitney Houston, Mike Wallace, Dan Rather, Gwyneth Paltrow, Loni Anderson, and Suzanne Somers. One night Jenny McCarthy, Ivana Trump, and Brooke Shields danced at a club known simply as 251, which has replaced Au Bar as Palm Beach's hot spot after midnight. Bruce Springsteen jams at 251 with his longtime sax player, Clarence Clemons.

"We see all of them at one time or another," sniffed Donald Bruce, who until recently owned a store on Worth Avenue that bore his name and sold Petrossian beluga caviar for $1,173 a pound. "They don't cause a ripple."

The town has only one supermarket—a Publix at 265 Sunset Avenue. When an elderly Palm Beach resident lost control of her car in the parking lot in March 1992, she hit a Rolls-Royce, a Mercedes, a Porsche, a Cadillac, and an Isuzu pickup truck. Alongside the celery and Pampers, Publix sells beluga caviar and Cristal champagne at $146.99 a bottle. "Caviar is kind of commonplace here," said Mort Kaye, who has been photographing Palm Beach parties for fifty years. The cookbook published by the Junior League of the Palm Beaches includes a recipe for caviar pie.

So that Publix would fit in, the town required the supermarket to adorn its exterior with murals, and prohibited it from displaying the standard large green Publix sign in the parking lot. Inside the Publix, women shop as their butlers push their carts. One of the town's more eccentric characters can be seen taking five minutes to examine the ingredients on a bag of jelly beans. Palm Beach is full of people sustained by trust funds but too cheap to buy their own soap, preferring instead to "borrow" it from hotel rooms.

"If you have material assets, you're called eccentric," Kooluris said. "If not, you're called crazy."

One afternoon, standing with me outside Publix, Dennis E. Spear, who was the caretaker at the Kennedy estate once known as the Winter White House, greeted Rose Kennedy's ophthalmologist, who was wheeling a grocery cart. "Frank Sinatra used to shove his cart from Publix," Spear told me. "In Publix, you see just about everybody."

At 5:00 P.M., when tennis games are over, the place becomes a pickup joint.

Being rich doesn't guarantee a place in line. In a famous incident, Pat Booth, a Palm Beach resident who wrote the *New York Times* best-selling novel *Palm Beach*, got in a shoving match with someone's maid. When a new line opened up, the maid got there first. Booth began maneuvering her cart to cut in front of her, according to two Publix clerks later interviewed by the police. The maid, who bit the tip of one of the novelist's fingers, claimed self-defense.

A mile and a half south of the Publix is Worth Avenue, Palm Beach's ultrachic shopping strip. A combination Rodeo Drive and

Mediterranean seaside town, what local wags call "Worthless Avenue" is lined with white stucco shops garlanded with climbing flowers. Conspicuous spenders from the sultan of Brunei to Adnan Khashoggi have no difficulty shelling out hundreds of thousands of dollars during a half hour's stroll along the glitzy strip, where stores include Ferragamo, Armani, Chanel, Louis Vuitton, Cartier, Tiffany, Van Cleef & Arpels, Calvin Klein, Valentino, and Saks Fifth Avenue.

In a reversal of the common attitude, the town tries to discourage businesses from coming to Palm Beach. The latest flap was Neiman-Marcus's plan to build a 57,000-square-foot store on Worth Avenue, across the street from the Esplanade shopping center and the existing 38,000-square-foot Saks Fifth Avenue, then Palm Beach's largest store. A "town-serving ordinance" requires any store with more than 2,000 square feet to prove that at least half its customers will be residents, their guests, or patrons of Palm Beach hotels. If every town had such rules, commerce in the United States would grind to a halt. But so far, no one has taken the issue to the Supreme Court.

At a public hearing on Neiman's proposed store, a witness for Neiman's claimed that, to be successful, the store would have to generate "only" $3,000 a year in sales from each of the town's residents. As spectators took notes with gold Mont Blanc pens, councilman Leslie A. Shaw questioned whether most shoppers would spend that much.

"Being a major shopping person," council president Lesly Smith interjected to laughs, "I can tell you that if you spend three thousand dollars at Neiman-Marcus, you possibly will have bought only a skirt and a blouse."

Lest the new department store attract unsuitables, the town agreed to let Neiman-Marcus come to the island if it would not advertise its new location for a year. The town also limited the store to 48,661 square feet—about the size of one of Palm Beach's larger homes. After the council approved the store's plans, Lesly Smith wryly said she would shop there but insisted, "I will shop in no more than 32,000 square feet of the store, and I certainly won't go to the third floor, which I opposed."

More recently, the town allowed Houston's to open where Au Bar used to be—but only on the condition that the restaurant would be called Palm Beach Grill.

The town-serving edict is one of an array of unusual—if not unique—rules designed to preserve Palm Beach as a sanctuary for the rich. Store signs must be so small—and rents are so high—that no fast food outlet wants to come to Palm Beach. Tennis-ball machines may not emit noises above prescribed decibel levels. Use of heavy construction machinery is banned during the season. A minimum speed limit keeps gawkers from tying up traffic in front of the palatial homes. It also allows the police to stop almost anyone unfamiliar with the island. Until legal challenges were mounted, Palm Beach had an ordinance banning topless (presumably male) joggers. Another law required employees to register with the police and submit to fingerprinting and photographing.

"You have to ask permission to take a deep breath in Palm Beach," longtime resident Donna Smith told me.

Despite the comparisons to Rodeo Drive and Beverly Hills, Palm Beach is far more exclusive. Rodeo Drive is sullied by such bourgeois stores as United Colors of Benetton—not to mention hordes of tourists bumping into one another as they pore over maps and peer into camcorders. Worth Avenue is lined with Rolls-Royces, Jaguars, Ferraris, and Bentleys. Along Rodeo Drive, the conveyances of the superrich are as uncommon as taxis in Palm Beach. When everyone has a chauffeur, who needs taxis? Neither Beverly Hills nor any other locale has the concentration of wealth and beautiful people that makes Palm Beach unique.

Because of the high rent, Palm Beach has no Starbucks and no CVS drugstores. "It's very hard to get your errands done here," said Pat Danielski, a local real-estate agent who bought a Harley-Davidson motorcycle jacket for her dog Skippy. "There used to be a hardware store here. I don't think you can buy a needle and thread."

But the Palm Beach Post Office does a land-office business for zip code 33480. "People have Palm Beach post office boxes because they want a Palm Beach address," said Danielski, whose husband, Frederick, managed the Colony Hotel for nearly two decades.

If the town requires conformity, that only reflects Palm Beach society. Along with its backward rules imposed on commerce, Palm Beach has a strict dress code—a blue blazer, open sport shirt, and loafers or moccasins, preferably without socks. Like a military uniform, the ordained dress says a person belongs. Charles Munn is credited with introducing the look to Palm Beach. Munn was a descendant of Carrie Louise Gurnee Armour, widow of the meat-packing king. In 1919 he and his wife, Mary Drexel Paul, moved into Amado, a home designed for them by Addison Mizner. After divorcing his first wife, he married Dorothy Spreckels of the California sugar family. Munn's family intermarried with the Wanamaker family.

Often called "Mr. Palm Beach," Munn entertained in the grand manner. Besides imposing his style in clothes on Palm Beach, he began the tradition of sending out a Christmas card listing the names and phone numbers of Palm Beach's inner circle.

At night, proper attire in Palm Beach is likely to be formal wear. To fulfill social obligations, Palm Beach women with sweet-tooth names like Brownie, Cookie, Sugar, Muffie, and Lolly each buy at least eighteen evening gowns from Martha Phillips or Fiandaca at $18,000 apiece, while the men must own at least three sets of formal wear from Maus & Hauffman at $2,750 each. Other essential items are several pairs of lizard shoes from Ferragamo at $900 a pair and a closet full of Valentino suits costing $2,500 each, according to James Jennings Sheeran's amusing compendium, *Palm Beach Facts & Fancies, Wit and Wisdom*.

On the island, spending substitutes for productive work. With nothing better to do, Palm Beachers spend millions of dollars collecting everything from vintage Rolls-Royce touring cars to the Howdy Doody marionette used for publicity shots for the *Howdy Doody Show* with "Buffalo Bob" Smith (price: $113,432, paid by resident Tamara Jeanne "T.J." Fisher).

"People spend hundreds of thousands at a time on linens alone," said Mary Kendall, a former clerk at Donald Bruce on Worth Avenue. At Mary Mahoney, a single cotton pillowcase—300 thread count with hand-stitching, made by Porthault in France—costs $390.

Businesses pamper the rich. Publix offers free valet parking. Palm Beach National Bank & Trust on Worth Avenue sends its tellers to customers' homes to pick up their deposits. For Valentine's Day, the bank sells roses made of money. For Christmas, the bank offers wrapping paper made of sheets of new bills. So that customers can safely store their jewels after attending social functions, the bank offers a special vault where valuables can be deposited after hours.

For the doggies, Worth Avenue features a special "dog bar"—a halfmoon-shaped tiled trough with a silver spigot providing fresh water. Palm Beach stores sell Chanel collars that cost $125 each, along with Gucci dog beds in lucite that cost $1,490. The fashionable Chesterfield Hotel threw a dog fashion show, complete with leather Harley-Davidson motorcycle jackets. The Chesterfield also supplies dogs with free beds and chow. Lucy, a well-muscled Chinese shar-pei who presides behind and beneath the Chesterfield's individual front desks, won't settle down at night until she's had three cheese-steak subs from her owner, Alice Shaw, the hotel's general manager. In a nightly ritual on the way home from work, Alice stops at the drive-in for Miami Steaks. At the ordering station, Lucy snuffles at the speaker and a disembodied voice says, "Please drive to the window." They know her.

A wealthy woman phoned Alice and said, "I heard Lucy has a designer." She and her friends wanted dresses made for their dogs. They had heard raves about Lucy's green velvet Christmas dress, made by a seamstress who makes drapery for the hotel. "She loves her clothes," Alice says of the dog.

The ideal Palm Beach club, so the joke goes, would serve dogs Evian water.

5. CASH DOESN'T TALK

Aside from shopping, the business of Palm Beach residents is charity balls—hosting them and attending them. It's where people go to see and be seen. Flagler set the tone by throwing lavish parties at his Royal Poinciana Hotel. For one party in 1898 commemorating George Washington's birthday, rich men were invited to dress as famous women—to wear wigs and heavy makeup and put on corsets and stockings under sequined gowns. Flagler himself dressed as Martha Washington.

But it was Marjorie Merriweather Post who turned grand Palm Beach parties into a tradition. Born on March 15, 1887, in Battle Creek, Michigan, Post was the daughter of Charles W. Post, who invented a hay stacker, an electric paddle, and a player piano. Afflicted with a stomach illness, Charles Post in 1884 mixed wheat berries, bran, and molasses to produce a caffeine-free coffee substitute called Postum. Beginning with an investment of $68.76 for kitchen equipment and ingredients, he achieved sales of $250,000 in three years. Next, he baked whole wheat and barley flour with yeast, then ran the loaves through a coffee grinder. He believed baking reduced the starches to grape sugar, so he called the product Grape-Nuts. Finally, Post developed a cornflake cereal, which he called Post Toasties. The products became the kernel of General Foods Corporation.

An only child, Marjorie was daddy's little girl. When women didn't attend such events, Post dressed his daughter in boy's clothes and tucked her hair under a cap so he could smuggle her into a Chicago prizefight. But in May 1914, suffering from depression, Post blew his brains out. At age twenty-seven, Marjorie inherited $20 million, including ownership of General Foods.

"I am not the richest woman in the world," she once said. "There are others better off than I am. The only difference is I do more with my money. I put it to work."

One example was Mar-a-Lago. Post spent $8 million to build what she called "a little cottage by the sea," which was finished in 1927. The home was in addition to a sixty-six-room apartment on Fifth Avenue at Ninety-second Street in Manhattan and estates in Long Island, Washington, D.C., Greenwich, Connecticut, and the Adirondacks. Not to mention a 316-foot yacht, the *Hussar V* (later named the *Sea Cloud*), a private railroad car, and an airplane.

Designed by Palm Beach architect Marion Sims Wyeth with the help on finishing details of Joseph Urban, Mar-a-Lago is a 55,695-square-foot Mediterranean-style complex. It has fifty-eight bedrooms, thirty-three bathrooms, three bomb shelters, a theater, a ballroom, a nine-hole golf course, tennis courts, and a private tunnel leading to beachfront property. A seventy-five-foot tower tops the structure on South Ocean Boulevard. The two-story, Venetian-palace living room provides a view of the ocean to the east and Lake Worth to the west. Some 36,000 Spanish tiles dating to the fifteenth century, Viennese sculptures, gold-leaf ceilings, and gold bathroom fixtures adorn the home. As Post explained, "Gold is much easier to clean."

For fifty years Marjorie reigned as the queen of Palm Beach. Until her death in 1973, she presided over endless parties, supper dances, and balls that lasted until dawn. It was Post who remarked, "There is more money, more champagne, and, of course, more affluence in Palm Beach than all the rest of America put together."

In 1921 Post borrowed costumes and a stage set from her friend Florenz Ziegfeld and threw a benefit to build the Good Samaritan Hospital in West Palm Beach. In 1929 she imported the Ringling Brothers and Barnum & Bailey circus for three days of performances. For her costume parties, she dressed in a gown from the court of Louis XV.

A superb dancer, Post regularly gave square-dancing parties. Promptly at eleven, the caller would instruct everyone to join hands. "May the Lord bless and keep you until we meet again," he would intone. "The party is over."

"Living in the grand style as Mrs. Post did, she had thirty-seven servants inside the house and twenty outside," James Torrie, a Scottish-born footman for Post, told me. "You had butlers, chambermaids, laundresses, cooks, parlor maids, footmen, and gardeners. She had so many sets of fine china, we would go for three weeks of dinners and parties without going back to the same motif."

A typical dinner consisted of twelve courses, beginning with caviar and blini served with Russian vodka and fermented lemon rind, on through filet of beef with stuffed mushrooms served with a 1961 Château Haut-Brion, and ending with soufflé Grand Marnier served with Dom Pérignon, 1962.

Back then, the balls were very private. Given by Post, the first charity ball was called the Hospital Ball. Later, Laddie and Mary Sanford started the Cancer Ball. Now anyone who can afford the $700 to $1,000 for two tickets to a charity ball can attend. The balls are usually held at the legendary Breakers Hotel. Razed by fire a second time in 1925, the Breakers was rebuilt in 1927 with walls and ceilings that reflect Italian Renaissance artistry. Set on 140 acres, the hotel has 572 rooms and 54 suites, 2 eighteen-hole golf courses, and 21 tennis courts. In a recent year, it spent $1.4 million on fresh flowers and served 12,317 bottles of champagne at banquets alone.

Almost every night during the season, as if they still lived in the prewar era of the *Titanic*, the celebrants dress in tuxedos and heavily starched formal shirts. Women don glittering tiaras, some so laden with jewels they cause headaches. Rolls-Royces pull up to the Breakers, and everyone dances to "Bad, Bad Leroy Brown" or "The Best of Times." During the season, more than one hundred charity balls are held to raise money for everything from the American Red Cross to the Mental Health Association and the Weizmann Institute of Science. Each ball spawns half a dozen luncheons, teas, and dinners given by the ball organizers in honor of themselves.

Then there are satellite organizations like the Young Friends of the Red Cross, which throws a New Year's Eve bash attended by the likes of Adnan Khashoggi and Lamia, one of his two wives, and their entourage. At a recent party, a reclining gold-painted young woman, straight from *Goldfinger* and wearing nothing but a G-string, promoted a James Bond theme. At other Palm Beach parties, silver-painted nudes substitute for floral centerpieces on the sumptuous buffet tables.

"Lee Iacocca had a party," said Ann Zweig, one of Palm Beach's top caterers, who did Burt Reynolds and Loni Anderson's wedding. "Iacocca wanted something that would be drop-dead. I said, 'May I do anything I want?' He had a billiard room with a billiard table. I covered it with a black top. I covered a nude artist's model with liquid silver from toe to head. I surrounded her with edible flowers. She didn't move for an hour. They couldn't tell if she was alive or dead."

"Nude girls in buffets is pretty normal," said real-estate agent Pat Danielski. Party givers often fly in their own caterers from New York. "They fly in the food—caviar, lobster, magnums and jeroboams of Dom Pérignon. That's expected."

Besides giving the doyennes a sense of purpose, the balls provide residents with an excuse to expand their homes. As chair of the International Red Cross Ball, the Cadillac of the charity balls, Betty Scripps Harvey hosted a party at her oceanfront home. In preparation, she added a glass-enclosed garden room and a kitchen just for the caterers.

To be sure, Palm Beach residents could write a check to each charity and be done with it. But then, said Cynthia Stone Ray, who was Rose Kennedy's secretary, "No one would get recognition for giving."

"Charity is part of what makes Palm Beach work," Danielski said. "Without the charity balls, there would only be half the number of hotels. That's their work. Some of these people wouldn't give money directly to the charities. They give the money so they can socialize."

"People will pay five hundred dollars a ticket to a charity ball when they would never dream of writing a check for five hundred, even though they're worth a hundred million," said Donald Bruce, a first cousin of the late Malcolm Forbes. "They want a party to go with it."

In the end, Palm Beachers cough up a mere $38 million a year at local charity functions. They spend as much as two thirds of that on the food and flowers for the parties thrown to raise the money. The town feels no need to make public the net figure, which is considerably less than $38 million. By comparison, Patricia Kluge receives $50 million a year as part of her divorce settlement with John Kluge.

If the charity balls provide an excuse to exist, they also provide an arena for the subtext of life in Palm Beach. The most striking young men and women in the world gravitate to Palm Beach to find wealthy mates. The line between them and the fresh-faced, well-dressed young call girls who show up at the bars of the Chesterfield Hotel, the Colony, or the Breakers is a fine one indeed.

"A maid will wheel a guy around in a wheelchair, marry him, and after he dies, she becomes the duchess of something," Kirby Kooluris observed.

On the other hand, Donald Bruce said, "You see single gals at night, and they might be living here alone and wouldn't mind a one-night stand."

Along with their homes, swimming pools, and tennis courts (Palm Beach has eleven hundred pools and one hundred tennis courts), residents buy into Palm Beach's rich history of scandal, beginning with Flagler, who divorced his mentally ill wife, Ida Alice, to marry his twenty-four-year-old, green-eyed mistress, Mary Lily Kenan. Marjorie Merriweather Post divorced E. F. Hutton after she caught him having sex with a young chambermaid in his own bedroom at Mar-a-Lago.

Palm Beachers pretend to be above it all, but I found they thrive on the latest gossip, making for lively dinner-party conversation or late-night prattle over scrambled eggs and truffles. The tales come with the territory, adding glamour and controversy. After spending eleven weeks at the FBI's National Academy in Quantico, Virginia, Michael S. Reiter, Palm Beach's assistant police chief, told me he was amazed that every officer in his class from thirty-one countries—including Russia, Poland, and Australia—knew about Palm Beach and its unique reputation.

During the Smith trial, the tabloids labeled Palm Beach the "Sin Capital of America." No one thought anything of it. Even James A. Ponce, the dignified historian of the Breakers Hotel and the town's unofficial historian, refers to the "panty-hose parking lot," where Patricia Bowman says she removed her panty hose at the Kennedy estate after Smith picked her up at Au Bar. Shuttling JFK and Jackie between Palm Beach and the White House, Marine helicopters had routinely landed on the same lot.

"There is a lot of night debauchery," Allen Heise, the strikingly handsome co-owner, with Jim Fazio, Jr., of 251 told me as we sat in the private bar above the club. Strippers from nearby clubs infiltrate 251, looking to lure wealthy men to the strip joints. With nothing better to do, the idle rich turn to sex. Despite AIDS, "orgies go on in homes or yachts or at pools," the thirty-six-year-old Heise said.

In her office on Sunrise Avenue, Ann Zweig said she has catered parties that turned into sex orgies in swimming pools. Trust-fund babies prowl for sexual conquests. Zweig laughingly recalled what happened when she mentioned to an heir to a major fortune in Palm Beach that Ivana Trump, who lives three minutes north of Mar-a-Lago in a $4.4 million home, needed a butler.

"Ivana Trump needs a butler? Me! I always wanted to make it with Ivana Trump," the man said.

"My God," Zweig said. "You don't know how to be a butler."

"What do you mean?" the man replied. "I've had one all my life."

The trust-fund baby applied for the job and was hired. He donned a white jacket and white gloves for a party.

"Amongst the guests was his mother," Zweig said. "He didn't stay long."

"Very often, men want me to furnish a mistress's entire home," said Michael Rosenow, the Palm Beach interior decorator. "It works both ways. We have married women who furnish a younger boyfriend's home." Men conceal the payments by charging them to their companies; wives have a harder time. "I've seen twenty to thirty thousand dollars in cash," Rosenow said. "Cash doesn't talk."

A few years ago the wife of one tycoon was caught having sex with a friend of her college-age son. More recently, the stepson of a wealthy dowager began having sex with his stepmother.

"There are a lot of powerful men, and the women maintain their lifestyles through these marriages," Cosmo DiSchino, the dashing hairdresser to Roxanne Pulitzer and formerly to Marla Maples, told me. "There is suffering from lack of attention. So the women get it from other sources all the time. They go out with tennis pros, physical-fitness trainers, hairdressers."

"I've been in real estate here forty years," said Earl Hollis, who owns Earl A. Hollis Inc. "Everyone has a skeleton in the closet."

Two blocks south of 251, around the corner from Publix, is Palm Beach's wildest landmark, E.R. Bradley's Saloon. Bradley's took its name from a casino opened in 1898 by Colonel Edward R. Bradley across from Flagler's Royal Poinciana Hotel. Colonel Bradley owned stables in Kentucky. Horses he owned and bred won four Kentucky Derbys. No matter what the weather, he wore stiff white collars and dress coats. At Bradley's Beach Club, eighteen Pinkerton guards with machine guns stood by as millions of dollars changed hands in an evening. The club saw larger takes than casinos in Monte Carlo.

Gambling was illegal in Florida, but the club managed to stay open, apparently because Henry Flagler did not want it shut down, according to James Ponce. Besides giving large contributions to political parties, Flagler was majority shareholder in the *Palm Beach Daily News*. His influence was so great that, so that he could marry his mistress, Flagler got the Florida legislature to pass a bill in 1901 legalizing divorce on grounds of incurable insanity. After his divorce, the legislature rescinded the law.

E.R. Bradley's Saloon is across the street from Bradley Park, once the site of the casino on the northwest corner of Bradley Place and Royal Poinciana Way. Until the Kennedys sold their home on the island, the bar was a favorite of Senator Edward M. Kennedy. Congressman Joseph Kennedy and other members of the family continue to patronize it. One recent evening, as I drank a Heineken, Rhonda Adams, a 1995 *Playboy* Playmate who was on the cover of the June 1998 Playboy *Classic Centerfolds*, pranced in, caressing her boyfriend's behind.

Despite the sign on the wall, ABSOLUTELY NO DANCING ON THE BAR, pretty young women get drunk and dance on the bar, a nightly ritual that starts at about eleven. They sometimes peel off their clothes, according to Rachel Butler, a statuesque blonde who worked at the saloon off and on for six years.

Butler grew up in Palm Beach, a town with unique rites of passage. Butler, now twenty-nine, said her father, who died two years ago, threw sex orgies and cocaine parties attended by some of the wealthiest people on the island. While she was expected to earn her own way, rich kids usually received Jaguars at sixteen.

"They have never held down a job," Butler said. "They're still doing drugs. Of all the places I've lived, I've never seen so much pain and agony as in Palm Beach. The people with the most money seem to be the most miserable."

At Bradley's, "chicks are always stripping, totally," Butler told me. "Sometimes they open their blouses and shake their boobs around. So many times they'll lift up their skirts, and they won't have any underwear on. They won't have to take off their skirt. They lift it to their waists . . . then they are groped."

Frank Coniglio, a former Washingtonian who owns Bradley's, said strippers who come over from Diamonds in West Palm Beach may be responsible.

After a stimulating evening at such Palm Beach nightspots, some people can't wait to get back to their homes or hotels. In the backseats of limousines, "sex happens fairly frequently," David J. Goodstal, a driver for Black Tie Limousines, told me. "A lot of times you have guys and a girl doing their business. They met in a club. People frequently don't put the divider down, or you can feel the car moving. Or you hear a woman screaming. I've had three guys and one girl, and two girls and one guy. Three guys and two girls or three girls and one guy."

Yet more than sex, "people here are concerned about their standing," Goodstal said. "It's about, 'Did we get in the paper last week?' Which ball you get invited to is very important."

"When I came here in 1953, I was taken to a dinner party," said George Stinchfield, a friend of Barton Gubelmann who owned a Worth Avenue apparel shop for forty years. "The hostess was a very wealthy lady. She said, 'Young man, where were you born?'"

"In Maine," Stinchfield said.

"I trust you were born in the summer," she said, implying a socially acceptable summer-resort area, like Bar Harbor.

"No," Stinchfield said. "I was conceived there. I hope that will do."

That attitude continues today. When Palm Beachers complain that the place has gone to hell, they really mean that in the old days "everyone was in his place," Dennis Spear, the caretaker of the Kennedy estate, told me over seafood marinara at Testa's.

Spear, with his lifeguard's tan, knows Palm Beach as well as anybody. Previously, he was youth-activities director of the Sailfish Club. When he took care of the Kennedy mansion, he often accompanied Ted Kennedy to Au Bar. On the night

William Kennedy Smith returned from Au Bar with Patricia Bowman, Spear locked up the estate. He is now caretaker for the new owners of the Kennedy mansion, John and Marianne Castle, who own Morton's steakhouses and are prominent on the island's social terrain. By day, Spear is a lifeguard at the Breakers.

One of the secrets of gaining access is appearing to already know a lot. Because of Spear, I was able to come across as knowledgeable. In the old days, Spear told me, "the blacks were across the bridge at night or in the servants' quarters." In those days, the police would not allow blacks to walk in Palm Beach after dark. "They had the same attitude toward Jews and Catholics. Palm Beach was very WASP."

Controlling much of the money are trust-department officers like Wyckoff Myers. For more than fifty years Myers has worked for the trust department of First National Bank in Palm Beach. Until recently, he was executive vice president in charge of the trust department, which manages $3 billion in assets of Palm Beach residents. As a consultant, Myers continues to handle smaller accounts—up to $75 million in assets.

Trust-fund babies try to outsmart trust officers like Myers. That's their job, living off inherited wealth. They wake up late, go to their clubs, have a few drinks, and urge people like Myers to give them more money.

One heir to an industrial fortune has homes in Palm Beach, New York, France, and Italy. He had a yellow Rolls-Royce Corniche convertible but wanted a red Ferrari as well. The trust department of his bank kept turning him down, considering the purchase frivolous. Finally, he bought the Ferrari using his American Express platinum card. The trust department automatically paid the charge.

"There is a large social aspect to the job," Myers told me at one of Kay Rybovich's get-togethers at the Sailfish Club. "When we choose replacement trust officers, once a guy gets through the qualifications level, and he can tie a neat knot in his tie, then we look at the wife. If she cannot handle a dinner-party conversation, the guy doesn't make it. All the years I was hiring new trust officers, I would never accept one with a Southern accent. You can't use a you-all type here with the Palm Beach establishment."

The *Palm Beach Daily News* acts as social arbiter. The paper is known as the "Shiny Sheet" or simply "the Shiny" because it is printed on smudgeproof high-quality paper. It runs pages of photos, taken at balls and private parties, of couples often grimacing through extreme plastic-surgery jobs. The paper is published daily from mid-September through mid-May and on Thursdays and Sundays the rest of the year.

No news is too trivial to escape the Shiny Sheet's notice. "Unlocked bike stolen from Publix," one headline said. The story reported that a twelve-year-old midnight-blue bike had been stolen from the supermarket's parking lot and that only one of the bike's twelve gears was working.

Although the paper doesn't print everything it knows, it understands the readership. One day, a banner headline screamed across the front page: EGGS OVER EASY: CAVIAR PRICES JUMP, SUPPLY DWINDLES. When Rolls-Royce announced that Palm Beach was one of the few locations in the country where its new $320,000 Bentley Continental Sedanca Coupé (top speed: 155 miles per hour) would be unveiled, the story and accompanying photos nearly filled the top half of the front page. When the bears drove down the stock market in September 1998, the headline over the lead story was: "PBers Calm as Market Fluctuates."

"Everyone tries to shine up to the photographers from the Shiny Sheet," Mickey Spillane, Palm Beach's best-connected and most respected public relations person, told me over lunch at the Chesterfield. "They want a photo shot with the author, the designer, the most important person there. It drives the photographers crazy. One photographer began activating his flash without taking a picture."

Not everyone likes to be in the paper. "The Old Guard is the WASP group," real-estate agent Pat Danielski said. "They don't like to be in the Shiny Sheet. The ones trying to make a social mark in Palm Beach are in the Shiny Sheet. Every time they see a camera, they jump."

Accomplished at little more than consuming, the socialites who populate the island look to external trappings to lend meaning to their lives, creating an artificial hierarchy as a way of measuring their own success. Based on wealth, breeding, manners, and dress, they determine who is in and who is out, who will be invited to the top parties, who will make the twelve-by-sixteen-inch card sent out by the Fanjul sugar barons. As in high school, those who are excluded—who are "unclubbable," as Palm Beachers say—are devastated. In Palm Beach, I learned, people are judged not by their accomplishments—most do nothing but cash checks from trust departments—but by the quality of their balloon decorations.

At the top of the A-list are a few doyennes vying to be known as social queen of Palm Beach. These are the members of the Old Guard who run the most prestigious balls—the International Red Cross, American Cancer Society, or American Heart Association dances—and who belong to the Everglades or the Bath & Tennis Club. Their place in society is guaranteed by birthright. In Palm Beach lingo, they are known as the "core people." Their names tell the story of the rise of American industry and business—Willie Hutton, grandnephew of E. F. Hutton, founder of the brokerage firm; Caroline Penney of J.C. Penney stores; Helen Cluett, whose husband was a founder of Cluett, Peabody & Company; Margaret Sanders of Colonel Sanders' Kentucky Fried Chicken; George Sturgis Pillsbury, the Pillsbury heir; Bunny duPont, of the chemical fortune; Joan Bove, cofounder of Clairol; Mary Alice Firestone Asher, who was married to Firestone Tire heir Russell Firestone, Jr.; Kathleen Ford, widow of auto heir Henry Ford II, and Marylou Whitney, wife of the late Cornelius Vanderbilt Whitney, who owned lumberyards and railroads.

Back when Marjorie Merriweather Post, Mary Sanford (of Bigelow-Sanford Carpet), and Sue Whitmore ruled Palm Beach society, the pecking order was clear. There was the Old Guard, the patricians who came from distinguished families of several generations of prominence, who threw lavish private parties, and who confused snobbery with genteelness. They had rank and breeding. By definition, they were on the A-list. No arriviste intruded. Life was good. As the *New York Herald* observed in 1902, "Not to go to Palm Beach is a serious thing from a social point of view. If you cannot go there, you should at all events say that you are going, and then retire from society for a time."

Nearly all WASPs, these children of tycoons now might invite some Catholics and perhaps a Jewish couple to their soirées. But the line is drawn at the Everglades and Bath & Tennis Clubs, where Jews cannot be members.

Jews maintain their own equally picky club, the Palm Beach Country Club at 760 North Ocean Boulevard, where the initiation fee is $150,000 and annual dues are $14,000. Its 350 members include A. Alfred Taubman, chairman of Sotheby's Holdings, the auction house; Abraham D. Gosman, founder of health-care companies, including CareMatrix; Nelson Peltz, who does leveraged buyouts; and Max M. Fisher, a top contributor to the Republican party and former vice chairman of Sotheby's.

Fisher's daughter Mary captured the attention of the nation when she appeared at the 1992 Republican National Convention to reveal that she had contracted HIV from her then-husband. George Bush, Gerald Ford, and Henry Kissinger all showed up to say wonderful things about Max Fisher at his ninetieth birthday party. But rich and powerful as they are, members of the Palm Beach Country Club are not part of the nobility, who measure their own importance by their ancestry. The aristocrats are still in charge, the upper crust intact, the future of WASPdom secure.

Growing up, I knew nothing about society. My father was a microbiologist at Columbia University's College of Physicians and Surgeons, my mother a concert pianist and composer who played at Carnegie Hall, my stepfather a physicist at the Massachusetts Institute of Technology. Our dinner conversations in the Boston suburb of Belmont revolved around the arts and science, not wealth or lineage. My parents valued only accomplishment. Yet like most people, I wondered how the other half lived.

My aunt, who lived in Scarsdale, was married to the country's largest importer and distributor of artificial flowers. At their dinners, the chitchat had to do with their live-in servants, their trips to Paris, and the weddings they would eventually throw for their daughters at the Pierre and the Plaza. I tried to imagine what their lives must be like.

Palm Beach would give me the chance to find out—on a much grander scale. Writing books allows me to explore different, secret, powerful worlds. I can live the lifestyle of others without actually becoming a part of it, ask questions I otherwise couldn't ask, and learn—as in a cultural anthropological study—about people engaged in pursuits totally different from mine.

Palm Beach fit all my criteria. In its own way, the town is as secret as the CIA, FBI, or Secret Service. Unless you know the combination, you don't get in. The residents are not only among the country's richest, they are among the nation's most powerful. And there is no question that the culture of Palm Beach is different. As F. Scott Fitzgerald wrote about the very rich, "They are different from you and me."

By the age of fifty-five, I had come to appreciate wealth. As Woody Allen said, "Money is better than poverty, if only for financial reasons." I was ready to have fun.

To introduce me, Kay Rybovich threw a series of lunches and dinners with such central players as George C. Slaton, chairman of Palm Beach National Bank & Trust, and Dr. Reginald J. Stambaugh, president of the Historical Society of Palm Beach. Kay is one of the women Kirby escorts to balls. I met her through David Miller, the art appraiser, who had been introduced to me by Cynthia Stone Ray, Rose Kennedy's former secretary.

At Kay's get-togethers at the Sailfish Club, anecdotes about relatives were halted with the question "And where were they from? And where were their parents from?"

"Germany in the 1880s."

"I respect that. Go on."

"My parents came from Sweden and Denmark, and nobody paid them anything, and they learned the language," Rybovich said. Referring to Hispanics, she said, "Why don't they learn the language? All I hear is Spanish, Spanish."

As the wine flowed, one of the diners said to Pam, whose mother, Edith Johnson, is a member of the Daughters of the American Revolution: "You know who runs the newspapers, don't you?"

"No."

"You know who runs the newspapers, come on. The Jews."

Wyckoff Myers wore a rosette in his lapel, a gold pin with a red cross "for British blood," he said, identifying him to the cognoscenti as a member of the Society of Colonial Wars. Their heritage predates the Sons of the American Revolution. "The Warriors celebrate with an annual black-tie ball at the Everglades that costs about seventy-five dollars a ticket, marvelous dance band, unlimited booze," Myers said. "Women in gowns, men in medals. They get to wear all their service decorations."

John Kluge may have boundless wealth—made by creating the Metromedia empire of radio, television, and cellular phones—but his name barely comes up in Palm Beach dinner-party conversation. His lineage is suspect, his money too new. Unless someone is idle, he is undeserving—a reversal of the more typical attitude toward slackers and welfare mothers. As if to prove the point that the working class is unworthy, Kluge's reputation in Palm Beach became momentarily tarnished when his then-wife, Patricia, had to resign as chairwoman of a Palm Beach charity ball. She had signed up Prince Charles and Princess Diana as the star attraction, but then the *London Star* revealed that Pat Kluge had starred in soft-core porno movies, stripped in London nightclubs, and engaged in lesbian and group sex during an earlier marriage. Ticky-tacky, as Palm Beachers would say. In 1990 the couple divorced. Patricia got a mansion in Virginia and the interest on $1 billion—about a million dollars a week.

Emulating their employers, even the help turn up their noses at such parvenus. Because he doesn't have enough servants, Torrie, the former Post footman, said of Kluge, "What kind of lifestyle does he have? I call him poor people with money. They don't have a clue about the life that should go with it."

For all its wealth, Palm Beach is relatively safe, with a crime rate a fifth that of West Palm Beach. As soon as outsiders cross the bridges into Palm Beach, they notice a Palm Beach Police Department patrol car angled strategically at key intersections. To those who don't live here, the officers seem to be staring directly at them. In fact, the police constantly run license plate numbers and follow interlopers to see if they have a burned-out license-tag light, bald tires, or windows tinted in violation of law. Even making a turn without signaling is an excuse to pull over the car. Regularly, the police find marijuana or cocaine.

If a crime is committed, the police throw up roadblocks at the bridges and check anyone leaving the island. A police boat patrols the shores twenty-four hours a day, and all-terrain vehicles scope out the beaches. If the CIA had such good security, it would have less espionage. Celebrities like Rod Stewart and Jimmy Buffett move to Palm Beach in part because the environment is safe for children. Many professional people bringing up families live on the north end of the island. Palm Beach women think nothing of strolling to nightspots at midnight wearing $500,000 strands of pearls and $1 million diamond earrings—unheard-of in Beverly Hills. Many residents don't lock their multimillion-dollar homes or their $300,000 cars.

The safety, the money, the sunsets, the lushness, the balmy weather, the unblemished streets, the lack of purpose all combine to create a feeling of floating. Instead of discussing the latest horror in Washington, Palm Beachers chat about the weather forecast. Sheltered on what Cleveland Amory called "an island of privilege, in many ways the most remarkable one left in this country," they tend to be trusting, open, almost childlike. When choosing jurors, prosecutors in the Palm Beach County State Attorney's Office told me they try to avoid Palm Beachers: They are too cut off from reality. Only the daily paper and television offer reminders that most human beings do not own matching Rolls-Royces.

For all the fussing about the erosion of standards, even Kay Rybovich and her friends concede that Palm Beach still has its moments. "There's a lot of money around," Rybovich said, even though, because of changing tastes, homes that once had thirty servants now have but fifteen, including gardeners, butlers, valets, chefs, personal maids, housekeepers, and chauffeurs.

"I've been on several charity committees. So many of our wonderful events are on the same night. I go out almost every night during the season," Rybovich said. "You can't go to everything. It gets hectic for all of us."

6. NOT OUR CLASS, DEAR

Kirby Kooluris, dressed in a blue blazer and tie, showed up forty-five minutes late for Brownie McLean's birthday party, called for 7:00 P.M. on July 13. George Heaton, a Minnesota developer, and his striking girlfriend, Denise McCann, were throwing the party for Brownie at the Brazilian Court Hotel at 301 Australian Avenue.

The hotel is said to be laid out with plenty of exits so Palm Beach men can visit their mistresses without being spotted by room clerks. A favorite of Gary Cooper, Errol Flynn, Howard Hughes, and Cary Grant, it is where David Kennedy, one of Bobby's sons, died of a drug overdose at twenty-eight.

Originally from Virginia, Brownie McLean was orphaned at the age of twelve when her parents—who traced their lineage to the first English settlers in Virginia—were killed in an auto accident. At eighteen she attended acting school in Manhattan. She became a cigarette girl at the Versailles nightclub. Later, Conover and Society Models Agency signed her as a model. She appeared in magazine ads as the Lucky Strike girl and the Jantzen bathing-suit model.

In 1946 Brownie married millionaire George Schrafft, and they moved to Palm Beach. They divorced a year later. In 1952 she married John R. "Jock" McLean, whose family once owned the *Washington Post*. She refused the Hope diamond as a wedding gift from him. Brownie knew nothing of the horrible deaths allegedly suffered by the diamond's previous owners, but she told me she was "spooked" by the way the blue diamond turned red as she approached it at Harry Winston's.

Instead of accepting the gem, she selected a thirty-eight-carat diamond. Ten years later, a jewel thief stole it when Brownie left it in her hotel room in Freeport. The thief was caught and confessed that a higher-up had paid him to steal the diamond from Brownie and kill her if necessary.

The McLeans lived in El Salano, one of Palm Beach's premier mansions at 720 South Ocean Boulevard. The 9,500-square-foot home has five servants' rooms, nine baths, a ballroom, and two pools. Brownie became a creature of the Palm Beach social scene.

When Jock died in 1975, Brownie rented the home to Larry Flynt, publisher of *Hustler,* who scandalized Palm Beach by using the place for sexually explicit shots for his magazine. Later Brownie leased the home to John Lennon and Yoko Ono. They eventually bought the residence in February 1980, ten months before the former Beatle was murdered. Kirby's friend Ben Johnson was the broker.

Now Brownie rents a condominium apartment in West Palm Beach, overlooking the Intracoastal Waterway. If she has come a long way since turning down the Hope diamond, she still reigns as Palm Beach's most beloved doyenne. The story on her is she will never say anything bad about anyone. If she really doesn't like someone, she says simply, "I don't know her."

Brownie organizes five-star trips to places like Morocco and Brazil, getting free accommodations and flights in return. She owns rental properties in West Palm Beach and an inn in West Virginia. Each November, she throws the Crystal Ball in New York to raise money for the Global Future Foundation. When I asked her what the foundation does, Brownie said it gives grants to the University of Houston's graduate programs in space exploration and the environment.

"Where is the foundation based?"

"Well, the foundation is in Houston, Texas," she said.

"Who runs it?"

"It's through the university, I presume," Brownie said. "I don't know. My interest is to create money for students. Not everybody wants to become a space student. But that's neither here nor there. You don't have to worry about that. It's just what I'm working on right now."

As it turned out, the foundation's address—number 115 at 277 Poinciana Way in Palm Beach—is the same as Brownie's Palm Beach address, a box at RSVP Pack and Ship, which ships packages and maintains mailboxes for customers. Eventually, Brownie told me she runs the foundation in return for a small fee—about $3,400 a year. In Palm Beach tradition, the foundation takes in $68,000 a year and gives about $5,000—7 percent of the proceeds—to the university. Almost all the rest goes toward expenses of putting on the balls. It's the parties—not necessarily the charitable results—that count.

"She likes to give parties, and people seem to have a ball, and frankly, last year, I had a ball too," said Dr. Larry Bell, who is responsible for the space program at the university.

No one at the party at the Brazilian Court knew about that—or cared. Nor did Brownie's guests know how old their hostess was. She still looked sexy, with an alluring figure and gigantic blue eyes, her cocktail chatter lively. Bill Allston sang "Happy Birthday," while Bobby Swiadon played the piano. And while the hors d'oeuvres at my first Palm Beach party were sparse, the drinks were plentiful.

"I don't like to have much food at cocktail parties," explained Brownie, who had invited me to the party after I called her about setting up an interview.

At Brownie's party, I spotted Kirby Kooluris chatting with Toni Hollis, one of the most successful real-estate agents on the island. When she was twenty-two, Hollis was a ballroom-dance instructor who gave lessons to other teachers. She met and married Earl Hollis, who owns a real-estate firm in Palm Beach. Under his tutelage, she became a real-estate agent. Now divorced, she works for Sotheby's International Realty.

Hollis often invites Kirby to private parties at Club Colette, a dinner club that counts as members some of the richest people in town. "By the end of the night, everyone wants to invite Kirby to their next party because he's so fun," Hollis told me when I went over to her. "I really love him. If you want to smoke grass, he'll smoke grass. If you want to tell jokes, he'll tell jokes. If you want to go dancing, he'll go dancing. Whatever you want to do, he'll do it. I wish I had six of him to put at a dinner party and spread around the table."

But Kooluris said he has to get himself "up" before going to a party.

"I came late for Brownie's party because I get these shy attacks," he said. Asked if he knew anything about Brownie's foundation, he said, "I'm on the committee for her ball, but I don't know anything about the foundation."

Hollis thinks nothing of spending $2,000 for dinner with a single client at Café L'Europe, an elegant continental restaurant with Rolls-Royces and Ferraris always parked around it. The owners of the restaurant, Norbert and Lidia Goldner, pamper their own friends with special dinners featuring truffles with every course (including the ice cream) and $2,500 trays of fresh white truffles.

Hollis openly discussed with me her breast implants and facial surgery, which make her look forty. In Palm Beach, augmented breasts are chic, plastic surgery openly discussed. And the hair—long, blown-out straight blond hair—is a near-necessity, part of the look. If nature hasn't given it, the real thing in the form of human hair extensions can be bought and woven in to your own to produce big, heavy hair.

"I had a boob job," Hollis told me. "I had it twenty years ago. Today, I wouldn't do it."

Every season, Hollis remarked, Palm Beach is the target of a new scam—a phony viscount selling shares in nonexistent hydroponic palm trees, dance instructors signing up ninety-year-old widows for a lifetime of dance lessons, or a faux baron who worms his way into the social scene by pretending he is about to build a mansion. The latest pretender is Stephen Howard Fagan, a part-time teacher at Harvard Law School's legal clinic who vanished with his two young daughters in October 1979 during a bitter divorce. Telling his children their mother had died in a car accident, Fagan assumed the name and Social Security number of a six-year-old Massachusetts boy who had died. The man surfaced in Palm Beach, where he bought a $1.6 million oceanfront mansion with his fourth wife, Harriet, who is wealthy. Barbara Kurth, the daughters' mother, remarried and ended up living in Charlottesville, Virginia.

Claiming he was a former CIA officer with a doctorate in psychology from Harvard, Fagan joined the Mar-a-Lago Club and became a member of the Palm Beach Opera's board of governors. On a Web site he reported that he was working on two books—one on nirvana, the other on family dynamics.

Calling himself Dr. William Martin, Fagan immediately won over his neighbors on South Ocean Boulevard by repainting his house, five blocks north of Mar-a-Lago. The house was an "awful hot-pink color," Mary Montgomery, a top social lion, said. "He also replaced the ghastly wood trim with stone. Everyone in the neighborhood was thankful someone with good taste had taken it over."

People "adored" him, said Montgomery, whose husband, Robert M. Montgomery, is one of nine lawyers who won a $13 billion judgment for the state of Florida against the tobacco industry. "Only a very few people who live in Palm Beach are actually born here, so in a sense everyone is a stranger," Mary Montgomery said after learning that police from Framingham, Massachusetts, had arrested Fagan on April 16, 1998, for allegedly abducting his daughters, now twenty-one and twenty-three. Fagan said he was trying to protect his daughters, to whom he was clearly devoted.

Fagan ultimately pleaded guilty to kidnapping his daughters and, as part of a plea agreement, received five years of probation and a $100,000 fine. He could have gotten twenty years.

If Fagan was successful at concealing his past, he was not as successful at penetrating Palm Beach society. For all his bogus CIA connections and his Bentley and red Ferrari, Fagan, living just five blocks to the south of Barton Gubelmann, never made it into the most prestigious clubs—the Everglades and Bath & Tennis.

Yet there are many aspiring Fagans, either living in Palm Beach or trying to. One morning, Hollis told me, a man called her and expressed interest in an $8 million house she had listed.

"When are you coming down?" she asked.

He said he didn't know. A few hours later, when Hollis called him back, a woman answered.

"When is Wayne coming?" Hollis asked her.

"Coming where?"

"To Palm Beach."

"He's fixing the radiator."

"Oh, he's not coming to Palm Beach? He was interested in the house I have."

"What house?"

"Well, I have a house here for seven or eight million."

"Are you crazy?" the woman said, and hung up.

Toni laughed as she repeated the story. Her laugh is like a ringing shout, raucous, unaffected.

Hollis recalled an open house she held at a $5.6 million oceanfront estate. Two men came by in a Cadillac, saying they were art dealers, in competition with Sotheby's.

"They loved the house," Hollis said. Instead of making an offer, they kept asking to see it again. Finally, with the owner's permission, Hollis gave them the key to the empty house. "I called them one day because they had made no offer. They said they were waiting for an art deal to be consummated." Hollis told them the owner wanted the key back. After three days, they returned it.

"Then I went to a big birthday party given by a wealthy friend of mine in Wyoming," she said. "He was having his art appraised. At dinner, I was seated next to the fellow appraising his art." Hollis told the appraiser she was from Palm Beach.

"You guys have your problems with the art scams," the appraiser said.

"What do you mean? I haven't heard about it."

"They get a real-estate agent with a very expensive-looking home," the appraiser said. "Then they wear her out. They get her to give them the key and hang this fake art on the walls. They call up their would-be clients and say they have this art. They show them the fakes hanging on the walls, and because the paintings are in an expensive home in Palm Beach, the clients think the paintings are authentic."

To Hollis, the scam sounded painfully familiar. "Palm Beach attracts this," she said.

For all her openness and colorful stories, Hollis did what I came to call the "Palm Beach Shuffle." She would pour out what she knew, then later become petrified that something she said would be taken the wrong way and impair her standing. Then she would not return calls, or she would claim when I reached her that she had to leave for an appointment. But every few months she would open up again, usually when I ran into her at a party. Then she would be as engaging and charming as ever, giving me tips on the island's secrets.

Kirby looked around the room. He knew almost every one of Brownie's two hundred guests. There was Conrad Hilton, Jr., grandson of the founder of Hilton Hotels, appearing to be enjoying himself. Hilton told me he was "on leave" from the company.

"Where else can you play golf or tennis with Al Haig?" Hilton said of Palm Beach. "Where else do you buy a house from a prince from some country that no longer exists? It's a small community. The intimacy can work both ways. It can mean you know your local barber and postal worker, but it can work in the opposite way. If you cough the wrong way, everybody hears about it."

Kooluris did not know Jane Grace, a newcomer who was wearing a striking teal-blue dress. Grace described herself as a fashion designer with her own company. Her dresses cost $3,000 to $10,000 each.

"I would never think of wearing a dress a second time to any function," she airily told me. "I have eight rooms for dresses, a cedar room for shoes and handbags. They have conveyor-belt racks."

Grace—not to be confused with a member of the Old Guard with the same name and homes in Palm Beach and Newport—said she was looking for a Palm Beach home of about forty thousand square feet. "The house with a ballroom I'm looking at is gorgeous," she said. "It could accommodate more than a thousand people."

When I asked how she could afford a forty-thousand-square-foot house, she became indignant. "Why are you asking such questions?" she asked. "Now you're getting into personal business. One thing has nothing to do with the other."

Seeking to document that she had a business, I pressed her for brochures or press stories about her company. Grace said they were in her "warehouse," and she would send them. She never did.

In another corner, I spotted Cheryl Marshman and her husband, Homer H. Marshman, Jr., whose father once owned the Cleveland Browns football team. Junior members of the Old Guard, the Marshmans belong to the Everglades and Bath & Tennis, as well as the Beach Club and Club Colette. He is a forty-four-year-old real-estate lawyer. Cheryl, in her thirties, is the prototypical trophy wife, with long blond hair, a brilliant smile, and a spectacular figure.

Homer grew up in Palm Beach. That usually means attending Palm Beach Day School, then being shipped off to prep school and visiting Palm Beach on holidays.

"When I was a small child, if I was out of the neighborhood on my bike, a policeman would stop me and say, 'What are you doing?'" Marshman told me. He would reply he didn't know. The policeman would say, "Since you don't know, why don't you get in my car, and I'll drive you home?"

Marshman remembers seeing John F. Kennedy walking on the beach or having breakfast at Green's Pharmacy, where tycoons, socialites, and chauffeurs sit side by side at the counter.

"I remember Nate Appleman, who made his money in oil and was a good friend of my father's," Marshman said. "At a party, my father mentioned to Appleman that I was struggling in Spanish in high school. He said the Spanish teacher was from Cuba and loved Cuban cigars. On Christmas morning, a chauffeur in a Rolls-Royce drove up to our house and presented me with a box of huge Monte Cristo cigars from Cuba. I gave my Spanish teacher half of them, keeping the rest for myself. He actually cried. He was so happy."

Marshman told his teacher, "I can get those anytime. Just let me know. I'm so happy someone will really enjoy them."

"I did very well in Spanish that year," Marshman recalled.

Before they married, Cheryl Marshman was a commercial artist in the advertising department of the *Palm Beach Post*, the daily that serves Palm Beach County. Then she became an Eastern Airlines flight attendant. She and Homer were flying to Cleveland, where Homer still has season tickets to the Browns games, when Homer persuaded a flight attendant to let him use the plane's public-address system.

"To the lady in four-B, if you're not doing anything for the rest of your life, will you marry me?" he said, for all the passengers to hear. "If the answer is yes, ring the call button."

"It took me a minute," Cheryl told me. "I was in shock. I thought he was a long way from committing. Finally, I pushed the button, and everyone cheered. The lady in the seat behind me leaned forward and said, 'If you hadn't pushed that button, I'd have pushed it for you.'"

Homer has served as junior chair of the American Cancer Society Ball and was on the committee that planned the Young Friends of the Red Cross New Year's Eve bash at the Breakers Hotel, which aims to attract younger patrons. "In Palm Beach, you can be 'young' pretty much forever," he said. "Unless you're over seventy-five or eighty, you can probably qualify."

One Halloween, Marshman told me, he went to a party at the Beach Club. Having recently accepted a few Jewish members, the Beach Club is less snooty than the Everglades and Bath & Tennis clubs. It includes members who cannot get into the other two clubs or don't want to be members of those clubs. The Beach Club and Bath & Tennis are the only clubs actually on the ocean.

At the Halloween party, Marshman "had had too much to drink," he said. "It was dark, and toward the end of the night, I saw what I thought was a woman dressed as a witch. I felt like dancing, and I said, 'Hey, do you want to dance?' I thought she said yes. Halfway through the dance, she said, 'Wouldn't you like to dance with one of these real pretty girls?' I looked at her and said, 'You look all right to me.' Everyone at my table was laughing, and I didn't know why. I came back to my table, and they said, 'We didn't realize you had switched.' I went right up to him and said, 'Are you a guy?' He said, 'Yes.'"

His dance partner was cross-dresser Neil Cargile.

As he edged toward the bar, Kirby Kooluris observed that it was a typical off-season party. While people like Barton Gubelmann were in Newport and others of the rich set were at homes in Southampton, Nantucket, Aspen, Paris, Monte Carlo, or London, other key members of the Old Guard were in attendance. Kirby pointed them out to me—Diana Busch Magnus Blabon Holt, heir to the $2 billion Anheuser-Busch fortune, for example, and Chesbrough "Chessy" Patcevitch. A regal woman with white hair and an aquiline nose, Patcevitch was wearing a striking black, gray, and white skirt. She is said to be heir to the Chesebrough-Ponds' fortune.

The legends are to be taken with a grain of salt. The late Sue Whitmore, a grand dame of Palm Beach society who chaired the International Red Cross Ball for twenty-two years, was said to be the Listerine heiress. In fact, her grandfather, Dr. Joseph Lawrence, invented Listerine in 1879. He named it after Lord

Lister, a surgeon who pioneered the use of antiseptics during surgery. In 1981 the rights were sold to the company that became Warner-Lambert. But Homer Marshman, Jr., her real-estate lawyer, said he was not aware of any royalties she earned from the invention.

Like women's breasts, everything in Palm Beach is enhanced. Thus, Patcevitch's first name may be Chesbrough, but her father was a lawyer and her grandfather was in the lumber business. Her late husband, Pat, was president of Condé Nast. "The source of my money is not Chesebrough-Ponds," she flatly told me.

In the old days, Patcevitch said, "It was all very simple, and there were no problems. Now all kinds of people have moved in," she said, referring to Jews. In fact, Jews now comprise more than half of the island's population. They generally live in a ghetto of condominiums on the southern end, which other Palm Beachers dismiss as being not part of Palm Beach. The ghetto includes South Palm Beach, a town of 1,300 half a mile long by less than a quarter of a mile wide. They call both areas the Gaza Strip.

"Are you Jewish?" Patcevitch asked me.

"Yes," I said.

"I don't know them when I see them," she said. "When I left Ohio when I was twenty-two, my mother said, 'We don't have any Jews in Ohio because they're too smart. They want to go east.' We didn't know there were any. It turns out there were a few, but it didn't bother anybody in any way." At the one-thousand-member Everglades Club, where she belongs, "they are perfectly willing to have nice ones around," she said. "The trouble is they work so hard, they lose their pleasantness. The Jews don't behave themselves. That's why they don't get in."

Meaning?

"They're rude and they're pushy," she said. "I don't know. Whatever they are."

Going back to my research on Joseph P. Kennedy, I knew that anti-Semitism and Palm Beach were synonymous. Kennedy railed about "kikes" and actually admired Adolf Hitler. Yet Palm Beach society more or less accepted Joe and Rose—Catholics though they were. Still, I had no idea how inextricably anti-Semitism was tied to the culture of the town. Nor did I want to know. The last time I had had personal experience with vocalized anti-Semitism was in junior high school, when a few bullies would confront me and call me a kike. Having lived in Boston and New York and now in a suburb of Washington, I was used to being with more or less sophisticated people. Now, I realized, I had a special challenge.

As a former *Wall Street Journal* and *Washington Post* reporter who has written books on everything from Adnan Khashoggi to the FBI, I was used to suppressing my own opinions in the name of journalistic objectivity. As it happens, while I am Jewish and proud of my heritage, I am not religious. Nor, over the years, have I had much use for Israel's intransigent policies toward its Arab neighbors and intolerance of the religious practices of non-Orthodox Jews. On the other hand, I look Jewish and have a Jewish-sounding last name. Both because I wanted to maintain my objectivity and because I would obtain little cooperation if I appeared to have a religious agenda, I tried to lean over backwards not to probe too deeply into anti-Semitism on the island. But I soon learned that I would be missing a big chunk of the story if I skirted a subject that made me uncomfortable professionally and that was personally painful.

As my research unwound and gathered momentum like a Slinky toy, certain members of Palm Beach society went out of their way to help—throwing dinner parties and letting me use their names as an introduction to others. As delicately as she could, one such member of the Old Guard told me that anti-Semitism is "a big factor here." She introduced me to another member of the Old Guard who grew up in Palm Beach and is a member of the Everglades and Bath & Tennis clubs. The town is "the last bastion of prejudice," she told me. "At our clubs, the unwritten rule [no Jews allowed] is very strong. It makes people uncomfortable. It hurts people. It's a great tragedy. There's a lot to learn from people who have come a long way."

The woman said she feels torn talking about it and asked not to be quoted by name. At one point, she recommended seeing *Gentleman's Agreement*, a movie portraying anti-Semitism in the late 1940s. Based on a best-seller by Laura Z. Hobson, the 1947 movie presents Gregory Peck as a magazine writer who masquerades as a Jew to report firsthand on discrimination in high society.

It tells the story, she said, if in exaggerated form. "The club situation is very hard to express, because it's as if I'm speaking against my own. The Everglades and Bath & Tennis are like my family . . . I don't like to sound disloyal, because I have never had bad treatment there. It's rather a sanctuary because the clubs don't change. It's wonderful to go back there and see that lovely setting that is the same. The food tastes the same, everything is done in the same way."

Because Jews are not admitted, she said, "we have seen circumstances where people have married, and the woman or man can stay a member of the club, but the new spouse cannot. It's split couples in two. The people in the club don't approve of the marriage. It may not be because of race or religion. I've seen people badly hurt by that. It's mean-spirited."

When anti-Semitic remarks are made, "you get caught off-guard in a conversation," she said. "If you're sensitive, it bothers you. It bothers me. I don't think I'm better than others, and I know a lot of people who think they are. I happen to like those people, but I don't like that about them." Prejudice is "the basis of all the problems we have all over the world," she added. "It's just encapsulated here. We're a little better dressed. We're not throwing rocks at each other and blowing each other up with car bombs."

The prejudice goes with the territory. From its founding, Palm Beach was a retreat for the well-born, and class distinctions remain in place. An occasional exception might be made for a celebrity. Because I appear regularly on television and have written twelve books, the Old Guard mistook me for one.

"Orderly" is the way the member of the Old Guard characterized Palm Beach. "I visited Aspen, and I swear to God I didn't know what to do because there was no structure," she told me. "I would go to a dinner and talk with a pleasant partner. The next night, I would go to another dinner party and that man was the waiter. A maid called me by my first name. I almost fell over dead. I couldn't adjust to that. I've always been properly addressed. That wouldn't happen here."

Yet she said, "This is not the real world. Any town that has a newspaper like the Shiny Sheet, you know you're not in the real world. People come here and act out the fantasy of what they think they should be doing."

For all the advantages of growing up in Palm Beach, "not one" of the boys she grew up with has been successful, she said. "They were not prepared for business life. They were beautifully dressed, beautifully educated. And out on the street, they couldn't make a nickel. When their looks were no longer quite as effective as they were when they were young men, what were they left with? The bottle, bad relationships. They were bad husbands and bad fathers. They didn't get out of their setting to look for answers. They had so much of a head start compared with someone who did not have all those advantages. How could they not have done more with what they had? They just sat around and said, 'I'm well-born, I'm good-looking, amuse me, life.' And life didn't do that for them. Now they're wondering what happened. Their Jaguar hit a palm tree, and they're getting arrested for drunk driving."

One might think that being rich would give residents the confidence to be more accepting of people. It doesn't work that way, she said. Palm Beachers have an array of terms for putting people down. "One term is NOCD, meaning 'Not Our Class, Dear.'" Or 'Basically Boca,' referring to Boca Raton, twenty minutes south on Interstate Route 95. "These are cutting, slamming remarks. I think they're horrible. Or, if a man is countrified, we say, 'The Full Cleveland.' Brown shoes, brown suit, brown shirt, brown socks, brown tie. When visitors come to Palm Beach and aren't part of the moneyed set that we're in, we don't want to hurt their feelings, so we take them to [a restaurant instead of a club].

They're all dressed up; sometimes their wives are wearing a corsage. They're not necessarily overdressed. There's a certain look. The dress here is specific."

She looked at my attire—blue blazer, white short-sleeve sport shirt, gray slacks, and plain black loafers. As I was leaving Barton Gubelmann's home, her assistant, Arthur "Skip" Kelter, had suggested the uniform.

"What you have on is perfect," the member of the Old Guard declared. "You're dressed for the entire season."

7. WILD BILL

After Brownie's party, Kirby Kooluris and I ordered the prime rib at Ta-boó. Bill, Kirby's boyfriend, was in jail because of the bike incident.

This was not Bill's first visit to jail, and Kooluris told me he had already been having problems with Bill. "When he's had a few drinks, he'll call everyone as late as he wants. It could be two A.M., and he wakes up someone's grandmother. It makes me furious. There are the telephone bills. He ignores me. It's like talking to a plaster wall. I'm used to people acknowledging that they got your point."

Lately Bill has been losing his glasses. Kirby buys him new ones. "Glasses aren't cheap," he said. "There won't be a real effort to find them. It's like having an eight-year-old child. Bill opens a beer in the car when I'm driving. If I lose my license, how the hell am I going to survive? I live on the north end of Palm Beach. My whole life would come to a screeching halt. He can't understand what the big deal is."

Once when Bill was drinking beer in his car, Kooluris drove directly to Palm Beach Police headquarters, a low-slung pink building on South County Road across from the town hall.

"I pulled two cops out politely. This is how confident I am about them. They know me. I said, 'Will you please explain to my pal the consequences of having an open beer can in the car, for me and for him?' They told him the law." The two could both get tickets, and Kirby's insurance could go up. Nevertheless, back in the car on the way home, Bill opened up another beer. "It's a passive defiance," Kirby explained. "He's not trying to punch you. He's like a teenager you'd like to strangle."

One day Bill threatened to kill himself. "Are you trying to hurt yourself? If you're going to do that, I will have no part of it," Kirby said, as he walked away.

When Kooluris runs out of solutions, "I say a little prayer for him," he said. Bill's response to that notion: "Was the line busy?"

But I was learning that Kirby sees another side to everything. In Bill's case, he was more than willing to forgive. Bill is "very bright," he said. According to Kirby, "You'd be giggling to yourself if you had a conversation with him. I know you would like him. He's not a show-off. He's very shy. He has a nice speaking voice, good manners, courteous. I think he has such little self-esteem that you almost have to speak for him at important occasions. If we were together and you asked him to order food, he would freeze because he would be thinking about not ordering something more expensive than what you ordered. He doesn't have the savvy to pick something maybe in the midprice range. Instead of responding, he will just sit there."

Kooluris finds that refreshing. "Bill is one of the most honest human beings I have ever known," he said. "He is so outraged when accused of something he didn't do that he acts like a wild animal. The demands from him are so modest. He worked all day painting the beach cabana. 'Can I have two dollars?' he asked. He fixed the light switch in the garden. He saved me seventy-five dollars, and he wanted a little knapsack."

A few days earlier, Kirby had visited Bill in the Palm Beach county jail. "You have to be there at one-fifteen," Kirby said. "Then you wait half an hour, then you go to another room to wait another half hour so you can have your one-hour visit.

They're supposed to give them a new razor every day. They didn't. I raised hell. I called the county and said they're promoting AIDS. They become nonpersons—one pair of socks, one T-shirt, one pair of undershorts. They don't get another one unless someone sends it. They wash them in the shower."

Aren't you worried about AIDS? I asked him.

"Every time he goes to jail, he has an AIDS test," Kirby said. "So he's okay."

After his visit to Bill, Kirby said Bill called him collect from prison. Then Kirby got a collect call from some "pretty gruff Negroid voices. They asked if I could make a three-way call for them. I had heard of scams. I said my phone isn't equipped for that. I said to Bill, 'What are you doing giving out this number?' He was bothered by the idea that someone had rifled through his possessions in his bunk."

Kirby continued, "He's mad as hell at me because I won't bail him out. I don't want him to get in any more trouble before he gets some sort of counseling. He feels that I don't trust him. Bill is threatening to stop the friendship if I don't bail him out."

Why would you want to put up with such a friend? I asked.

"There is security in landing someone like Bill," Kooluris said. "There is security in feeling that if he does these sorts of things with me, he really likes me and trusts me. Around here I'm with so many people who are important but have no heart. They are just amusing themselves by having an entourage. I don't know if I'm going to break up with him. Certainly it's not a relationship when a guy doesn't know what he wants and is hanging around waiting for someone to give him a home. Imagine what it does to me that I can't give Bill a stinky little apartment in Lake Worth for three hundred dollars a month. Then he could get a job. Instead of having him live with me, I would like Bill to make dates with me, so I wouldn't have the responsibility. I can't do that. I went to the bank today to get a loan. We have the same problems everyone else does. You just add a few zeroes."

Kirby mused about the incongruity of his life. "I have this albatross, the house I live for," he said. "I have to sleep in people's moldy basements because I want to keep this house. Bill said, 'Do you want to have a twenty-four-carat bedpan?' He's right. What am I doing all this for? For what?"

As for Bill, Kirby said, someday he'll have to face the music. "The most honest thing I said to him was, 'I'm not a believer in tough love. But what I've done so far hasn't worked. I care enough about you to try to see if that works.' But it might consume our friendship."

8.   A NIGHT AT TA-BOÓ

In mid-July, a blond, skimpily dressed woman with 44D bouncing breasts came prancing past the long bar and stopped at Franklyn de Marco, Jr. The Palm Beach strut. All the women have it, but it's especially noticeable at Ta-boó, where it's de rigueur for the women to straighten up and stick out their chests—enhanced or not—when walking past the bar. Everyone is looking, they're on display, and they know how to work it. They wear short skirts and simple, expensive clothing—no prints. Low-cut dresses are everywhere, the boobs bought and paid for.

As co-owner of the restaurant, De Marco has a front-row seat. Back in the sixties, De Marco was in the Navy working for the National Security Agency when he realized the Washington real-estate market was booming. In 1966 he started his own mortgage-brokerage company and began buying properties. He built up a portfolio of office buildings, apartments, and hotels. When every-one was buying at high prices in the 1980s, he sold and moved to Palm Beach.

People move to Palm Beach for the same reason students want to go to Harvard or Yale and reporters want to work for the *New*

York Times or the *Washington Post*. "This is a unique product. No other place has the cachet. It's a phenomenon," said Sherman Adler, a regular at Ta-boó who formerly was executive assistant to John MacArthur, a penny-pinching insurance tycoon whose money funds the genius awards given by the John D. and Catherine T. MacArthur Foundation.

"Each city has its Asheville Tool and Die," Adler told me. "The owner gets older and decides to sell. He buys a home at the top of the hill. He buys a mink for his mother and a Jaguar for Mary Alice. Then he tires of that. He wants to prove to everybody he has made it, so he comes to Palm Beach. He wants to show his former girlfriend or grammar-school teacher or mother he is a success. He then launches into the social set."

If he succeeds in the competitive environment, he builds a bigger house. If not, he becomes discouraged and returns to Asheville. "Then a new wave comes in and redecorates the house and changes the shrubbery and goes through it all again," Adler said. "The houses just get bigger."

De Marco succeeded. A cross between Dustin Hoffman and Danny DeVito, De Marco has intelligent brown eyes and is balding, robust, quick on his feet. He is the consummate host. De Marco's pink stucco home with white trim in Palm Beach has marble floors, a four-car garage (he has a white Rolls-Royce Corniche convertible and a silver Wraith, not to mention a Mercedes convertible), and eleven bathrooms. The living room overlooks the pool, which overlooks his dock and Lake Worth. Across the street is the smaller house De Marco bought for his parents. An aspiring Adnan Khashoggi, De Marco keeps his refrigerator stocked with at least two pounds of beluga caviar, which he serves as others serve popcorn, only with Möet & Chandon Brut Imperial Cuvée champagne. He is building a fancier house.

From June to early July De Marco stays in Aspen at the Ritz-Carlton. Then, after a few weeks back in Palm Beach, he rents a condominium on a wharf in Nantucket for $500 a day, returning to Palm Beach in late September.

A few years back, De Marco showed his mother and father around Nantucket and introduced them to Nelson Doubleday. When De Marco asked his mother what she thought of the island, she said, "I've never seen so many rich people acting so poor." Walking on the historic cobblestones nearly wore out her shoes. "All this money," she said. "You'd think they'd pave these streets."

In 1988 De Marco began dating Nancy Sharigan, a dewy-eyed blonde. Back when she was twenty-one, Sharigan and her husband drove their black Mercury convertible to Palm Beach for their honeymoon and ate at Ta-boó. She was enchanted. The restaurant had been a local landmark since 1941 and a favorite of Frank Sinatra. Legend has it that Ted Stone, the original owner, dismissed suggestions of off-color names for his new restaurant by saying, "No, that's taboo."

With her husband, Sharigan owned four restaurants, in Annapolis, Philadelphia, and Delaware's Rehoboth Beach. Having separated from her husband and started going with De Marco, Sharigan was thinking about opening a restaurant in Palm Beach. Ta-boó had fallen on hard times and had just closed. De Marco arranged a meeting in the vacant restaurant with Sharigan and Burton Handelsman, who owns or manages more than half of the property on Worth Avenue. They struck a deal, and in October 1990 Sharigan and De Marco reopened Ta-boó.

Even though it's the only restaurant right on Worth Avenue, they call Ta-boó an American bistro, meaning its prices are not out of line: $9.50 for a bacon cheeseburger of ground filet and sirloin, served with hot potato chips; $12.50 for linguini with shrimp and wild mushrooms in Parmesan cream sauce; $5.25 for a bowl of black-bean chili. While the fourteen-ounce New York sirloin strip steak is not prime, at $22.95, it's dry aged and superior to the more expensive prime strip at the Breakers' Flagler Steak House. Nancy trains the servers not to turn up their noses when a customer orders a cheeseburger or a pizza at night instead of shrimp cocktail and rack of lamb.

In 1995 Franklyn and Nancy ended their personal relationship. Three years later, she married Robert Simmons, an aggressive former broadcasting executive with a ninety-three-foot yacht, but Nancy and Franklyn continued their business partnership. The two men avoid being in the restaurant at the same time and refer to each other as "What's His Name."

Sharigan tends to the restaurant operations and menus, while De Marco schmoozes the customers and handles relations with the town. At night, always on the lookout for attractive women, he sits at the end of the bar in his uniform—navy sport jacket, white shirt, khaki pants, and red power tie, or one of the dozens of silk Nicole Miller novelty ties he owns. He can't believe he makes so much having so much fun.

By the time I met with Franklyn, I had already interviewed Kevin O'Dea at length. Kevin told me that if I hit it off with him, I would learn more about Palm Beach society than Kevin knew. Franklyn moves in those circles. I invited Franklyn to lunch at his restaurant and picked up the tab.

From some of his questions, I could tell that he wondered if I had an agenda—perhaps to expose anti-Semitism in Palm Beach. When I told him that my second book was on Adnan Khashoggi, and that I had obtained Khashoggi's cooperation and attended his parties in his villa and on his 282-foot yacht in Marbella, Spain, Franklyn relaxed. If I got along with an emissary of the king of Saudi Arabia, I was clearly not a threat. In fact, going back to Fred C. Ferris, a Lebanese-American friend in high school, I have always had Arab friends. Beyond that, if I could move in the league of the ultrarich, that meant I was almost one of them.

The latter point is critical. If I appeared to be intimidated by wealth, my tongue hanging out, I would lose the access I had gained. Like dogs that sense when strangers are afraid of them, the rich can tell if people are envious of their wealth. Occasionally, I let slip that when vacationing in Palm Beach with Pam, I stayed at The Four Seasons, where in high season the daily rate is more than a round-trip ticket to California. To the people I interviewed, that meant that I was comfortable in their milieu. Rich as they are, I took them to the best French restaurants.

Franklyn later joked that, given my investigative background, he thought it wiser to cooperate rather than not to. In any case, soon I was on Franklyn's party list, not only in Palm Beach but in Nantucket and Aspen.

Drinking champagne at lunch, Franklyn told me, "People love being friends with the owner of a restaurant." The phenomenon clearly amazed him. In fact, I learned, everyone wants to know Franklyn. Hoping for special treatment or just a word of recognition, people tell Kevin O'Dea, "I'm a friend of Franklyn." At the restaurant, employees call them FF's. Not realizing that Franklyn hates to be called Frank, customers say, "I'm a friend of Frank," or "I'm a friend of Mr. Marco." When they get the name right, they say, "I'm a good friend of Mr. De Marco." At which point O'Dea has had to say, "Okay, he's standing right next to you." O'Dea still calls De Marco "Mr. D," while Nancy is "Miss S."

Having majored in philosophy at the University of Virginia, De Marco is given to citing Plato. It sounds good, but he could be making it up as he goes along, à la Palm Beach. Never married, De Marco said of women, "They can't be very bright. Someone looking for a husband has obviously never had one. Why would you want one? Why do they want to get married? It boggles the mind. Marriage is an unnatural act." He is equally perplexed by men. "Most men confuse love with laundry," he said. "They want somebody to do their underwear. If anything, marriage limits how much sex you get."

Franklyn has flattery down to a science. In front of his date, foxy blond Betsy Fry, a successful real-estate broker from Easton, Maryland, he said to another woman, "You're the second-most beautiful woman in the room." He enjoys taunting a husband while flattering a wife: "What's a gorgeous woman like you doing with this guy?" The most interesting response Franklyn has gotten to that line came from a drop-dead beauty who replied, "He's the only one who asked." She was married to a troll. "Men are afraid of really beautiful women," Franklyn explained.

If he knows a woman, Franklyn freely offers his fashion tips: "I don't like women in pants. Look at her dress. Get something like that. Or a pleated skirt. I love pleated skirts."

Whoever his girlfriend is, his taste prevails. He tells her very specifically how to dress, buying her whatever she needs to complete the picture he has in mind. His dominance extends to other women as well. Periodically he gets into a jag about panty hose, his bête noire.

Most Palm Beach women go bare-legged. They may be wearing Armani or Chanel, but they won't wear stockings with it. Some won't wear panty hose even with formal ball gowns. As a side benefit, less clothing in the subtropical heat reveals more of the body. When Franklyn spots a woman who has veered from the norm, he says, "You're not wearing panty hose, are you? How can you stand it? Go bare-legged." When the woman protests, he tells her, "Then get some thigh-highs." He asserts his concern that panty hose may cause female troubles. The Florida heat and humidity bring on vaginitis and worse, and thigh-highs are a preventive measure.

None of this is any of his business, of course, but he's so outrageous that women listen just out of curiosity and disbelief. How far will he go with this obsession? He'll talk about it every time he sees the woman and observes she is still wearing hose. Then the woman begins to suspect his real motive has something to do with a fantasy: that he just wants to feel "access" to every woman in the room.

De Marco insists on a strict dress code at the restaurant—one that applies only to men. They may not wear T-shirts. "It can get arbitrary," O'Dea said. "A guy can come in with an old polo shirt. He has a collar. Maybe he has on shorts and is off the boat. We would seat him at the bar. Then a guy comes in with a two-hundred-dollar Armani silk T-shirt and two-hundred-dollar pants. So I say, 'No T-shirts allowed.'" One customer was offended. "I know you look fine, but Mr. D. is extremely rigid on that," O'Dea told him.

Sharigan and De Marco worked night and day to make the five-thousand-square-foot restaurant a success. As part of an antiquing process, she applied glaze to the woodwork herself. After two years, De Marco and Sharigan hired managers to help run the restaurant. As night manager and maître d', Kevin O'Dea oversees the restaurant's operations during its busiest times. He may say the restaurant works as a team: Richard Whitaker is day manager and Marc Mariacher is general manager, but Kevin is the front man. Along with Franklyn, Kevin gives the restaurant its personality.

Kevin is earnest, engaging. "A touch of class," the female customers at Ta-boó say of him. He has a narrow face, framed by combed-back hair, and a perpetual healthy-glow tan. Besides swimming, flirting is O'Dea's game: "I'm a terrible flirt, I admit it." He has mastered the maître d' skill of the deft touch in the middle of the back, no more than a tap; he knows exactly how much pressure is acceptable so the woman is scarcely aware she's being touched. He looks patrons full in the face, with a direct gaze. He is lean like a long-distance runner with none of the haggardness, and given what he's been through, that alone is a feat.

O'Dea studied art at the University of Denver, then migrated to a commune in Oregon and on to an apartment at the corner of Haight and Ashbury streets in San Francisco. Hosting at his apartment whoever was the "guru of the month," he dabbled in psychic healing and developed a following. Then he began scheduling rock groups, finally moving to New York, where he started a construction business. Finally, he began helping his brother restore brownstones.

When O'Dea was eleven, his father died of leukemia. It was a long, painful illness. O'Dea created in himself emotional walls to block the hurt. "It set up a pattern," he said. "I never let myself grieve. I would block the emotions with interior mechanisms and alcohol. Eventually, I became a full-fledged alcoholic. It got bad in New York. I was thirty-two. I had a codependent woman I lived with there for eight years to take care of me. I more than experimented—LSD, everything, and lots of it. In New York it was work hard and play hard, go to the local bar. Eventually, I was waking up drinking. I drank twenty-four hours a day.

Without a drink, I couldn't go more than four hours without shaking."

O'Dea's family had moved to Palm Beach. They rescued him, taking him to a treatment center in Wellington, Florida. Afterward, he took a job working for Palm Beach County. In 1991 he became a host at Ta-boó, where his sister Kim was general manager. Soon Sharigan and De Marco made him night manager, knowing that he was in Alcoholics Anonymous.

Palm Beach has more than its share of alcoholics. O'Dea makes himself available for those who are serious about quitting drinking. For nine months he chaired AA meetings on Saturdays at Dempsey's. The bar and restaurant at 50 Cocoanut Row is a favorite of Barton Gubelmann and Frank Shields, Brooke's father, who owns Johnnie Brown's, a gift shop on Worth Avenue.

"Going public is one of the hardest things," O'Dea told me, just twenty minutes after we first met. "I live my life based on prayer and meditation." A former Catholic, he says he has "no particular religion. I pray to the deity. People babble about spirituality. This is personal. It's inside stuff. I found redemption here. Of all places, working in a bar in Palm Beach."

Ta-boó is "an upscale Cheers," said the well-endowed woman who had stopped to chat with De Marco at the bar. "You know everyone. You feel comfortable. Franklyn wants me to be safe. You don't get that anywhere else but here."

With her on this steamy night was an equally scantily clad friend from Venezuela. Acting like a dog in heat, De Marco escorted them to a table and sat down with them. The two women were wearing white, tissue-thin dresses that only came to their tailbones. "When they walked in, every man, woman, and child looked up," O'Dea said. A lady asked him, "Who is that at that table? Is that guy Mafia?"

"No, that's Franklyn de Marco. That's my boss."

Then she wanted to know about the two women. "Are they twins?" she asked.

A woman with her chimed in, "No, they both went to the same doctor."

As De Marco ordered beluga caviar, O'Dea sat down with him and the two knockout women. When the blonde announced she was going to the bathroom, O'Dea said, "I'm going to escort you."

"Oh, you're going to help me," she said.

"Yeah, I'll hold your hand."

"Oh, no more than that," she said.

When she came back from the bathroom, the woman was stroking O'Dea's leg as she talked. He kissed her neck. Having topped off their meal with black Sambuca, the women left at eleven-thirty. De Marco put the bill on his account.

O'Dea introduced me to Wrendia Devary, a pretty brunette who had just opened Basilicus Sanus, a club in West Palm Beach. Devary grew up in Palm Beach and had come to Ta-boó as a child. "In those days, there was no problem about children going into bars," she told me as she drank her Chardonnay. "They kept stuffed animals in the back. They were famous for banana daiquiris. They had bananas hanging behind the bar. For the kids, they made a virgin banana daiquiri. Before I was seven, I sat at the bar."

As a teenager, Devary said, "We went to dance parties, pool parties, house parties, tennis parties, golf parties, polo parties, charity parties. Every day there was an excuse for a party. Someone would come into town. The parents would go to dinner. The kids would take over the pool house and party. Or we would go down to the beach and have our own parties."

Now that she's older, nothing has changed. "We pick our disease every year. We go to a certain number of these functions," Devary said. "You see what everybody is doing, what people are wearing, how they try to outdo each other in terms of the decorations, entertainment, and the themes. Before the season, you get a flock of invitations. There is tremendous pressure to make the right decisions. Which event are you going to attend, who might be offended if you don't, which ticket to buy?"

Devary has been all over the world. "I have never seen a place where on Monday night you can walk into a restaurant or bar and see people in tuxedos. Sometimes there are two or three balls in one night, and you go from one to the other. The season is getting longer and longer because there are only so many days when events can be booked. In the winter, the listings in the Shiny Sheet are pages and pages. It's overwhelming."

Devary said some charities, like the Lord's Place, a homeless shelter for families, actually have asked for checks in return for staying home. "They say, 'Save the money you would spend doing your hair and nails and buying gowns and send it to us.'" The invitations suggest wearing "your favorite nightshirt" instead of formal attire on the "night of your choice." According to Devary, "the nonparties are not too popular." In fact, the Lord's Place has discontinued its nonevent. Devary added, "Going to the balls is Palm Beachers' contribution to society."

Most people in Palm Beach aren't making money. "They've already made it. They're spending money. They inherited money. If you walked into a bar or club, and you asked what someone did, they would know right away you are an outsider. Because people here don't do anything. They come here to spend the money they've already made or inherited. It's actually a comedown for anybody to work."

Residents appreciate characters as comic relief from ennui. Wrendia used to scope out women's rooms for Neil Cargile. "The men wouldn't let him in the men's room," she said. "I would let him in the women's room, after checking. I would say, 'Okay, go in,' and I'd stand guard outside the door."

She told me, "If you eat caviar every day, sooner or later you get bored with it. I don't know anybody who wants to dress in black tie seven nights a week." Palm Beach is a "community that caters to the virtues and the vices of the residents. That's why I like it."

About midnight, Prince Simon Mihailesco Nasturel Monyo of Rumania walked in. He was sporting a blond beard, sneakers, navy polo shirt, gray slacks, and glasses rimmed with twenty-four-carat gold. Alain Cohen, a highly regarded buyer and seller of antiques, introduced him to me. A descendant of Rumanian kings, Monyo is a Palm Beach artist whose sculptures of little boys and girls sell for $2,000 to $100,000. He lives in the Colony Hotel and can easily be spotted around town because he always drives a yellow-and-black Rolls-Royce. Altogether, he owns five, plus a BMW motorcycle, all specially painted yellow and black.

"I made my first million in Toronto," Monyo told me through a thick accent. "In 1966 I bought my first Rolls, a Corniche. I'm still driving it today. Then I bought more." He has a 1973 Corniche, a 1973 Corniche convertible, a 1975 Corniche, a 1979 Silver Shadow, and a 1935 Rolls with a sunroof. The 1935 model is worth over half a million, Monyo said. The cars' colors were an idea he got from his father, who owned a 1945 yellow-and-black Rolls.

Monyo came to town in 1980, attracted by the spectacular women. "I don't pick up girls," he explained. "They pick me up."

Way back, before he became a successful sculptor, Monyo was a lifeguard in Fort Lauderdale making $40 a week. Now he says he has to make at least $1 million a year just to break even.

Back then, "I had no Rolls-Royce," he said. "I had a bicycle. Those were the happiest moments of my life. Beautiful ladies talked to me. I discovered I was good-looking. We made love in the sand. Nobody knew who I was. Now I don't know if they want my money, my cars, or my sculpture."

A busboy came up to O'Dea. He said he had just cleared table 24 near the front of the restaurant, and the woman sitting there had left a pair of Victoria's Secret red thong underpants on the banquette. The busboy put the underwear in a doggie bag and handed it to O'Dea. O'Dea put it in a takeout bag. Now the woman was sitting on a bar stool talking to Franklyn, her legs spread wide. Her boyfriend stood nearby, apparently unconcerned.

"I have known her seven years. She is gorgeous," O'Dea said later. "I knew her underpants were sitting there in a doggie bag on a counter. I was almost going to say, 'Here's your to-go bag.' But I wasn't sure what was up. Jokingly, I said to one of the servers, 'Go drop something in the middle of the floor so I can pick it up.'"

O'Dea walked by her again. "One of her legs was up on a bar stool," he said. "She was face-to-face with Franklyn. She was teasing him. He was trying to pay attention to what she was saying." O'Dea told De Marco what was in the doggie bag. De Marco said he already knew. She had told him, "I left them for you."

Just then, one of O'Dea's regular customers came up to him.

"See that little lady over there?" he asked O'Dea, motioning to a bejeweled woman near the rear of the restaurant. "She's wrapping up half a hamburger to take home. I happen to know she is one of the largest stockholders in General Motors."

Sitting at a side table in front of the bar, a salesman with Braman Motorcars, the local Rolls-Royce and Porsche dealer, said one of his customers bought a Porsche for his mistress. "The girl called and said, 'I'm coming in to pick up the car,'" he recounted. "She had no idea what she was picking up or whether it cost ten thousand or two hundred thousand. I gave her the car, along with a check issued by us using his funds for ten thousand dollars for the insurance and upkeep."

Later that night, a crew filming a movie with Amanda Donohoe of *L.A. Law* came in. They ordered Louis XIII brandy, which sells for $120 an ounce. The starlet began dancing with the crew. When O'Dea came out of the kitchen, Donohoe had crawled over the bar and was riding a bartender, her legs wrapped around him. When she had finished her fun, O'Dea pulled her over.

"You had to pick the only gay bartender we have here," he said.

A hostess motioned to O'Dea and pointed to an older, regal-looking woman.

"This lady said she's a good piano player. Can she play?"

"Sure," O'Dea said.

Next time O'Dea walked out of the kitchen, the woman was playing the piano and singing a beautiful aria.

9. THE LEOPARD LOUNGE

In late July a man wearing khaki Bermuda shorts with a white short-sleeved dress shirt and a striped tie was lounging at the small but perfectly appointed pool of the trendy Chesterfield Hotel at 363 Cocoanut Row—the spelling of *coconut* the locals prefer. The sumptuously decorated sixty-four-room hotel, three blocks from the ocean and two blocks from Worth Avenue, was a favorite of Bill Blass, Catherine Deneuve, and Margaret Thatcher. The man in the shorts got up to drink from the water fountain.

"It's warm," he said to no one in particular.

"They have ice water near the bowl of oranges," I told him.

The man introduced himself as Dr. Robert D. Williams, a psychiatrist practicing in Palm Beach, Miami, and San Francisco. Williams had an improbable blond mane, oily and sun-bleached, which he had inherited from a Southern grandfather. Conceding that his attire was a little odd, he said it was a style he was introducing to the town. As he spoke, he absently stroked his nostrils or his temple with an index finger. He had puffiness under the eyes and needed a shave. But Dr. Williams seemed to know almost everyone in Palm Beach and had a good grasp of what makes it tick. I wanted to spend more time with him. Strangely, Williams did not have a business card. He wrote his phone number on a scrap of paper.

Later, the doctor met with me at the Leopard Lounge, the hotel's classy bar. From the tablecloths to the trim on the drapery, from the rug to the wallpaper, from the chairs' velvet trim to the flowerpots, from the waiters' vests to the leopard orchids on every table, everything in the Leopard Lounge has spots—the inspiration of Beatrice Tollman, who owns the hotel with her husband, Stanley. By day the lounge is a meeting place for business types; by night it is a place for dancing, Leopard Lounge lizards, and hopeful well-endowed women. Overhead is a freehand ceiling painting of red satyrs and their angelic, nude big-bosomed consorts, against a white background. Looking carefully, one can also see that two of the male figures have erect penises.

Lino Mario Prebianca painted the ceiling in return for food and drink. Prebianca was an Italian architect who had thirty people working for him in Toronto. After he and his wife divorced, he sold the firm and moved to Palm Beach, where he claimed to be a member of society. He began drinking and died on Easter 1996.

"He told me he had one-point-two million in the bank twelve years ago," said Louis Fourie, a friend of his. "He had nothing when he died. He just partied." When he painted the ceiling of the Leopard Lounge, "he used the piano as scaffolding, moving it around at three A.M. In return, they let him run a tab."

The Leopard Lounge has replaced the Colony Hotel as the place to go for continued revelry after social events. Rod Stewart and George Hamilton are regulars, Whitney Houston drops in, and singers like the McGuire Sisters sometimes entertain free while staying at the hotel.

One night around midnight, Mimi Humphrey, a flight attendant on private jets rented by rock groups, was at the bar. Looking like she just climbed out of a *Playboy* spread, she sat on my lap. "I'm pretty much one of the best," she said. "Travolta loves me, and Stallone loves me. I could go on and on and on. I'm the flight attendant of the stars."

Michelle Gagnon, one of the Leopard Lounge's two knockout blond cocktail waitresses, told me Neil Cargile used to come in and make out with his girlfriend, Dorothy Koss, in the courtyard. Gagnon is what men call a tall drink of water. She has an instantaneous, dazzling smile, very white teeth. Her platinum hair and bright lipstick give her a somewhat theatrical look. Her lipstick matches the red carnation on her black blouse; her black skirt is very short—any shorter and the world is her gynecologist—and she wears black hose and very high heels on which she manages to expertly negotiate the room. The other cocktail waitress, twenty-five-year-old Liana Verkaden, has a model's build and naturally blond hair down to her behind. She spends her life warding off advances.

"The guys are nuts for her," Gagnon said of her colleague.

"We had one woman walk into the lobby one evening," Gagnon said. "I guess she had had too much to drink and went into her room. She thought she was on the way to the bathroom, but she walked out of her room and got locked out."

Stark naked, the woman went out the fire escape, came out the front, and came in the front lobby. "The night manager told her there was no skinny-dipping," Gagnon said.

At about seven one evening, Gunilla von Post, who wrote a book about her love affair with John F. Kennedy, was having a drink at the lounge when a woman noticed her chihuahua peeking out of her handbag. (Dogs are not allowed in Palm Beach eating establishments.) A dead ringer for the Taco Bell dog, it was named Lara, from the character in *Doctor Zhivago*. "The woman bought Von Post Cristal champagne, at two hundred ten dollars a bottle," Gagnon said. "Then she wanted to buy the dog and offered her ten thousand dollars."

When Von Post refused to sell, the woman went off in a huff.

"You don't sell your babies," Von Post told me later.

Gagnon said tipping is not necessarily related to a customer's wealth. "Some who have lots of money are pretty chintzy. Others tip well and expect you to bend over backwards every time you see them."

One customer orders a drink and gives Gagnon $100. "I pay for the drink, and the rest is mine. Nice," she said. Another customer, a seventy-year-old-woman, comes in with a black man who plays steel drums on Wednesdays from five to nine. "The man is about forty," Gagnon said. "She drinks martinis, and he drinks whatever she sends him. Neither one of them talks. Every time I go over there to talk to her, she orders another drink."

A Saudi billionaire picked up another cocktail waitress at the Leopard Lounge, and she never returned. "He flew her to L.A., and they went shopping on Rodeo Drive," Gagnon said. "He bought her a wardrobe of Versace. She was just a kid. I used to get those offers when I was younger. You have your ideals, and you're not for sale. Now I look back and think, 'What if I had?'"

Now that Neil Cargile is gone, Lord Beaver is the chief topic of conversation. I first heard about his lordship from Allin Mansfield, a salesman with Braman Motorcars. Mansfield was having breakfast at Green's Pharmacy with a blond female companion. He told me I should hang out at Dempsey's bar, and the first time I went there, I wound up sitting next to Beaver himself. As Beaver explained it, he got his moniker after an incident at Dempsey's.

"A young lady was loaded, and she pulled me into the ladies' room, and we got it on," Beaver said. "She was tall, thin, and beautiful. Blonde, from Massachusetts. She turned to me and kissed me. I took her panty hose off. I put her in the sink. I was doing a service," he said.

Beaver thought the door was locked. The seventeen-year-old daughter of George Dempsey walked in. "She raised hell," Beaver said. Dempsey banned Lord Beaver from the restaurant. But Beaver claimed Dempsey asked for the woman's name and number.

I asked Dempsey about Beaver's claim.

"I did not ask for her number," Dempsey said. "I knew who she was. She was a hostess at Charlie's Crab. All I know is my daughter came out shrieking."

Even after the ban, Lord Beaver occasionally showed up at Dempsey's. "I never would embarrass him by saying, 'Get out,'" Dempsey said.

For his part, Beaver asked that I not use his real name. "I'm trying to get over this," he said.

When Lord Beaver is introduced, Palm Beach socialites accept his title as authentic. "When I first heard of Lord Beaver, I honestly for months thought he was a British lord," Denise McCann, a witty friend of Brownie McLean, told me. "When I actually spoke to him for the first time at the Chesterfield, I curtsied and said, 'Glad to meet you, Lord Beaver.' He was very gracious. I learned later about the story."

Lord Beaver is "involved in more scandals than anybody," Gagnon said. "He comes in often and does the old wallet shuffle when he goes to pay the bill. The wallet comes out, and there's never any money in there, basically. It goes back in, he comes back out with the wallet to see if something has miraculously appeared and there is money in there. He barely has money for cabfare. At one point he got a hundred dollars' credit from the food-and-beverage manager. Somebody else finally paid that off."

Usually, Lord Beaver comes in with a "sponsor," meaning someone who will pay his way. "That's what he tells us right away. He has a lot of good friends who don't mind. Some get fed up with the sponsor situation, or they'll run the other way when he comes in."

Beaver used to drive a car that was "held together by duct tape," Gagnon continued. "Somebody finally got rid of it for him. Now his sponsors take him around."

When people come to the Leopard Lounge, they think everyone is a billionaire. Lord Beaver plays the part, dressing elegantly with an ascot.

"One night he was sitting at the bar," Gagnon said. "Some women from Boca were there. These women saw him dressed to the nines with the ascot. He has that deep voice and can bullshit anybody. They thought they had found somebody. Little did they know he was hoping they'd pick up his bill."

"It's a town of eccentrics," Gillian Haughtaling, who formerly owned Jeannie's on Worth Avenue, told me at the bar at the

Leopard Lounge. "The more eccentric you are here, the more you're accepted."

As he ordered bottled water at a side table near the bar at the Leopard Lounge, Dr. Williams reflected on what he had seen in his psychiatric practice. He said Palm Beach is an "exterior society. People are very concerned about their position" and about how much money they have in relation to others. "They want to be players," he said. "There is a lot of insecurity and anxiety. The women are very threatened by younger women. Men like younger women. When they marry a second wife, they marry down in age. They also compare with people with more money. Seating at balls is important. If someone is not seated at the right place, it's a reflection of her standing. You don't want to be in Siberia."

Getting into the right clubs is critically important, too. "At a dinner party, I sat next to one man who had been rejected by a club. He had plenty of money. The wife was too outspoken. You have to take the temperature of the water before you jump in. The aggressiveness might mask shyness." People who want to be accepted by clubs try to "feel above other people, so they won't feel vulnerable." The younger set gets help. "You have Special K, a mixture of drugs. They have dance drugs that include anesthetics," he said.

Williams turned out to have no telephone listing in Palm Beach. Nor did he seem to own a car. After our initial meeting, he asked for a lift to the Palm Beach post office, where he keeps a box. Asked for his address, he wrote down 95 North County Road. It proved to be the address of the main Palm Beach post office. Asked later where he lives and has his office, he mentioned an address on Orange Grove Road. At another point, he said he lived on Chilian Avenue. Yet he constantly referred to patients he was treating in Palm Beach.

In his practice, Williams said, "I use a more spiritual approach to create an inner strengthening. I'm interested in the joy of life, sharing that with people, because there is so much grimness with people working too long hours. Even in the midst of the most difficult moment, you can meditate with peace. These feeling traces are stored."

For a subsequent breakfast meeting at the Chesterfield, Williams arrived fifteen minutes late. This time he was clean-shaven. He wore a white Valentino shirt, a purple Gucci tie, and turquoise shorts. Apologizing for being late, Williams said he had been treating a patient for "stress." He said he had spent the weekend with another woman who suffered from low self-esteem. The comment brought to mind the psychiatrist in Carl Reiner and Mel Brooks's "2,000-Year-Old Man" routine. Dr. Haldanish, the Yiddish-accented psychiatrist, explains that he got a woman to stop tearing paper by slapping her hand when she did it.

"Wouldn't that require you to be with her at all times?" the interviewer, Carl Reiner, asks.

"I lived with her for a while," the psychiatrist, Mel Brooks, explains.

Dr. Williams said he considered his extended house calls to be separate from his patient work. "I believe in integrating the art of nature, therefore walking meditation, calming the mind, creating an inner richness," he said. If the words didn't scan, at least health insurance wasn't paying for it.

"I do a lot of it for fun," he said. "God has been good to me, and it's my way of giving back."

I asked Williams if he really is a psychiatrist. He said he obtained his medical degree from the University of Oklahoma. "I'm an adult and child psychiatrist," he said. "I did two fellowships." He would not say when he graduated. "I don't want to go into that. That will date me." Eventually, he said he graduated in 1970—a fact the university confirmed.

"Are you licensed in Florida, or were you licensed?"

Finally, Dr. Williams admitted he was no longer a practicing doctor. "I don't keep a traditional practice," he said. "I do these other things. I'm not licensed."

New York State confirmed that Williams was licensed in 1974. His license lapsed in 1993. Eventually, his story began to make more sense. Williams had visited Palm Beach since the early 1980s. In 1987 his girlfriend died, which was a pivotal point in his life. In 1992 he decided to start over in Palm Beach.

Williams had said earlier, "A lot of people come here because something else fell apart. They try to reinvent themselves here." That appeared to be what Williams himself was doing. Apparently, he had enough money to live on. In a phone conversation overheard in the lobby of the hotel, he seemed to be transferring $4,000 into one account, $20,000 to another.

Ann Zweig, the caterer, said she understood he was on the boards of several hospitals.

"How do you know?" I asked.

"He told me," she said.

A few weeks after meeting with Williams, I was at Ta-boó when a well-toned woman of about fifty struck up a conversation. "I know who you are," she said when I introduced myself. "You're staying at the Chesterfield Hotel."

Jane Hardy described herself as a former ballerina and a friend of Dr. Williams. She lives on Chilian Avenue, around the corner from the Chesterfield. "My girlfriend called me and said, 'This is a guy who needs to hang his hat,'" Hardy said. "He left today. He stayed about two months. He is a mystery man. He had a relationship with a rich woman. All I know is her name, Barbara, and that she died. He's been suffering ever since."

Then, as if reporting on the weather, Hardy said, "I stabbed my husband ten years ago."

"Really?" I said.

Yes, she said, laughing. "It felt like a knife going into butter." He didn't die, she reassured me.

"Were you prosecuted?" I asked

"I served thirty days in jail, had two months of house arrest, and paid a ten-thousand-dollar fine."

Hardy wanted to show me a manuscript she had written about her crime. I told her I had another appointment shortly but could take a brief look. We walked to her apartment, and I began quickly flipping through the pages. I'm a speed reader and can rapidly pick up the information I need to know. But she became enraged.

"I've poured my soul into this, and you're glancing at it like it's garbage," she said, looking as if she were about to attack me.

I left as quickly as I could.

10. BORN RICH

Friends of Sir Bobby Spencer, first cousin of Lady Diana, threw a birthday luncheon for him in mid-July at the Sailfish Club. Ann Anderson, a friend of Barton Gubelmann and the longest-standing member of the Everglades Club, took me. As the debonair Spencer blew out candles over a chocolate cake Anderson brought, the conversation turned to the Kennedys, who have withdrawn their full-time presence on the island but continue to visit during the season.

Until they bought a home on the island, Rose and Joe stayed at the Royal Poinciana Hotel. Then, on June 30, 1933, Joe bought a five-bedroom, red-tiled home at 1095 North Ocean Boulevard for $100,000, along with adjacent property for which he paid $15,000. Built in 1925 and added onto in 1933, the Palm Beach home had a heated pool. Addison Mizner, the island's mansion architect, had designed the Spanish-style home for Rodman Wanamaker II, founder of Wanamaker Department Stores.

When John F. Kennedy was president, the home was known as the Winter White House. Joe and Rose Kennedy never maintained the place. It was not air-conditioned and was furnished in what looked like Salvation Army castoffs. The concrete steps were crumbling, the paint and stucco fading and peeling, tiles were missing from the roof, and wood was rotting in the gate. At night, huge water bugs took over.

Most of the children never liked the Palm Beach home, and although he was acquitted, the rape trial of William Kennedy Smith soured the family on the island. In May 1995 they sold the home for $4.9 million to New York merchant banker John Castle and his wife. The Castles spent more than $6 million to renovate it. In the garage they found that bees had deposited three hundred pounds of honey in the rafters.

Almost everyone on the island has a story about one Kennedy or another not paying his bill. Bill Suther, who owned Bill's Tuxedo Rentals, recalled that Jack and Bobby Kennedy returned their tuxedos in a taxi, neglecting to pay the driver. Robert W. Neumann, a former FBI agent who is Palm Beach County sheriff, joked that after the Kennedys left, crime went down 30 percent.

At the Sailfish Club luncheon, Charles Van Rensselaer, the last writer of the Cholly Knickerbocker society column at the New York *World Telegram & Sun*, said he used to walk along the beach with Rose Kennedy. Until Tom Cunneen's recent death, Van Rensselaer lived with Cuneen, a partner in writing a gossip column for James Sheeran's *Palm Beach Society* magazine. "He was my boyfriend," he had told me earlier. "People liked us because we were monogamous. After he died, several people mentioned that."

Rose Kennedy got so tired of Van Rensselaer saying he wished he were Catholic that she said, "Why don't you become one? If you do it before Christmas, I'll be your godmother.'" So he converted in 1975.

Another luncheon guest, Beatrice de Holguin Fairbanks Cayzer, said she attended Marymount Convent in Tarrytown, New York, with Rosemary Kennedy, the supposedly retarded daughter of Joseph P. Kennedy. "She was not retarded at all," Cayzer said, confirming what the surgeon who performed a lobotomy on Rosemary was quoted as saying in my book *The*

Sins of the Father. The surgeon, Dr. James W. Watts, said Rosemary was mentally ill. Getting one of his sons into the White House might be difficult if it came out that his sister was mentally ill. So Joe made up the story that Rosemary was mentally retarded, a less embarrassing category. On that prevarication, the family built an entire industry—however laudable—of helping the retarded.

At the Sailfish Club, Anderson pointed out members of the prominent Fanjul family dining a table away. The Fanjuls—Alfonso "Alfie," Jose "Pepe," Alexander, and Andres—publish the Christmas card listing members of Palm Beach's ruling class. Outside of Palm Beach, the Fanjuls are controversial. They are constantly being accused of causing environmental pollution in the Everglades through the operations of their Flo-Sun Inc., which accounts for 45 percent of American sugarcane production. A *Wall Street Journal* profile said Alfie and his family "aim to be to sugar what the Rockefellers once were to oil." They agreed that their stock-brokerage firm would stop doing business after the Securities and Exchange Commission accused it of contributing to county and state political candidates who could influence the award of municipal securities business. Alfie Fanjul, a big Democratic-party donor, happened to call President Clinton when he was trying to break up with Monica Lewinsky in the Oval Office. But here, where they live behind the walls of multimillion-dollar estates and drive Ferraris and Porsches, the Fanjuls are respected.

As Bobby Spencer fended off questions about Diana, the guests at the luncheon traded gossip. In Palm Beach, "please keep it quiet" is taken to mean: You can tell all your friends, but don't call Shannon Donnelly, the Shiny Sheet's savvy society columnist. There was a mix of favorite Palm Beach expressions: "My best friend I grew up with . . . I love, love, love . . . It's not important . . . She's a good seat . . . She has a dicey reputation . . . Frightfully . . . Substrata." The latter refers to people who reside just below the A-list.

Who is George Heaton, who gave the birthday party for Brownie McLean? someone at the table wanted to know.

"George Heaton is not social," said Anderson, whose father, John T. H. Mitchell, founded an advertising company. "He is just nice, decent people." Later, talking about a house, Anderson spoke in the local staccato: "He restored it completely. Art Deco. Nice boy."

If the Everglades Club is exclusive, Anderson asked rhetorically, what about the Palm Beach Country Club, where only a few Christians are members? "You can't get in the door at the Palm Beach Country Club," she said. "Why don't they admit that they don't want us? The Palm Beach Country Club is very snooty. Very snooty. They don't want any Christians. I've been there a couple of times as a guest," Anderson went on. "I went there because I knew the president. They have delicious food but not much liquor. Cocktails but hardly any alcohol at dinner."

Barton Gubelmann told me Anderson "knows Palm Beach as well as anybody." But I later learned that Ann's characterization of the Palm Beach Country Club—a common one of the Old Guard—was not quite accurate.

Anderson said the Bath & Tennis Club, which was started by Marjorie Merriweather Post for her guests, began allowing Jews as guests because the son-in-law of an officer is Jewish. "Silly, silly," she said. "You can only bring Jews a few times to Bath & Tennis. Isn't that funny? What else do you know?"

"Whether it's true or not, someone was just ousted from the Bath & Tennis for handing out her real-estate card," said Denise Lee, a descendant of Robert E. Lee. Lee picked up a British accent while attending school in England. "I go along with the club's rules on those kinds of things. I'm a member of B&T."

The talk at the Sailfish Club turned to Kirby Kooluris and his boyfriend, Bill.

"Kirby is adored by all," Lee said. Expressing a common view, she added, "I'd like to strangle Bill."

That evening, Denise Lee gave a party with her French friend Nicole Humphries to celebrate Bastille Day. Kirby Kooluris brought me. If anyone was aware of the irony of the privileged celebrating French Independence Day, no one mentioned it.

The party was held on the top floor of Lee's stark white condominium building at 400 South Ocean Boulevard. Designed by Edward Durrell Stone, the building overlooks the ocean. "The Hugh Bedford Vanderbilts live here, the second cousin of the king of Spain, Garrison duPont Lickle," Lee said.

I sat with Kirby and Judy Schrafft, widow of the late George Schrafft, whose family founded Schrafft Candies. George Schrafft had previously been married to Brownie McLean. "I was George's fourth wife," Schrafft told me. "There was Suzie, Brownie, then Liz. It took five years for her to get a divorce. She married Gordon MacRae, who sang in *Oklahoma!* As soon as they were divorced, we were married."

Schrafft is a rare commodity in Palm Beach, a "real person," according to Barton Gubelmann, someone who is "not phony." Stately and serene, Schrafft wears three necklaces with symbolic pendants: an ankh, "from Egypt," an eye, "for the Mediterranean," and a cross, "garage sale. I should say a house sale. I love those things," she said.

"I'm an oddball because I know a lot of different levels of Palm Beach society," Schrafft said. "I do diving trips, diet trips, rustic things, I have a funky house. I don't live luxuriously. I don't care about wonderful cars and jewels. I live to go to Third World countries and work on my environmental stuff." Her usual dive is between 80 and 90 feet but sometimes extends to 110 feet. Her new book, *Other Places*, recounts some of her adventures.

Schrafft lives just north of Wells Road, which bisects the island and is one of the markers real-estate agents use to denote home locations. The first area extends from the inlet at the north of the island to Wells Road. The second goes south to Worth Avenue. The third—called the Estate Section—extends to Sloan's Curve, south of Mar-a-Lago and the Bath & Tennis Club. The fourth section goes to Manalapan, a town of 333. Because Manalapan and South Palm Beach comprise such a small part of an island dominated by Palm Beach, the island generally is referred to as Palm Beach.

Schrafft said the color of her house offended some of her Palm Beach neighbors, who thought it was mustard or orange.

"My house is painted field daisy, not mustard or orange," she insisted. "I'm going to paint it the same color again. I got a letter when I moved in, on Howard Johnson's stationery, saying it's not an appropriate color for Palm Beach."

Judy said she wrote a letter of reply and stuffed a copy in every mailbox in her neighborhood. "I said it's not orange, it's not mustard. It's field daisy."

Just then, Brownie McLean showed up with Peter Rock, who often accompanies her to parties. Tall, with blond hair and a ready laugh, Rock is a walking telegraph office, transmitting the location of the latest party to everyone on his list.

"Brownie will kill me," Rock told me when he saw the tables laid out with plates and silverware. "She hates sit-down dinners."

"I've always been friends with Brownie," Schrafft said. "The fact she was once married to George has never affected our relationship. We call ourselves 'the Two Mrs. Schraffts.' She is fantastic. She never changes. Fun, always upbeat, beloved. Brownie hasn't blown her money like Gregg Dodge."

A Palm Beach legend, Dodge was married to Horace Dodge, Jr., an heir to the Dodge motorcar fortune. His father, Horace Dodge, Sr., worked in a blacksmith and machine shop owned by his father. One day in 1901 Henry Ford walked into the shop with plans for an engine. If they would build the engine for his self-propelled buggy, Ford proposed giving Horace senior and his brother John 10 percent of Ford Motor Company. The Dodges shook hands with Ford, and the American auto industry was born.

Gregg was a luscious showgirl and model who appeared on the cover of 150 magazines and was a Miss America contestant. She was briefly engaged to Joe DiMaggio. She and Horace spent millions of dollars a year, living among the Rockefellers, the Mellons, the Biddles, Wideners, Wanamakers, and Vanderbilts. The Dodge home was Playa Riente, Horace's mother's place at 901 North Ocean Boulevard. Gregg and Horace threw lavish parties at the home and on Horace's 325-foot yacht, the *Delphine*.

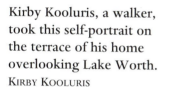

Kirby Kooluris, a walker, took this self-portrait on the terrace of his home overlooking Lake Worth. KIRBY KOOLURIS

Lorraine Hillman, at Ta-boó, said, "I can't find a guy in Palm Beach." MORT KAYE STUDIOS, PALM BEACH

Ingrid Tremain tried on $40 million in jewelry from Graff Jewelers of London at the Palm Beach International Art & Antique Fair. MORT KAYE STUDIOS, PALM BEACH

Franklyn de Marco Jr., left, co-owner of Ta-boó, and Kevin O'Dea, the night manager, have front row seats on Palm Beach debauchery. The women are, from left, Mia Morrison, de Marco's girlfriend, Betsy Fry, and the author's wife, Pamela. LUCIEN CAPEHART, PALM BEACH

Nancy Sharigan, co-owner of Ta-boó, oversees the restaurant's operations. —MORT KAYE STUDIOS, PALM BEACH

Barton Gubelmann, queen of Palm Beach society and honorary vice chairman of the International Red Cross Ball, chatted with the author and his wife, Pamela, at the ball. DAVIDOFF STUDIOS, PALM BEACH

Celine Dion, center, sang at the Mar-a-Lago Club during the season. With her were Donald Trump and his girlfriend, model Melania Knauss. COURTESY OF THE MAR-A-LAGO CLUB

Gianna Lahainer postponed her husband's funeral 40 days in part so she could enjoy the season. COURTESY OF GIANNA LAHAINER

Liana Verkaden, left, and Michelle Gagnon see the super-rich at play in the Leopard Lounge of the Chesterfield Hotel. MORT KAYE STUDIOS, PALM BEACH

After her divorce from Herbert Pulitzer Jr., Roxanne Pulitzer went with Count Jean de la Moussaye, known as "the count of no account." MORT KAYE STUDIOS, PALM BEACH

Palm Beach adopted architect Addison Mizner's Mediterranean style.
HISTORICAL SOCIETY OF PALM BEACH COUNTY

Marjorie Merriweather Post hosted square dancing parties at Mar-a-Lago.
HISTORICAL SOCIETY OF PALM BEACH COUNTY

When John F. Kennedy was president, the Kennedy home was called the Winter White House. DAVIDOFF STUDIOS, PALM BEACH

Mary Sanford was queen of Palm Beach society. Her husband, Laddie, kept his mistress in a home on the north end of the island. MORT KAYE STUDIOS, PALM BEACH

A member of the Everglades Club, Chesbrough (Chessy) Patcevitch said, "The Jews don't behave themselves. That's why they don't get in." John Bailey is her escort at the Coconuts. MORT KAYE STUDIOS, PALM BEACH

Prince Simon Mihailesco Nasturel Monyo of Romania parked one of his five Rolls-Royces on Worth Avenue. RONALD KESSLER

Royal palms line Royal Palm Way, where many of the town's fifty banks have their offices. PAMELA KESSLER

Island architect Addison Mizner designed the fountain north of the town hall. PAMELA KESSLER

Donald Trump's captain, Mike Donovan, took a mid-flight break from piloting Trump's Boeing 727-100. PAMELA KESSLER

The author and his wife, Pamela, flew with Donald Trump on his Boeing 727-100 from New York to Palm Beach and back. The cost of fuel was $40,000.

Marjorie Merriweather Post's Mar-a-Lago is home and club to Donald Trump.
COURTESY OF THE MAR-A-LAGO CLUB

Guests enter
Mar-a-Lago through
a reception hall that
opens onto the living
room. COURTESY OF
THE MAR-A-LAGO CLUB

Brunches are held
in Mar-a-Lago's
living room.
COURTESY OF THE
MAR-A-LAGO CLUB

Parties are held around the pool at Mar-a-Lago. Lake Worth is in the background. COURTESY OF THE MAR-A-LAGO CLUB

Donald Trump now uses Marjorie Merriweather Post's bedroom. COURTESY OF THE MAR-A-LAGO CLUB

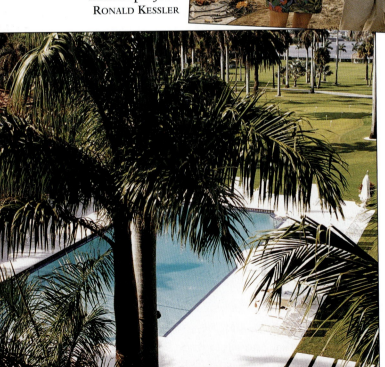

The author and his wife, Pamela, at right, sat in on Donald Trump's strategy meetings with lawyers, architects, and staff at Mar-a-Lago.
RONALD KESSLER

Donald Trump inspected his new Trump International Golf Course in West Palm Beach with the author's wife, Pamela, and Jim Fazio Sr., the architect of the $40 million project.
RONALD KESSLER

The pool can be seen from the upper cloister at Mar-a-Lago.
RONALD KESSLER

Angelia Savage manages Donald Trump's spa at Mar-a-Lago. A former Miss Florida, she was number three runner-up in the 1996 Miss USA contest. Ronald Kessler

Donald Trump held a party at Mar-a-Lago for contestants of the regional Hawaiian Tropic beauty pageant, held in Miami. Don Camp

The author and his wife, Pamela, chatted with Anthony P. Senecal, Donald Trump's butler, and Vilda B. de Porro after Donna Summer sang at Mar-a-Lago on New Year's Eve. Davidoff Studios, Palm Beach

Before performing at Mar-a-Lago, Jay Leno chatted with, from left, the author, Donald Trump, the author's wife, Pamela, Lorraine Hillman, and Lorraine's friend Sharon Dresser. DAVIDOFF STUDIOS, PALM BEACH

Mar-a-Lago sprawls over nearly 18 acres. SMITH AERIAL VISIONS

Manfredo Horowitz, right, represented Harry
Winston with overseas clients such as the
sultan of Brunei. At his birthday party are, from
left, real-estate agent Earl Hollis, his wife, Gloria,
and Manfredo's wife, Jasmine.
MORT KAYE STUDIOS, PALM BEACH

Homer H. Marshman Jr.
proposed to Cheryl over a
plane's public address
system, and she became a
trophy wife. MORT KAYE
STUDIOS, PALM BEACH

Lady Trisha Pelham,
whose family owns
Sherwood Forest, found
her autistic son, Dorian,
improved after being in an
experimental program
using the drug secretin.
KIRBY KOOLURIS

Kirby Kooluris, left, escorted Helen Boehm to the International Red Cross Ball. To the right are the author and his wife, Pamela, and Mayor Paul R. Ilyinsky and his wife, Angelica. DAVIDOFF STUDIOS, PALM BEACH

The Old Guard soured on Betty Scripps Harvey, who chaired the International Red Cross Ball for three years, because she donated $750,000 one year to make the ball a success. MORT KAYE STUDIOS, PALM BEACH

Jay Rossbach, left, chairman of the Palm Beach County chapter of the American Red Cross, and his wife, Linda, attended the International Red Cross Ball with Candy Van Alen, general chairman, and her brother, Wallace Alig. MORT KAYE STUDIOS, PALM BEACH

At age three, "I would go everywhere in limos with my nanny," said Heather Wyser-Pratte. She now goes with Allen F. Manning, a bastion of the Old Guard. LUCIEN CAPEHART, PALM BEACH

Brownie McLean rejected the Hope Diamond because it "spooked" her. LUCIEN CAPEHART, PALM BEACH

The $12.1 million estate of Abraham Gosman includes his 81,000-square foot home on the ocean. SMITH AERIAL VISIONS

Karen Lane, the town dockmaster, knows everything that goes on in town. At the end of the dock is the *Taipan*. RONALD KESSLER

Rod Stewart flew Liana Verkaden, a cocktail waitress at the Chesterfield Hotel's Leopard Lounge, to his concert. COURTESY OF LIANA VERKADEN

Danielle Brunet, whose stage name is Dania Deville, scandalized the Old Guard by stripping naked at the Poinciana Club. ©STEPHEN SOLOMON

Philip J. Romano with his wife, Lillie, bought a home in Palm Beach along with two Rolls-Royces after founding Fuddruckers and other national restaurant chains. MORT KAYE STUDIOS, PALM BEACH

When Horace died in December 1963, he and Gregg were separated. According to Gregg, the separation was a "contrivance" to obtain more income from his trust. In any case, he left $14 million in unpaid bills and no money for his wife. There followed the usual litigation. Finally, she received a suitable multimillion-dollar, tax-free settlement. Then Gregg married Daniel Moran, a former New York City plainclothes detective whom Horace had hired as a bodyguard. Not long after moving into a new home next to Estée Lauder's, Moran shot and killed a burglar who had scaled a wall and was standing on the top-floor balcony.

Two years later, Gregg and Moran bought Jessie Woolworth Donahue's beach house. Donahue's father was F. W. Woolworth, who founded the chain of dime stores in 1879. In 1978, high on liquor and Valium, Moran killed himself with a .38 revolver. He and Gregg had accumulated some $2 million in unpaid bills.

"Horace's mother was very good to me," Gregg Dodge told me over dinner at Ta-boó. "She thought of me as her daughter. She insisted that we marry in her home, Playa Riente. His allowance was a hundred fifty thousand a year. Every time we needed to pay bills, we would play canasta with her. We would lose, then ask for money. It's very hard to say no to someone at two A.M. That would take care of a million or a million and a half in bills. That was our lifestyle. It's something they had been doing before I came on the scene. It's Palm Beach foreplay."

Dodge began enumerating the homes she owned with Horace: "We owned homes in Palm Beach and in Grosse Pointe. We had a one-hundred-and-twenty-eight-room estate in Windsor, England, and a thirty-three-room villa in the South of France. When I was married to Danny, we had the Donahue property on the ocean in Palm Beach, a duplex at 834 Fifth Avenue in New York, a home in Greenwich, and a house in Southampton on eight acres." She later remembered other homes, including an apartment at the Waldorf Towers she shared with Horace.

Wasn't it a nuisance to own so many homes? I asked.

"Why do you think I'm not living in the grand manner any-more?" Dodge said. "Because the staff was always eating, and I was always dieting."

Gregg Dodge now lives in a rental apartment on a lake in West Palm Beach. She hopes to start an international society magazine. Because she could not afford the dues, she let her membership in the Everglades and Bath & Tennis clubs lapse. Dodge looks as stunning as ever, but many of her former friends in Palm Beach don't cross the bridge to see her.

"When you don't have the money you had, you don't enter-tain the way you did," she said as I drove her home. "Society is like an ongoing film. A new set comes in, and the others leave. The tables are always filled, but with different people."

Schrafft told me that if Horace Dodge—known in Palm Beach as "Horrible Horace"—had outlived his mother, Gregg would have received half the Dodge fortune. "Instead, the money stayed in a trust for the children," she said. "But Gregg Dodge is a survivor, very bright. Nice laugh, good sense of humor.

"This is a high-gossip town," Schrafft said. "There are a lot of people here who don't have a lot to do. So they gossip." Secretly, Palm Beachers may relish the town's reputation as the most sin-ful spot on earth, but they also fear being ostracized. "If they say too much, they'll be criticized. There is still that closed-mouth policy. Nobody wants the town's dirty laundry hung out. It's really a small town," she said.

Occasionally, because of a lawsuit or a criminal charge, the behind-the-scenes hits the press. Schrafft recounted the story of socialite Nancy "Trink" Wakeman, heir to the John Deere for-tune, and her husband, William. During a drunken fight on September 5, 1967, at their home at 120 El Brillo Way, Trink accused William, a former model, of having an affair. When he denied it and lunged for her, she took his .22 revolver from a drawer.

"If you lay a hand on me, I'll shoot you!" Trink warned.

"You wouldn't dare shoot me, you haven't got the guts!" he yelled back.

Trink pulled the trigger, and a single shot ripped through his back. She called for help. An officer asked him what had happened. "Poosie shot me," he said, using his nickname for Trink. Bill Wakeman became a paraplegic.

Trink admitted to police that she had shot her husband, but Wakeman would not testify against her. When asked about her actions, he took the Fifth Amendment. But a six-man jury found Trink guilty of aggravated assault. She was sentenced to five years of probation. Wakeman consulted leading medical experts and decided to undergo a risky operation to restore his spine. A few minutes after he was returned to his hospital bed, his heart gave out. Trink was by his side when he died. She continued to give parties but never spoke of the shooting.

Schrafft said she doubted Betty Scripps Harvey would appear on the Palm Beach social scene again. Harvey is the widow of Edward Wyllis Scripps, the oldest grandson of E. W. Scripps, who founded the Scripps-Howard newspaper and broadcasting empire. She is descended from the founders of the Knight newspaper chain. For three years Harvey headed the International Red Cross Ball. In the last year, she contributed $750,000 herself. However generous, contributing such a large sum to help make the event more successful was a no-no, something akin to robbing a bank.

"She pretty much shot herself in the foot around here," Schrafft said of Harvey, whose spokesman later said she wouldn't discuss it. "She alienated the hierarchy of the Red Cross, including Barton Gubelmann. She contributed her own money to make the bottom line impressive. She brought in minor royalty."

In fact, while Harvey increased total contributions, she also increased total expenses. The Red Cross paid $15,000 to fly in Princess Chantal, the great-great granddaughter of King Louis Philippe of France, and her entourage. The Red Cross also paid for their suites at the Breakers and limousine service.

"She was trying too hard," Schrafft explained.

Then Harvey's son Barry filed a $50 million lawsuit against her, alleging he was wrongfully fired by the family newspaper chain. No one liked that, even though Palm Beach residents are constantly suing their own family members or being sued by them. Harvey said her son's claim stemmed from the "ingratitude of a privileged son." She said Barry stands to gain $10 million from gifts from his parents and profits from the sale of the Scripps League, a chain of sixteen daily newspapers and thirty other publications. The suit was tossed out of court.

That spat is dwarfed by the feud Palm Beach resident William Koch has had with two of his brothers over ownership of Koch Industries, the nation's second-largest privately held company. Koch, who spent $68 million to win the America's Cup Sailing Trophy in 1992, contends the $1.1 billion he and other shareholders received in 1983 in return for giving up their claim to the company was based on questionable accounting. William has been fighting his brothers in court for more than twelve years. His courtroom costs are $5,000 an hour. So far he has collected zero.

"People with money are not happier," Schrafft said. "They are more comfortable. They have the same problems as anyone else. But they don't have to worry about the electricity being cut off."

"A lot of these people get divorced and marry their next-door neighbor, get divorced and marry another next-door neighbor," Kooluris offered at the Bastille Day party. "I don't think their marriages are very important. The last wives wind up with the fortunes and are a lot younger."

Returning from the dessert table, Kirby reported on the latest development with Bill. "I have a feeling that the court system is beginning to notice his case," he said. "The last time at a deposition, where they take you to the courtroom for ten minutes to see if you're still breathing, I said to the public defender who sat down next to me, 'Have you read his history? He's not holding people up. He's reacting to situations.'"

Bill told the judge he would stop drinking. "The judge said, 'Everyone finds religion after they're in jail.' So we'll see," Kirby said.

Interrupting the conversation, an accordion player played "I Love Paris" and "La Marseillaise." The celebrants joined in. For diplomacy's sake, he played "Dixie" and "The Battle Hymn of the Republic." Everyone joined in again.

"I dread the season more and more," Schrafft said. "Every year it becomes more frenetic. There is more pushing and shoving, clawing. I leave for Christmas and New Year's. Last year I went to Yemen. This year I'm going to Senegal, then to Mali with my friend Mickey. I've been to Somalia and Micronesia. In Palm Beach every night is another disease, another cause. You can't drive. You can't get a reservation, can't get a parking space. It's silly."

As the party broke up, Albert M. Littleton invited Brownie McLean, Peter Rock, and a few others to follow him to his triplex.

"Are you coming with us?" Brownie asked me.

Downstairs, the caravan of cars was right out of high school, except Littleton was driving a Rolls-Royce. Littleton—who also has a Bentley—formerly owned the Culligan water-treatment franchise in Tennessee. Now he just has fun.

Pouring a domestic sparkling wine in his apartment, Littleton said, "For a single man, Palm Beach is incredible. It's like shooting fish in a barrel. I go to Ta-boó, to the Chesterfield. Did you hear about the man who went to a cocktail party? A woman turns to him and says, 'Where are you from?' 'Here, in Palm Beach.' 'I don't understand,' she says. 'You're so pale. Why don't you have a suntan?' 'I've been in prison for fifteen years,' the man says. 'Oh, you're a single man,' she says happily."

Just after arriving in Palm Beach a year earlier, Littleton attended a dinner at the Beach Club. He sat next to a woman who asked where his wife was.

"I'm not married," he said.

"May I have your card?" she asked.

The next day, Littleton said, "Five of her girlfriends called me."

To prepare for the Crystal Ball she organizes in New York, Brownie throws another party in Palm Beach. Littleton suggested she could hold it in the atrium of his condominium building. Brownie played him along. She became more animated when Littleton extolled the virtues of serving minimal food at cocktail parties—preferably goldfish.

"Get them in, get them out," Littleton said.

"What are goldfish?" I asked.

"He's doing a book on Palm Beach, and he doesn't know what goldfish are," sniffed Juliet de Marcellus, a French countess who traces her lineage to Charlemagne. She is the sister of Yvelyne "Deedy" Marix, a former mayor of Palm Beach who was a proponent of mounting video cameras at bridges to record license plate numbers of anyone entering Palm Beach. Littleton explained that Goldfish are Pepperidge Farm crackers.

Littleton told me he knew Neil Cargile from Nashville. "I gave him the name SheNeil," he said proudly. "He was as crazy in the nineties as in the forties. He was a wild man. I sold him my Rolls in 1983 in Nashville. He bought the car from me, and I threw in Trish, my girlfriend. I introduced them. I said to her, 'Why don't you follow the Rolls?'"

I asked Littleton if Cargile dressed as a woman back then. He said he did but not as often. He thought Cargile went off the deep end after he flew to New Orleans in his plane. A passenger got out and, walking into the turning propeller, was killed instantly. "They found so little of him that it took seven years for the insurance company to pay off," Littleton said. "I think Neil flipped out after that."

But Tommye Elrod, Cargile's second wife, told me Cargile had begun cross-dressing long before the accident. If anything, Cargile was more traumatized by the death of his son Neil, she said. The son, from Cargile's first marriage, died of a brain aneurysm when he was thirteen. "I don't know if that was a factor," Elrod said. "I was seeing him when his son died, before we were married in 1973. I can't say that caused him to run around and dress up." Cargile began his peculiar behavior in the late 1970s. At first, he only dressed for costume parties. "It got out of control," Elrod said. "There wasn't any way I could stop it. He said he was having a good time. He loved the attention. If any-body should know why he did it, I should, because I analyzed it a million times."

In 1981 they divorced. "I couldn't believe he would go to that extreme," Elrod said. "It was the biggest factor in our breakup. Also, he wasn't home a lot. He was heterosexual. He had girl-friends and everything else."

For all his eccentricity, Cargile was an authentic entrepreneur, very successful in business, she wanted me to know. "He was a brilliant engineer," his former wife said. "He had a company called American Mining and Machinery. They built dredges and shipped them all over the world. He also did gold mining. He played polo and he flew."

Jean M. VanWaveren dated Cargile and let him live in her guest house on South Ocean Boulevard. Her Mizner house just attracted a $7 million offer, which she turned down. She also has homes in Nantucket and Greenwich, Connecticut. As she put it, "I was born rich. My father's company—Tecumseh Products—dominated the world market in air-conditioning compressors."

VanWaveren said she didn't know about Cargile's cross-dressing until Franklyn de Marco told her about it. "I didn't know what a cross-dresser was," she said. Cargile thought that it was "a kick. He kept it hidden from me."

A month before he died of malaria, the Palm Beach Police arrested Cargile for drunk driving after he left Ta-boó. A public defender was assigned to represent him.

"He never paid attention to his business," VanWaveren said. "He got malaria and dropped dead. It was sad. He was kinky. A lot of people are kinky but keep it at home."

Barton Gubelmann was not happy. She had lunched with Candace Van Alen, a longtime friend who had been named general chairman of the International Red Cross Ball for the coming season. Van Alen has homes in Newport; Greenvale, New York; and Saint Croix but not in Palm Beach.

Candy's late husband, Jimmy, was a legend in the tennis world, having founded the Tennis Hall of Fame and devised the Van Alen Simplified Scoring System. That's not enough, Barton told me in mid-August in the drawing room of her Newport home on Narragansett Avenue. Called Starboard House, it is one of Newport's oldest stone villas, a high-ceilinged Victorian with sweeping grounds, a grand staircase, a library with floor-to-ceiling books, and an antique teapot collection. "Piss-elegant," she calls it.

"I have known her since 1938," Gubelmann said of Candy. "I visited her in California during my honeymoon. I visited her family home on the Hudson. We have traveled together, we shopped together." As Skip, her assistant, poured a French Chardonnay, Barton said, "She has never lived in Palm Beach, except this last year when she was there for six weeks or something, renting a house. She does not have the following in Palm Beach they need. They need a pretender, a person who wants to be somewhere and who will spend the money to do it. Candy is not going to spend the money. It takes a lot of money to cut a swath."

Gubelmann had told Van Alen that the Red Cross Ball needed an injection of life.

"She wants to run it like it was run thirty years ago," Gubelmann said. "It ain't going to work. She has to find the young people who will go. Nobody my age wants to go to a dance. Candy is my age. Anybody over eighty wants to stay home."

It's called the "International" Red Cross Ball because ambassadors are guests of honor. Ambassadors may be considered minor functionaries in other parts of the country, but in Palm Beach they are accorded divine status. Yet lately, according to Barton, the ambassadors themselves haven't been up to snuff.

"I told her we've had a perfectly awful crowd of ambassadors," Gubelmann said. "New-country ambassadors, not the English, French, Spanish, Italian ambassadors, or the ones from Danish or Nordic countries. They have South America and all those new countries created since World War II. Marjorie Merriweather Post didn't like to see that. I'm worried. She doesn't want to listen to anything I have to say."

On top of that, "Nobody wants to go to the party, because Mrs. Scripps ruined it. She gave them seven hundred fifty thousand dollars to put on a show. I was on the board. I've done more to make money for the Red Cross than almost anyone in Palm Beach. But nobody knows Candy. I don't know why I should go work for her. Candy is very negative about my advice. I think she thinks she is smarter than I am, which she probably is in many ways. But she hasn't lived in that crazy little town all those years. You learn a lot. You know who will go and who won't. I'm not going to call a lot of people I don't know just to get them to go to a party. I said let's give it a younger approach. Let's change it. Let's get the right people. Candy doesn't know them. I'm trying to figure out why they chose her."

As she puzzled over this, I asked her about Celia Lipton Farris, who is worth several hundred million dollars. A successful British musical-comedy star with Hollywood ties, she married Victor Farris, an industrialist and inventor of the paper milk carton and the Farris valve, used in oil refineries and military ships. Celia tried to impose a healthy diet on Victor, but he would sneak out and grab a bowl of chili at the counter at Green's Pharmacy.

Now widowed, Celia lives on El Vedado Road in a home once owned by Consuelo Vanderbilt, who became the duchess of Marlborough. Before Vanderbilt bought it, the home was owned by John Wendell Anderson, who helped finance Henry Ford's first assembly line, and by Audrey Emery, an American whose first husband, the grand duke Dimitri of Russia, helped murder Rasputin, the so-called "mad monk." In memory of her late husband, Farris gave several million to build the Victor W. Farris building at Good Samaritan Hospital in West Palm Beach.

Farris, a striking blonde with an hourglass figure, has five servants—including a former Palm Beach County deputy sheriff—and a saltwater swimming pool that must be emptied and refilled every two days. By day, she wears designer fashions by Escada.

When she twice chaired the American Cancer Society ball at the Breakers, Farris brought in Bob Hope, Gloria De Haven, Anthony Quinn, Douglas Fairbanks, Jr., Ginger Rogers, Tom Selleck, Glenn Ford, Jane Powell, and Petula Clark. The tables were laden with ten-piece place settings—four forks at the left of each plate, three knives at the right, and two spoons and a fork on top—with crystal for champagne, red and white wines, and water. For another fund-raiser, Farris threw a reception at her home for Prince Phillip, who sailed over on Her Majesty's yacht, *Britannia*. For the event, she had a tent constructed over her pool. For an AIDS benefit, she brought in Elizabeth Taylor. More recently she was the executive producer of *Palm Beach People and Places*, which ran on PAX-TV. Much as she has embraced Palm Beach society and its tinsel, Farris is more interested in her own singing, acting, and television-production career.

Being rich is difficult, Farris told me. People are always looking for money. Money and fame arouse jealousy. She wishes her money came from her own career instead of her late husband's estate. "I like earning my own living in the theater better than the situation I'm in now," she said. "I'm always cautious, because two women in town with a lot of money did go broke."

Farris made it clear that she is part of the Old Guard, even ticking off her own name in the black book when indicating which listees are considered Old Guard.

"It's become a society of money and celebrity," Farris said. "Before, it was people who were truly well-known, like the Kennedys. Of course, he was president. You had Charles Munn and his wife, the Winston Guests, the Drexels, and the duPonts. Those were the true American society people. Now they come in here and build enormous houses. People are trying to impress everybody with these great big houses. Mr. Kluge has an enormous property. I don't know, frankly, where they are going to get the help, my dear, unless you've had them for years. You don't want strangers in your house."

Farris went on: "There are people who come in here and get their faces in the paper immediately. They think they are somebody, and they're not. They live elsewhere. They don't even live here. I am a resident. There's a big fat difference in the people who come down from New York in the winter and the ones who live here. They come in for three months, spend their money like mad, and get publicity."

Yet photos of Farris, usually posing with Bert Sokol, a former hotel owner who booked people like Jay Leno, appear constantly in the Shiny Sheet. When I asked to see her, Farris FedExed a packet of biographical data and press clippings. In Newport, Barton called her a "pretender to the throne."

"Sometimes I call people like that Nescafé Society," said George Stinchfield, Barton Gubelmann's friend, referring to Celia.

At a dinner at the Sailfish Club, Helen Cluett, who was married to William G. Cluett, whose grandfather founded Cluett, Peabody, turned up her nose when I brought up Farris.

"Socially, she is a zero," Cluett said.

Despite her earlier claims, when told what Barton and Cluett said about her, Farris said she never aspired to be a socialite. She laughed when told she has been described as a pretender to the throne. "It's pretty hard to ascend to a throne when you're busy working," she said.

"Celia Lipton Farris is wonderful," said Charles Van Rensselaer of Cholly Knickerbocker fame. "People who say she's not part of society are jealous."

In Newport, Skip drove Barton, Pam, and me in Barton's Mercedes to a French restaurant. She would have gone to the New York Yacht Club, but she was mad at the club over the way it had handled one of her parties.

"I was asked to bring you to a party tonight," Gubelmann said. But she decided against it because she didn't want to run into a friend who was expected to be there. "The friend did something I didn't like," she said. It had to do with a request to write a letter recommending someone to a club, she said vaguely. "Instead of getting in a fight with my friend, it's better to stay away."

While Gubelmann tolerates Celia Farris ("She says, 'Barton, I'm so glad to see you,' and I say, 'I'm glad to see you, Celia,'"), she has no use for Roxanne Pulitzer. "Roxanne is a piece of trash," Barton said. "There's one in every town, there's one on every corner. She's just something Peter ran into."

No Palm Beach dinner party is complete without a mention of Roxanne—her whereabouts, her current marriage, her hairdo, her workouts. Palm Beachers may say she was born in a trailer park—actually, she lived with a friend in a white trailer while putting herself through college—but the sordid details of her divorce from Herbert "Peter" Pulitzer, Jr., the grandson of newspaper publisher Joseph Pulitzer, gave residents juicy gossip to feed on for years. The publicity—not to mention the *New York Post*'s claim that she slept with a trumpet—magnified the town's reputation as the Babylon of America.

The divorce proceedings included testimony by Roxanne about threesomes she and her husband had had with Jacqueline T. Kimberly, the wife of James H. Kimberly, an heir to the Kimberly Clark tissue fortune. According to a psychic who had once advised Roxanne, Roxanne told her that during her marriage to Peter, she had had sex with a real-estate salesman and a handyman. In court, Roxanne denied it all.

Then the *New York Post* headlined a story: "Pulitzer Sex Trial Shocker: I Slept with a Trumpet!" It was all a misunderstanding, Roxanne said. She had been given the trumpet as a gift, and she had kept it in her bedroom. When covered with black tape and taken to bed, it was supposed to call forth spirits from the dead. It had nothing to do with sex.

Gubelmann notwithstanding, most of the Old Guard is sympathetic. Roxanne simply was not prepared. Having married Peter Pulitzer, she found herself on the A-list, attending functions at the Everglades and Bath & Tennis clubs. "I became acutely aware that the Palm Beach dress code didn't cover much that was in my wash-and-wear wardrobe," she said. "A two-hundred-dollar pair of Gucci loafers, de rigueur for just kicking around, or a three-hundred-dollar Louis Vuitton handbag, were essential to fitting in."

At Peter's suggestion, she signed up for tennis and French lessons. She began reading books on the *New York Times* nonfiction best-seller list. She learned, however, that tennis elbow was the "one type of dinner party conversation which was of almost universal interest. For all its social pretensions, I learned that Palm Beach has few intellectuals."

In Roxanne's Palm Beach, the fast crowd would attend a swank soirée, "climb into their Ferraris and Porsches, snort Colombian crude, and zoom off to whatever disco joint happened to be in at the moment. . . . Then it was on to the home of whoever had the largest stash of drugs in the larder," according to her autobiography, *The Prize Pulitzer*. "By the dawn's early light, they would stagger home and into bed—some with their original partners, some with different ones."

One afternoon, Roxanne brought a Jewish friend to the Bath &
Tennis Club for a few matches on the courts. When she got
home, Peter told her the club was about to suspend him. "I didn't
know the rules," said Roxanne, blue-eyed and blond, with silky
smooth skin. "I was too young to realize. So they called my husband. They were all mad and said, 'We're going to suspend you.'
He talked them out of it. I was so upset that I couldn't take my
friend there, and I thought it was so wrong that, after that, I
played tennis with her at Sea View, a public court. I still went to
parties there with him. Herbert tried to explain it to me. I could
see he was embarrassed as he tried to tell me. There are rumors
that the Pulitzers were Jewish way back in Hungary. They're not
going to kick him out, because his father founded the Bath &
Tennis."

Roxanne told her husband she didn't even know what a Jewish
person looked like. He looked at her and said, "Well, Roxanne,
what was her name?"

"Rosenbaum."

"Didn't that give you a clue?"

After her divorce and the publication of her book, Roxanne
had a long affair with Count Jean de la Moussaye. Known in
Palm Beach as "the count of no account," he is a French race-car
driver who traces his lineage to Louis XIV. In 1992 they attended
the International Red Cross Ball together. The dalliance landed
Roxanne in court again. In divorce papers, the count's wife,
Francine, accused him of having an affair with Roxanne.
Meanwhile, Moussaye told *Penthouse* admiringly that Roxanne—
who went on to pose nude for *Playboy*—was an "animal fuck."
She "loves sex so much she has to have it three times a day."

A former Chicago detective testified that he saw the count
"straddling" Roxanne in the front seat of his red Porsche outside
a West Palm bar. Admitting to the affair with the count, Roxanne
testified that Francine taught her own daughter to call Roxanne
the "slut," "the whore," and "piggy." The daughter "says it with a
smile" to her mother, Roxanne said. "I don't think she means it
or knows the meaning of at least two of those names."

But Francine charged that Roxanne had turned the children against her. She said her daughter Alix had said to her, "You're a bitch! Roxanne's my new mommy!" Moreover, she alleged the count had had a string of other affairs during their marriage, including one with Kirsten Thompson, a lingerie model who posed nude on top of his racing car in a videotaped session. The model said on TV that she had had sex with the count three times, once immediately after the modeling session.

For her part, Francine admitted that she swam nude with a female friend and showered with her, but she denied an improper relationship. After separating from the count, Francine said, she found God. In the middle of her affair with the count, Roxanne married boat racer John Haggin. This led his mother, Palm Beacher Naoma Haggin, to cut him out of the $200 million family fortune. Seven weeks later the marriage was over.

Roxanne's personal trainer, Roger Stewart, took responsibility for the whole mess. After he led her though months of intense training and body building, Stewart said he could see trouble coming because he knew Roxanne's improved body could be dangerous. "It's all my fault. I warned her this would happen," he said.

When told of her trainer's comments, Pulitzer breathed a sigh of relief. "Finally," she said, "someone is admitting some blame."

Roxanne later married Harald Dude, a German real-estate developer who gave her a seven-carat diamond engagement ring. They live in Aspen and on the polo grounds in Wellington, an enclave for the horsey set on the mainland. Palm Beach's first lady of divorce often hangs out at Ta-boó. "I like to sit in the front room," she said. "I like to people-watch."

In the Leopard Lounge, Pulitzer told me that during her marriage to Herbert, she may have been into drugs and threesomes, but that doesn't compare with the activities of other Palm Beachers. "I'm much more normal than these people, I think. Yet I have the reputation of being so wild. That's the scary part." During the divorce, she said, "people stopped inviting me, especially the Old Guard. Peter will always have that name and that in. They circle the wagons. You do feel shunned a bit. I had lost custody of my kids, and I was trying to get it back. Some tried to make up for not inviting me, so they would be nicer in public than they should be. I think there was a certain amount of guilt. But they didn't want to cross him. They still wanted to be invited to his parties."

If Gubelmann is not a fan, it's because she is "very good friends with my ex-husband. The crowd split," Roxanne said without rancor.

What makes Roxanne different from other Palm Beachers is not her sexual appetite or sordid affairs but the fact that she is devoid of pretense and blind to class distinctions. From waiters to reporters, she treats everyone with respect. "I don't like the term 'little people,'" she said. "But I know more of the working people, the maître d's. I can always get a great table. They pamper me. I could call the police for anything. If I'm ten miles over the speed limit, they tell me to slow down." Unlike most Palm Beachers, she said, "money has never been a motive for me. The only nice thing Herbert said on the stand about me was 'I can say one thing, she never married me for my money.' I take care of myself. Never had a prenup, never asked for one."

Roxanne's directness is disarming. When I asked if she has had breast-enhancement surgery, she said, "I haven't had breast implants. I had inverted nipples. In 1978 I had something done to correct the nipples. But I never had implants or had them enlarged."

Now, she said, "I have a pretty nice lifestyle. I travel a lot. I'm not into flash and clothes. Give me a nice car and vacations. I have a Porsche. I drink Cristal. We eat at Renato's and Café L'Europe the most." She is close to her sons, who agreed when they were twelve that their parents should have joint custody. As for the count's comments about her sexual prowess, she said, "Well, I hope so. I've always known that. I don't need anybody to tell me that, thank you very much. Doesn't everybody know when they're good? The stupidest question is when somebody asks after they have made love, 'Was I good?' If you have to ask that, you're not. I know when I'm good and when I'm bad," she said without a trace of irony.

When she is in town, Pulitzer has a standing 3:00 P.M. appointment on Tuesdays and Fridays with Cosmo DiSchino of Cosmo & Company hairdressers. Until she moved to California, DiSchino did Marla Maples's hair. He also provided hairdressers for Mar-a-Lago until the club hired its own. Arnold Scaasi, designer of gowns for the elite, is a regular when he's in town. Roxanne told me to use her name when calling Cosmo.

"These young women come from all over the world looking for older, rich guys," DiSchino told me. "During the season, they come in droves. The older guys get the pick of the litter. You constantly get the threat of the man being caught with the younger women, and the women getting caught with the men. Everybody gets caught. A divorce lawyer caught his wife with the trainer. They were doing it all over the place. He said if they stay married, she has to sign a *mid*-nuptial agreement. If she is caught again, she gets nothing." In Palm Beach, he said, "husbands buy their mistresses fifty- or sixty-thousand-dollar diamonds in cash. They wouldn't want their wives to see the credit card charge." Everyone wants bigger and better. "It's no longer the role of the man to chase women," he said. "The women are in control. If they're beautiful, it's so much easier. The bombshells pick up the men with money faster."

In the season, women offer DiSchino more money for appointments. "There is constant bribery," he said. "The rivalry is over who gets done by whom. I'm booked six days a week. They will double the fee, two hundred dollars instead of one hundred for a wash and a blow dry."

For all their wealth, at least 90 percent of Palm Beach women are "very unhappy," DiSchino said. "Look at how unhappy they are with their own looks. They are in a race to maintain themselves. There are constant face-lifts, touch-ups, implants, collagen work, and vein-reduction therapy. When you have your hand behind the ears under the hair, you see the nips and tucks. In Palm Beach, men give implants as a gift, just like giving ten thousand dollars in diamonds. Instead, they give them bigger breasts. Sixty to seventy percent of the women have some of it."

12. Do You Know Who I Am?

Late in July, two cops stopped three bikers in front of Chuck & Harold's, next to Testa's, both sidewalk restaurants where people-watching is prime. The police told the bikers to get off their motorcycles. Lacking anything to accuse them of, a cop said to one of the bikers, "Do you know you're supposed to have the visor on your helmet down?"

In the future, maybe the bikers will think twice about crossing the bridge from West Palm. But there's another side to policing Palm Beach. It takes special knowledge and diplomacy. As assistant chief Michael S. Reiter told me, "You have to know the difference between a one-hundred-year-old Tiffany pattern and one in production now. You run into virtually anybody here."

Anybody who is anybody, that is. Reiter was in charge of investigating the death of David Kennedy, one of Bobby's sons, who died of a drug overdose in room 107 at the Brazilian Court Hotel on Australian Avenue. After Patricia Bowman accused William Kennedy Smith of raping her on the Kennedy estate, a detective on the case called Reiter. "There's somebody who says she is the victim of sexual battery, and his name is Smith, and he's a member of the Kennedy family," the detective told

Reiter. "There isn't anyone in the family by that name, is there?"

"Oh, yes there is," Reiter replied.

The next day, Reiter tried to interview Ted Kennedy at the Kennedy estate. Although the senator was at home, a Kennedy minion told Reiter he had left. That's the way it was on the island. There were always powerful, wealthy people who thought the Palm Beach Police were their private security force. In fact, any resident who is too drunk to drive may call the police for a ride home.

In 1989 some residents suggested at a town council meeting that the police set up video cameras to record the license numbers of everyone entering Palm Beach. The plan called to mind a 1940 law, maintained for forty-five years, requiring that all workers on the island obtain identification cards issued by the police. They had to submit to being fingerprinted and photographed as well.

Rochelle Vana came up against it in April 1983 when she began working as a $12,900-a-year waitress at the Sailfish Club. She was told to fill out forms at the police department. As the fingerprinting ink was being readied, she burst into tears. The experience reminded her of her husband Rosti's life in Soviet-controlled Czechoslovakia. He had fled the country in the 1950s.

"This is America, not Russia," she told the officers, then ran out.

Around the same time, Ignatius Wallace, a black man who had been unemployed, got a job delivering ice at the Breakers Hotel. The police told him the fee for the ID card was $4. He did not have it. The requirement reminded him of conditions in South Africa, where blacks had to carry a "pass card" at all times.

The American Civil Liberties Union took up their cause. The litigation raged for two years. In June 1985 Garry Trudeau portrayed the situation in "Doonesbury." In one strip, a Palm Beach matron tells a friend that the friend's domestic worker is in trouble with the law.

"I'm dreadfully sorry, dear, your Mr. Royce didn't have an ID, so he was detained," the socialite says.

"You mean arrested? For being an undocumented black man?"

"Ordinarily, dear, it's a good system," says the first woman. "In fact, our employees all love it. It gives them a sense of security, of belonging. The cards make them feel like members of our big Palm Beach family."

"Are they?"

"Don't be silly, dear," she says. "It's just something they can show their friends."

In December 1985 a U.S. District Court judge ruled the registration law unconstitutional.

When a resident suggested installing video cameras at the bridges, Chief Joseph J. L. Terlizzese opposed it. He doubted the license plate numbers would show up clearly. "And we can't continue to build fortresses and barriers around ourselves," he said. "Next thing you know, we'll be building machine-gun nests."

Terlizzese retired as chief in March 1998 after nearly twenty years in the job. He had brought discipline and training to the department. Before Terlizzese took over, "if a black person came over the bridge, he was stopped because he was black. That does not go on anymore," Sanford P. Lopater, a former Palm Beach Police sergeant, told me.

Residents think the police check the license plate numbers of anyone crossing the bridges. In fact, the police are more discerning. "Cops who have been on the road a while develop a sixth sense," Lopater said. "You get a feeling if something is not right," he said. "If you see a beat-up car in Palm Beach, it's going to get some extra scrutiny. If a car is cruising up and down side streets and the tag shows he is not from the area, I will pull him over to see if he is lost or to let him know I'm there in case he's up to something. Of course, in Palm Beach there are plenty of sight-seers. They ask, 'Where is the Kennedy house?' or 'Where is Trump's house?' I might say, 'May I help you find what you're looking for?' If he gives some kind of crap answer, my level of suspicion goes up." If they really want to know where Trump's house is, he tells them.

When Terlizzese retired, the local press said he had cut out gratuities to police. That was only partly true. According to

Lopater, the police still receive free or discounted meals from many local restaurants. The practice, though banned by police regulations, is winked at, so long as a tip is left.

"We just work it so we have to leave some money," Lopater said, claiming the practice is common among local police departments. The Palm Beach Police had no comment.

Now a police sergeant in Atlantis, Florida, Lopater had to quit the Palm Beach Police Department during an internal investigation into his friendship with Count Jean de la Moussaye, Roxanne Pulitzer's former boyfriend. In April 1995 the Palm Beach Police arrested the count in a cocaine bust at his home at 404 Cocoanut Row. They found 3.4 grams of cocaine in his pants pockets. He pleaded not guilty but was deported over a previous conviction in Paris for selling stolen jewelry that belonged to the French and Spanish royal families. The count pleaded guilty to that charge but fled to the United States. He failed to appear at a July 1994 deportation hearing in Miami.

Back in 1989, according to Lopater, the count called him, and Lopater went to his apartment. "When I got there, he was lying in bed as if he was ill," Lopater told me. "He told me he had a cocaine habit. He couldn't break it."

"Do you have any cocaine in the apartment?" Lopater asked him. "If you're strong enough to dump it in the toilet, I know you're strong enough to break the habit."

The count did so, according to Lopater. But in 1995, while investigating the count, the Palm Beach Police asked Lopater about his relationship with him. Lopater volunteered the 1989 incident. What with Lopater's failure to arrest the count for possession or to report the incident to the department, along with making personal calls to the count from a police cruiser and giving him a ride, Reiter warned Lopater that the department was leaning toward terminating him. Before he could be fired, he quit in April 1995.

During his eleven years with the department, Lopater said, he often found couples having sex on the beach or even on the benches that overlook the ocean. "It happens all the time," he said. "I found one couple on the beach in the middle of having sex but not moving," he said. "When I shone my flashlight at them, they started moving again." Drunk, they had apparently fallen asleep while in the act.

"I pulled over a resident for making an illegal left turn at a posted sign," Lopater said. "I walked up to him. At first he got out of his car. He walked toward me. We like the violator to stay in the car. I got on my PA and asked him to get back. He started screaming at me about Gestapo tactics."

"You've made an illegal left-hand turn," Lopater told him.

"Of course I did," the man said. "I do that every day."

Within ten minutes, the driver was in the mayor's office, saying Lopater had had no right to pull him over and "should have known" who he was. Indeed, every Palm Beacher could wear a badge: DO YOU KNOW WHO I AM?

Another officer stopped a young woman on a traffic violation. "Before his shift was done, she went to the police station and complained he had fondled her breasts," Lopater said. "He was a rookie and was still on probation. If this complaint had been true, it would have ended his career. But they had just recently installed video cameras in every police car. They viewed the tape, spoke to the officer, and called her back in. They said, 'We need you to sign the report.' They went over it carefully with her. She signed. Then they showed her the videotape, which showed none of what she had claimed. She said, 'I would like to change my story.' They arrested her for filing a false report."

One afternoon, Lopater said he was dispatched to look into a complaint by a member of the Old Guard that his next-door neighbor routinely parked illegally in front of his own house. "The neighbor was parked where he should have been parked, but he was Jewish. He didn't like that. He was screaming up and down about the man's car being parked illegally," Lopater said. "Then he started calling him a Jew and a kike. The old Palm Beach is very prejudiced, Anglo-Saxon Protestants. They are the Old Guard who say no one else belongs here. They usually are people with family money. The new Palm Beach is people who have made it on their own and have attained the ability to live here."

The man's tirade continued for almost ten minutes. "My backup had left because he didn't want to hear it," Lopater said. "Finally, I said, 'I'm Jewish, and I don't like hearing that stuff. So if you'll excuse me, I'm going to leave now. There is no parking problem.'"

The man stopped his harangue. "He tried to say some of his best friends are Jewish," Lopater said. "But I was already walking away. He later called the mayor to complain about me being impolite because I had walked away. I was called in. The captain wanted to find out what had happened. He said he would handle it."

Occasionally, Lopater said, "We would get calls to go to a house, and they would say don't come to the mansion entrance. Use the service entrance. I would never do that. These people are something else. There are some very nice people in Palm Beach, and then there are people who thought we were servants."

13. ONLY IN PALM BEACH

Unlike most other resorts, Palm Beach has no downtown area with traffic jams and tourists, no pizza joints or fudge factories. Outsiders are easily spotted by their pale faces, their fast walk, or their dress—Bermuda shorts or blue jeans. Soon the police are watching them. In Palm Beach long-legged women in skimpy dresses or short shorts stroll around as if in their own backyards.

"I have a chocolate Lab," Karen Lane, Palm Beach's dockmaster, told me. "I can walk him around the block at two A.M. and feel perfectly safe."

That feeling of invulnerability was shattered when Michael Pucillo, a respected local lawyer who lives on Dunbar Road, called 911 on the evening of June 13, 1996, to report that he had just found his seventy-one-year-old mother, Geraldine Pucillo, tied up and lying facedown in the shower at her home at 130 Seaspray Avenue. She had been strangled to death.

In the previous two decades, only eleven murders had been committed in Palm Beach. Over blueberry pancakes at Testa's, Palm Beach residents asked themselves why anyone would kill someone like Geri Pucillo. With her late husband, Costanzo "Gus" Pucillo, Geri had owned Petite Marmite, for more than three decades Palm Beach's most chic restaurant. Located on Worth Avenue, the restaurant claimed among its patrons John Lennon, Liberace, Bing Crosby, Jayne Mansfield, Richard Nixon, the duke and duchess of Windsor, and John F. Kennedy.

Geri was an orphan who had been raised by a succession of families in Boston. She met Gus, who had come over from Italy, in 1947. They married and moved to Florida. Trading free meals for rent, the immigrant and the orphan opened Petite Marmite as a small café under a banyan tree in 1949. Their investment was $1,900. Eventually, they bought the land, adding parcels as the restaurant became more successful. The entrance to Petite Marmite, or "the Petite" as Palm Beachers used to call it, was through an arched passageway called the Worth Arcade at 315 Worth Avenue, just in front of where Bice Ristorante is now.

The restaurant served classic European cuisine, what was termed continental when that was something good to be, before the word gathered quotation marks and the dishes became household words, utterly passé: Beef Wellington, chicken tetrazzini, shrimp scampi. The restaurant prided itself on its fresh seafood—whole lobster, raw oysters, sole, pompano. It prominently displayed an example of a marmite, the earthenware stockpot in which a clear, savory soup known as *petite marmite* is prepared, and for which the restaurant was named. Petite Marmite always led the list of recommended Palm Beach restaurants, before Chesler's, Ta-boó, and Testa's, Palm Beach's oldest restaurant.

If Gus and Geri were an American success story, they did not forget those less fortunate. They quietly gave loans to their employees to buy homes. They sold chicken-salad sandwiches and minestrone out the back of the restaurant at reduced prices so employees of other Worth Avenue businesses could enjoy the same food consumed by Palm Beach's elite.

As the proprietor of Palm Beach's most distinguished restaurant, Geri was a mother figure, dispensing food and making sure notable customers got reservations at the last minute. When Earl T. Smith, a former ambassador to Cuba, ran for mayor of Palm

Beach in 1971, Geri volunteered for his campaign. Lesly Smith, his wife, became Geri's friend. "Geraldine Pucillo meant perhaps as much to the town as Princess Diana did to the rest of the world," Lesly, now the Palm Beach Town Council president, would later say.

Practically everyone in town knew Geri, who had been president of the Worth Avenue Merchants Association and went to mass at Saint Edward's Catholic Church every Sunday. But Gus and Geri had no time for charity balls. They considered the very concept of society to be nonsense. They dressed conservatively and insisted on pronouncing their last name "pa-SIL-o," considering the Italian pronunciation, "pa-CHIL-o," to be pretentious. Of all the people in Palm Beach, Geri was the last one anyone would think would be murdered.

Since she was the detective on duty when Mike Pucillo called for help, Diana Burfield was assigned to the case. A former hairdresser, Burfield had been a police officer nine years and had never worked a murder. The Palm Beach Police Department has two divisions, one that deals with law enforcement and one that provides support, including communications, administration, and a beach patrol with lifeguards. The law-enforcement division has seventy-seven sworn officers, including detectives like Burfield. Mike Reiter headed it.

The autopsy report showed that Geri had defensive knife wounds on her left thumb and right hand. Apparently, she had been accosted in her bedroom. She had tried to defend herself with the knife. The perpetrator then ripped the cord from the phone, tied her hands with it, and threw her in the shower, where he strangled her with an orange dress. Wounds on her forehead meant she had tried to raise her head as she was being strangled. Either to make sure she was dead or to rinse off forensic evidence like prints or hair, her attacker had then turned on the shower. No prints were found on the knife, and a palm print in the shower could not be matched with anyone's in the family.

"This was a whodunit homicide, very atypical in Palm Beach," Reiter told me. "Usually, we see domestic situations." The last was in January 1991, when Joseph Vannier shot and killed his fifty-seven-year-old wife, Arlene. In the Pucillo case, Reiter said, "We had a limited number of clues and had to figure it out backwards."

The Palm Beach Police devoted nearly all the department's investigative resources to the case—besides the lead detective, Burfield, at least fourteen other detectives and supervisors working twelve-hour days, six days a week. They checked on reports of suspicious people and defendants who had been sentenced or prosecuted by Deborah Pucillo, Michael's wife. She was then a county judge and had previously headed the major-crimes unit of the state attorney's office.

The couple figured out that $16,700 in jewelry—including a heavy, eighteen-carat-gold bracelet from Italy—was missing. The police circulated flyers listing the items to pawn shops and jewelry stores in the area. Notices posted in public places offered a reward for information about the jewelry.

On June 28 Richard Hanna, owner of the Palm Beach Pawn Shop in West Palm, told the police that Kim Duane Cain, a boisterous, thirty-two-year-old man, had tried to pawn a gold bracelet at the shop two days after the murder, without showing identification or submitting to fingerprinting as required by state law. Hanna knew Cain as a regular customer. Hanna refused to buy the item but suggested that Cain—an exterminator with Tillman Exterminating—might be able to sell the item to a jewelry store without showing identification.

On July 10 Eric Miles Newton, a local sort of Forrest Gump who lives with his father, saw the notice about the missing jewelry posted at the Palm Beach Kennel Club. Here, in a cavernous gray arena in West Palm Beach, wrinkled men and women puffing on cigarettes and wearing brightly colored plaid shorts place bets on which of eight greyhound dogs will win a three-minute race. Admission is a dollar. In between dog races, they watch horse racing on television monitors, sipping their Buds and looking as if they had just stepped off a cross-country Greyhound bus. There is not a blonde in sight. The contrast to Palm Beach could not be more stark.

Like Lurch, the manservant in *The Addams Family*, Newton, forty-three, had a deep, monotonal voice. He told a friend, a deputy sheriff assigned to the track, that he had seen the notice about the missing jewelry. He said a friend of his who worked for Tillman Exterminating had paid him $50 to sell an eighteen-carat-gold bracelet at a jewelry shop. According to Newton, Kim Cain told him the bracelet belonged to his ex-wife, and he didn't want her to find out he had it.

Cain lived in two worlds. One was the $10-an-hour life of an exterminator. The other was the opulent Palm Beach life he saw every day but could never have. As a way of bridging the gap, he fantasized about striking it rich. A man with a mustache and receding black hair, Cain went to the track almost daily, wearing his white Tillman Exterminating uniform with KIM emblazoned in blue over his left breast. Usually, Cain bet $10 to $100 per race. He liked to brag about his wins but never mentioned his losses. As it turned out, Cain was $7,000 behind on child-support payments to his first wife and had pawned his third wife's camcorder so he could continue to bet at the dog track.

Cain would pay Newton $1 to fetch him a hot dog or to cash in his winnings for him. What Newton didn't realize was that in claiming Cain's winnings and so listing his own Social Security number, he became liable for income taxes on the money.

When Cain found out he couldn't sell the bracelet without submitting identification and fingerprints, he had Newton sell it at Ruby's Jewelers for $578. Cain accompanied him to the jeweler, and Newton showed his own identification and submitted his own fingerprints. Besides giving Newton $50 for helping him, Cain told him he would cancel Newton's debts to him. Newton didn't realize that, in fact, he owed Cain nothing.

As it turned out, Cain had inspected Geri's home for termites six months earlier. And the palm print next to Geri's body matched his.

The Palm Beach Police arrested Cain, and he drew Marc Shiner as his prosecutor. A New Yorker who had stayed in Florida after attending Nova Law School in Fort Lauderdale, Shiner had been with the major-crimes unit of the state attorney's office—the same one Debbie Pucillo had headed—for nine years. Yet Shiner had rarely been in Palm Beach. On his $60,000-a-year salary, he told me he considered the place too expensive. Shiner, thirty-five, wore gold-rimmed glasses and brushed his dark hair back. Perennially skeptical about police, victims, lawyers, and witnesses alike, Shiner's reflexive comment was, "You never know."

Cain's lawyer happened to be Joseph D. Farish, Jr., who represented Roxanne Pulitzer in her divorce from Herbert "Peter" Pulitzer, Jr. Farish also represented Trink Wakeman during her trial for shooting her husband; the wife of Count Jean de la Moussaye in their divorce; and Mary Alice Firestone when her husband, Russell Firestone, Jr., divorced her. A former high school cheerleader who dated Burt Reynolds when at Palm Beach High School, Mary Alice had the habit of having casual sex with the help. Farish's investigators learned that Russell was having his own fling with his secretary. They took pictures of the couple half naked in Russell's office.

At Cain's trial, Shiner told the jury that Geri Pucillo often left her back door open after going out to water her orchids. Cain may have entered thinking she was not home. With the radio tuned to an easy-listening station, neither heard the other. When Geri caught him taking her jewelry, Cain decided to kill the only witness to his crime. He tied her up so he could think about what to do, then strangled her in the shower.

"She was alive and struggling when her hands were bound," Shiner told the jury. "She was struggling the whole time she was being murdered."

After hearing two weeks of testimony, the jury made up its mind in fifteen minutes. The exterminator had ended Geri Pucillo's life. He got life without parole.

For Palm Beach residents, the outcome confirmed their worst fears. Living symbiotically with their help, they are constantly serviced by landscapers, painters, construction workers, and caterers. The morning sounds of Palm Beach are droning pruners and buzz saws, and raking and sweeping, hypnotic and constant.

In Palm Beach, something is always crawling into something or crawling out. Ubiquitous curly-tailed lizards saucily race across the pavement with their tails up, flattening their tails when resting on a sign or a rock for the short wait for a flying bug. Major buildings like the Everglades Club are completely wrapped in red-and-white striped tents while exterminators fumigate them. After air-conditioning repair people, exterminators are the island's most prized workers.

"Wherever there's money, people want to get it," commented David Goodstal, the Palm Beach limousine driver. "That's what happened with this poor woman."

While the murder momentarily stunned Palm Beach, it did not register as an event within the Old Guard. Geri Pucillo was not one of them. In Palm Beach, even bank presidents are considered tradespeople, members of the working class. As a restaurant owner, Geri Pucillo was part of the help.

Now some of her closest friends refuse to talk about her for publication. The memory of the way she died is too unpleasant, the whole episode too upsetting. To say something nice about their friend would be too great a sacrifice.

Only in Palm Beach.

"We have no graveyards or hospitals," Kirby Kooluris said. "All that glitters is not gold. If you really have a problem, Palm Beachers will hear it for maybe five minutes. 'You'll be able to take care of it. You have it in you.' This is not a place where you want to need anything."

Seven months after Geri Pucillo was murdered, jewels valued at $12 million to $15 million were stolen from two locked cases in the bedroom of Kathleen duRoss Ford, the widow of Henry Ford II. The heist was said by the Palm Beach Police to be the "largest single residential burglary" in United States history.

If the crime was up to Palm Beach standards, so was the victim. A former model who resembles actress Kathleen Turner, Ford is the daughter of a Chrysler autoworker. At fifteen she married David duRoss, a Chrysler plant worker who moonlighted as a trombone player. He died in a car crash four years after their marriage. She met Henry Ford II at a party at his Detroit house in 1969, when Ford was still married to his second wife, Cristina. After divorcing Cristina, Ford married Kathleen in 1980, and they built a $4.3 million waterfront home on North Lake Way in Palm Beach. After Henry Ford died in September 1987 at the age of seventy, she inherited $3 million and the income from a $350 million trust, estimated at $15 million a year. Not to mention homes in Palm Beach, London, and Grosse Pointe Farms, Michigan.

In Palm Beach style, Kathleen Ford and Ford's children from his first marriage became embroiled in a quarrel over the family fortune. In a videotape made in 1984, Ford explained that his primary concern was for "Kate." He wanted her to "live the rest of her life as she has during her lifetime with me." He told his three children they would not inherit any of his property upon his death.

According to an audit produced during the litigation, Ford's expenditures included $200,000 a year for security at their three homes. Despite this outlay, on January 11, 1997, the diamonds, rubies, and emeralds disappeared from Kathleen Ford's Palm Beach home.

As a member of society, Ford merited sympathy. Weeping as her attorney read a prepared statement, she held a press conference in January 1997 and offered a $500,000 reward. "The jewelry is a reminder of my life with my husband and the good times we shared for so long," she wrote in a statement. "The sentimental value to me of the stolen jewelry far exceeds its monetary value."

When jaded jewelers along Worth Avenue saw pictures of the missing gems, even they were impressed. "Sheesh," commented appraiser Allan Cohen of Mayor's Jewelers.

"A lot of this is major jewelry," said Jay Bauer of Trianon Jewelers.

With the help of a jeweler who spotted the missing gems pictured on a Web site, the FBI and Palm Beach Police eventually arrested Alvaro Valdez, forty-six, and his "fence," Barry Marshall, fifty-two. They pleaded guilty to federal charges of conspiracy and transporting stolen merchandise.

The jewels were not insured. Often, the rich do not want to put up with the security precautions imposed by insurers. But the police and FBI recovered nearly $8 million of Ford's jewels. The Old Guard never questioned why Ford would keep up to $15 million in jewels in her home. When Ford put off paying a promised reward to the jewelers who turned in the culprits—prompting a story in *People* magazine—Palm Beachers shrugged. The jewelers were part of the help; they could wait.

14. PENIS PASTA

Having served sixty days, Bill was released from the county jail on September 1.

"He called me and said, 'Come and get me,' Kirby Kooluris told me. "I felt I had to. You just don't turn your back on a friend. But he has to obey rules. My rule is no beer." Kirby also told Bill to sleep in the cabana, which he owns on the ocean side of the island.

Of course, sleeping overnight on the beach is not allowed, but the ordinance is hard to enforce. "How does one define sleep? He wants to watch the sun rise," Kirby said. "I'm truly trying to help Bill. It's not easy if a person doesn't want to help himself. If he comes over, it will be a matter of days before the beer cans come out. Then I'll be hoping he'll go to sleep by one or two in the morning."

Kooluris said he often wonders aloud why he puts up with Bill.

"Why do I get suckered?" Kirby asked. "I need that feeling of usefulness—somebody to take care of. I should have someone who is not so wounded by life. He says, 'I'll never have anything.' He's given up. It's disarming."

Is Bill manipulating him? I asked.

"He very well could be," Kirby said. "He doesn't understand that very generous souls have a limit."

Just then Bill came in from the cabana. Kirby offered him blueberry pancakes.

"I just got out of the can," Bill said. "Did he tell you about being accused of stealing a bike? Now I'm out on time served. I have another case going on. I was arrested. I go to court in October. I haven't drank since I got out. But that doesn't say much because I've only been out two days."

Bill continued, "I like the police here. It's West Palm that's the problem. They get freaked out. You mention 'gun' over there and jeez. It's like two different countries. I was drinking with this guy on the street. I had a rough day that day. I bumped into this guy and he said, 'Can I bum a beer from you?' I said, 'Yeah.' This prostitute walked by and said to the police, 'Those guys have a gun.' They swarmed me."

Bill asked me about the book on Palm Beach.

"This is not like a Washington exposé," I said.

"What's an exposé?" Bill asked.

I couldn't believe he didn't know what the word meant. "It's something that reveals wrongdoing, scandal, that kind of thing," I told him.

"Wrong with the law, or like cheating on the wife?" Bill asked.

But Kirby saw Bill's vacuousness as disarming. "Isn't he refreshing?" Kirby asked me later. "My pal who lives up the street warned me about Bill. What they see is a police car in front of the house. They don't realize that it wasn't for something awful."

The police are understanding. When Kirby called them after Bill became violent when asked to stop making calls at two in the morning, Bill asked if he could have a sandwich before the police took him away. When Kirby made him a sandwich, Bill asked for mustard on it. The police patiently waited, then dropped Bill at the north bridge and told him not to return for a day.

"A lot of Bill's problems aren't Bill's fault," Kirby asserted.

That's not how Kirby's friends see it. In addition to the fabulously rich doyennes he escorts, Kirby has a circle of beautiful platonic female friends, all a contrast to Bill. The friends include Monica von Hapsburg, an archduchess from Austria; Gunilla von Post, who was one of John F. Kennedy's lovers; and Lady Trisha Pelham. Pelham is a former Hollywood actress whose father was the duke of Newcastle. Her family owns Sherwood Forest in England and once owned the Hope diamond.

Trisha is Kirby's date when he wants to show off—a Joan Collins look-alike, he calls her. "I need you," Kirby tells her. "I really love girls' company," he explained. "I've had beautiful girls as friends. A few I slept with. But it always had to be someone important when it came to women. I love powerful women. It turns me on. With men, I love the wild kid, the wild animal."

Lady Pelham has skin like double-Devonshire cream and an aristocratic accent like butter. She is connected, always has been. Pelham married the manager of a rock band, Delaney & Bonnie & Friends. John Lennon and Ringo Starr were among their friends. "We showed John Lennon around the island," Pelham told me after Kirby introduced us. "We took him to Ta-boó." She and Ringo celebrated their July birthdays together "for years." So often did she go for drinks with a certain Southern playwright that she refers to him simply as Tennessee.

After divorcing, Pelham, now fifty, played a Hells Angel biker girl in the 1985 movie *Mask* starring Cher. In the movie, a teen suffers from a disease that inflates his head to twice its normal size.

Trisha has tried to explain to Kirby the importance of British titles—why she is referred to as Lady Pelham, yet, since she is not part of British royalty, why people do not curtsy when they meet her. Her full name, she told me, is Patricia Pelham-Clinton-Hope, "as in the diamond."

According to legend, ever since a thief was said to have stolen the Hope diamond from the eye of a statue of the Hindu goddess Sita, a curse has followed its owners. Originally 112 carats, the dark blue diamond was smuggled to France in 1668 by a French adventurer. Not long afterward, he supposedly met a slow and painful death when a pack of wild dogs attacked him in India.

The stone ended up in the possession of Louis XVI and Marie Antoinette. They were guillotined. The gem was stolen and wound up in Amsterdam, where jeweler Wilhelm Fals recut it. He is said to have died of grief after his son stole the diamond from him. Out of guilt for what he had done to his father, the son is supposed to have committed suicide.

In 1830 Henry Philip Hope, a London banker who was a member of Trisha's family, acquired the gem. From then on, it has borne his name. A Greek merchant bought the diamond in Turkey for a wealthy sultan. According to the legend, the Greek and his family were killed when their car went off a precipice. Finally, Evalyn Walsh McLean bought the diamond in 1911. She had her husband, Edward B. (Ned) McLean, owner of the *Washington Post*, committed to an insane asylum. After her death in 1947, New York jeweler Harry Winston acquired the flawless 45.52-carat gem. In 1958 Winston gave it to the Smithsonian Institution.

In *Blue Mystery: The Story of the Hope Diamond*, Susanne Steinem Patch suggests that most of the misadventures are fairy tales. In her exhaustive study, published by Smithsonian Institution Press, Patch—the sister of Gloria Steinem—demonstrates that many of the people said to have been done in by the diamond never even owned it. Only after Evalyn Walsh McLean acquired the gem did the legends of bad luck begin to sprout. Still, the diamond spooked Brownie McLean.

"So," Trisha Pelham said, "both Brownie and I have this connection to the Hope diamond. My father was Lord Henry Edward Hugh Pelham-Clinton-Hope, lord of the manor of Worksop, then there's a whole bunch of other titles—earl of Lincoln, duke of Newcastle-Under-Lyme." The family's original name was Cavendish. "They and the Newcastles descended from the same woman, who married six millionaires and buried all of them," she said. "She was Beth of Hardwick, who was Mary Queen of Scot's jailer."

William John Robert Cavendish, the marquis of Hartington, married Kathleen Kennedy, one of Joe Kennedy's daughters. Then she fell in love with Pelham's great uncle, Peter

Fitzwilliam, a thirty-seven-year-old married British lord. They died together in a plane crash. One of Pelham's ancestors killed the king of France on the battlefield. Another ancestor was the "Lord of the Bed Chambers to William the Conqueror. He was deeded land when they landed in England. He built Kenilworth Castle. His great-grandson swapped that with the crown for Sherwood Forest, which we still own. Lincoln green was the color Robin Hood wore. That is our family color. When they had jousting, we had a Lincoln green pennant. We have had two prime ministers and a minister of war in our family."

As Pelham sees it, titles are like doctorates. "Guys would go to battle and do great deeds. They would find the most beautiful girl in the village and carry her off and have children with her." In effect, "they were doing selective breeding. Titles are badges of honor for deeds done. They are sort of like doctorates, except titles are handed down from generation to generation."

Kirby doesn't get it. When he hears about the dukes and the earls, he wonders what the fuss is about: "Hmm, do I get any money?" he jokes.

In fact, Palm Beach prizes hereditary titles as much as it prizes ambassadors. No party is complete without a prince or princess, a viscount or a baroness, a marquess or an earl. While members of the British royal family are frequent visitors, most of the titled are pretenders to the throne of a nonexistent country or have bought their titles for anywhere from $2,000 to $500,000. While feudal baronies or lordships of the manor may be legitimately purchased—often by credit card—many are sold by scam artists and are worthless, according to Antony Cartaya Boada, a Palm Beach and Miami attorney who specializes in peerage law and is author of *Instant Aristocracy*.

Pelham is amused by the notion of working the nobility angle. When she spoke of getting a tour of the Mar-a-Lago Club with no intention of joining, she said, "It's time to take the duchess out for a walk."

Pelham's social life is limited by her need to care for her eight-year-old autistic son, Dorian. "Autistic children have a terrible time learning to talk," Pelham told me. "Their hearing is excellent, but the wiring of the brain stem causes them to hear things in a strange way. A beep or a gong sounds like a bomb. They can't distinguish between two voices, so they hear words in the wrong way."

Screaming is Dorian's only form of communication. "So I can't take him places," Pelham said. "I have him in a special school program. I bought my house without a pool to protect him. I call him the Terminator. After an hour with him, I have to change my clothes. I'll feel this thing on my back, and he's taken a pen and is drawing there. It's a twenty-four-hour job."

Kooluris spends hours playing with Dorian with a Slinky or reading to him. Kirby seems to derive as much enjoyment from the Slinky as Dorian does. Or he has Dorian admire himself in a mirror. "After playing with Kirby, he knows two or three new words," Pelham said.

Despite their divorce, Kirby is always saying nice things about Joan, to whom he was married for eight years. Joan's husband, Tony, is a psychic healer and columnist. Pelham really wanted to meet her, so Kirby brought her over. "She is a perfect china doll. I looked at her and said, 'You were married to Kirby?' She giggled in this charming way and said, 'Do you believe that?'"

For Pelham, the fact that Kirby is a walker and gay is not a problem. "It's great having Kirby because he's my closest male friend that I can treat like a girlfriend," she said. "We always roar with laughter. I call him Puck from *A Midsummer Night's Dream*. Kirby takes care of me. He's like a big brother. Every woman should have a guy like Kirby in her life." He may be "slightly off kilter," Pelham said, but so is everything else in Palm Beach.

One night Pelham called Kirby and told him, "I'm making dinner for you. Get over." He came over, and "he's digging into the pasta and says, 'I don't understand why you were so insistent on my coming.' Then he looks at the pasta. It's penis pasta a friend gave to me." Shaped like a penis complete with testicles, the pasta was about an inch long.

"He was the only person I could make it for," Trisha told me.

"Do you wish Kirby were straight?" I asked.

"I couldn't stand it if he were straight," she said. "He's too much fun being gay."

"Trisha is classy," Kirby said. "She is the real thing. She is a wonderful soul but vulnerable. The reason she hasn't remarried is that some nice guy will ask her out, but she wants him to have fifty million dollars. She has money, but she is used to rich people. I don't think it has to do with being a materialist. It's just habit."

For last season's Red Cross Ball, Kirby fixed Pelham up with John McCoy, a friend. For the event, women wear tiaras and men wear medals. "I find the Red Cross Ball to be a playground for little girls with too much money so they can wear the tiaras that they don't own, that they don't have a right to wear," she said, referring to the fact that jewelers along Worth Avenue lend Palm Beach women tiaras for the ball. "Really, if they knew what it really meant to wear a tiara, and who can wear one—but none of them have the right. European aristocracy can. I can," Trisha said.

When McCoy picked her up for the ball, he was sporting a medal. She asked what it represented. He said, "I bought it on Worth Avenue. I'm trying to figure out what it is."

Riding in the car to the ball, Pelham said, "Okay, this is the deal. Your grandfather was in World War I. He was a double agent. He did such a good job for the Germans that they presented him with this medal, called the Red Baron."

"Great," McCoy said. "I love it." At the ball, they spotted Kirby with Helen Boehm. One of the wealthy women Kirby escorts, Boehm owns the Boehm Porcelain Studio, which makes unique porcelain figures displayed in the White House and Buckingham Palace. When Boehm asked about the medal, McCoy told her the story.

Boehm was enthralled and motioned to a newspaper reporter that he should hear the story. "He was writing it down," Pelham said. "I was hysterically laughing, trying to disappear."

In Palm Beach, "You say anything and they believe you," Pelham said. "But then people look at me and don't quite believe who I am. They become confused because I have an American accent."

When Kirby first hooked up with Bill, Pelham warned Kirby about him. "From the beginning, I said, 'Don't do this,'" she said. "I kept telling him what would happen. He'll drink and be arrested." Kirby is a "wonderful, wonderful character with so few street-level smarts because he's lived in a wonderful world where nasty things like being arrested for being drunk don't happen," Pelham said. "When he sees trouble coming, he doesn't recognize it. He doesn't want to hurt anybody. He has a wonderful heart. It gets him in a lot of trouble. So he's wasted almost two years of his life on Bill."

15.   POSEURS

"You're beautiful. You're just the look we want."

A woman who said she represented a modeling agency in Miami was trying to recruit Holley, a willowy blond hostess at Ta-boó, at four-thirty on a Friday afternoon in early October. Just turned twenty, Holley is gorgeous and sweet, if a bit vacuous. "Hi, my name is Holley," servers mimic her. "My favorite color is clear, and I like to watch the wind blow." A store across the street lends her $500 skirts just so she'll show them off.

The woman said she would return that evening with the owner of the agency, who was from Morocco.

At 10:00 P.M. Ta-boó was crowded, the disco music enveloping. Even off-season, on Friday and Saturday nights the restaurant is packed. As promised, the woman showed up. She took Holley outside and introduced her to a swarthy-looking man in a Mercedes limousine. A van was parked behind the limo. The man wanted to take Holley to Miami. Holley walked back into the restaurant and found Jonathan, a server who was her boyfriend.

"These people want to take me in a limo and talk to me about modeling. Doesn't that seem a little strange?" she asked him.

"What do you mean?" he said. "That's crazy."

Jonathan rushed over to Kevin O'Dea, who was at the center of the restaurant booking a reservation. Jonathan told O'Dea he was afraid they would abduct her. So O'Dea walked outside, where Holley was talking to the man in the limo.

"I can't go now," Holley was saying.

O'Dea imagined Holley being taken to Morocco, pressed into sexual slavery.

"Are you her boyfriend?" the woman asked O'Dea.

"No, I'm her boss," O'Dea said.

The woman jumped into the limo, and the limo and the van took off.

Almost every week, someone tries to pull a scam on the restaurant. One afternoon a man phoned O'Dea claiming he was editor of a magazine doing a feature on Palm Beach. "We're going to be down Friday night, and we would like dinner for three," he told O'Dea.

O'Dea had never heard of the magazine and thought the request strange. Usually, reviewers and travel writers pay for their dinners and don't give advance notice. O'Dea ignored the request. Then the man called Ta-boó co-owner Nancy Sharigan.

"Didn't you get our fax?" the man asked her.

"Frankly, we don't know your magazine," she said.

The man offered to bring some copies.

"Okay," she said, "You can come for dinner, but you can't order Dom Pérignon."

Later, Nancy had second thoughts and wanted to call the man back to cancel the invitation. O'Dea said, "Let's see what happens." As it turned out, the man never showed up. Kevin called his counterparts at Galaxy Grille and Amici to warn them.

One afternoon a knockout blonde came into the restaurant and claimed that the night before a waiter had spilled red wine all over her white leather dress. She proffered a dry-cleaning bill. Normally, the restaurant doesn't pay for dry cleaning unless a customer calls O'Dea over immediately. Then he hands out a signed card saying the restaurant will pay. But this woman was so appealing that O'Dea paid her anyway. When he called other restaurants—Bice, Galaxy Grille, and Amici—he found out that the same woman had been in with the same bill.

Some claims are legitimate. "One night a server spilled a whole tray of drinks on someone," O'Dea said. "The man had on a brand-new fifteen-hundred-dollar jacket. It had sloe gin, which is red, all over it. My dry cleaner is wonderful. On his third try, he got it cleaned. That saved us fifteen hundred dollars. I gave him a gift certificate for dinner for two."

One evening at eight-thirty, a busboy hit a chandelier with a chair he was moving. The chandelier began swinging back and forth, then crashed to the floor, just missing a diner. The next night, the man came in.

"Remember me?" he said to O'Dea. "Are you going to give me a hard hat tonight?"

O'Dea ushered him to a nice table and ordered him an expensive wine.

When people leave things at the restaurant, it's not just keys and wallets stuffed with $20 bills. A Russian couple came in one night for dinner. After leaving, they returned at ten.

"The woman was hysterical," O'Dea told me. "The guy was stoic. She had left her purse. It had eight thousand dollars cash in it. We went through the laundry, everything. We never found it. But forty-five minutes later, they came back and said they had found the purse on Worth Avenue near the Colony Hotel. The strap had broken."

Another woman came back to the restaurant one evening around midnight and said she had lost her bracelet. Studded with diamonds, emeralds, rubies, and sapphires, it was worth $100,000. More important, it had been her grandmother's. The woman was devastated.

"If we don't find it by the morning, we'll call the police," O'Dea told her. "They can try to track it through pawn shops."

Just then, a busboy came up.

"Is this it?" he asked.

The elated woman tipped the busboy $200.

Besides comparing notes about scams, O'Dea keeps in touch with bartenders at other restaurants to trade information on deadbeats and heavy drinkers who should not be served. One of O'Dea's contacts, Richard L. Brown, a man with a mustache and a cheery round face, has been a bartender at Chuck & Harold's for more than fifteen years. Chuck & Harold's and Testa's, next to each other on Royal Poinciana Way, both have outdoor tables. Both were favorites of the Kennedys. Sitting at one of the outdoor tables is like sitting beside a runway at a fashion show. No where else can one see such a concentration of striking women. Still owned by the Testa family, the Italian restaurant has better food than Chuck & Harold's, including an extraordinarily fresh fish soup; seafood marinara with lobster, shrimp, mussels, sea scallops, and fish over linguini; and an awe-inspiring strawberry pie. When Palm Beach couples want to announce that they are having an affair, they go to Testa's to be seen having breakfast outdoors along the sidewalk. Chuck & Harold's, with a roof that opens to the sky, is more elegant than Testa's, with an inviting L-shaped bar near the front.

Every night some of the most dazzling women in the world show up at the bar, looking for wealthy men. "They use their charms to entice these men," Brown said. "I see a lot of these girls—very pretty, very young, and very smart. I've seen fifty-year age differences. Every once in a while, one of them hits the jackpot. Or they may not get married to them but they get a nice settlement. Maybe they have an affair that is an embarrassment to the family."

Men confide to young women details of their finances, telling them their net worth or that they own a jet or a yacht. "They tell this to a girl who has walked in here with a short skirt and is showing her ass and breasts," Brown said. "They tell these young girls more than they tell their accountants, to get their attention."

Few prostitutes work Palm Beach. "Too many women are willing to give it away for free," Brown told me. "They're willing to sleep around."

AIDS has had little impact. "You see people getting ready to have sex after four drinks," Brown confided. "It's amazing. That has never changed. I can guarantee you it's completely unprotected sex. They come back and tell me about it. I say, 'What are you doing? You could catch something. Are you nuts?' I've seen girls doing it in the bathroom and under the table."

Most of Brown's customers have inherited money. "Their goal is just to keep it," Brown said. "They are not entrepreneurs. They are more conservative. A lot have their money in bonds instead of stocks."

A son of a very wealthy Palm Beach family kept giving Brown checks that bounced. "We're not supposed to accept checks at all," Brown told him. "This can't continue. The manager will go to the police.'"

"My father died," the young man explained, "and the estate is being contested. No money is coming in."

"Why don't you get a job?" Brown asked.

"Richard, I've never worked a day in my life, and I never will," he told the bartender.

The restaurant got in touch with the attorney representing the young man and made arrangements to extend credit tied to the proceeds from the case. "He was willing to risk jail time rather than get a job to tide him over," Brown said.

When customers have had too much to drink, Brown cuts them off. But one Saturday, when Brown started his shift at 5:00 P.M., the previous bartender didn't warn him that a customer had been drinking most of the afternoon.

"He was starting to argue with his girlfriend, using language I didn't like," Brown said. "'Excuse me, sir, don't use that language in this restaurant,'" Brown said.

"Gimme my goddamn bill," the man said.

Brown gave him the bill, which was for $26. He had already paid the previous bartender $180.

"All I got is twenty dollars," the customer said.

"I'll take it," Brown said.

The man glared at Brown and looked as if he were about to hit him.

"Do you want me to call the police?" Brown said.

The man began walking out of the restaurant, then turned back.

"You're an asshole," he shouted at the bartender.

Three hours later two state troopers came in and asked Brown to step outside.

"The man had just flipped his car over and killed his girl-friend," Brown said. "I thought he had just had a couple of glasses of champagne. I didn't realize he had been drinking all day. If I had known that, before the guy left, I would have called the police. Somebody died that day due to the actions of people at the restaurant who were not taking care of a customer the way they should have."

Because they tend to be better at cutting off customers, Brown prefers working with female bartenders. "Stacy would put her hands on the guy and say, 'We think you've had too much to drink. Can I bring you a cup of coffee?' We take their keys," Brown said.

The female bartenders at Chuck & Harold's tend to be dazzling. Holli, a Pamela Anderson Lee look-alike, told me men constantly say to her, "Let me take you away from all this. You shouldn't be here. You should be on my yacht."

Celebrities love Palm Beach because the local press—the Shiny Sheet and the *Palm Beach Post*—are respectful. "There are no journalists chasing people as in California," Brown said. "We've had them all—the Kennedys, all the personalities of our time—and they are completely left alone. Nowhere else in the world are celebrities insulated from journalists and photographers. Rarely does anyone even ask for an autograph."

To make sure they have privacy, Chuck & Harold's seats celebrities at a table in the back away from other diners. But that's not always what they want. When Sylvester Stallone came in one day, he was seated at a back table. "Nobody approached him," Brown said. "He asked to be moved. So we put him in the middle of the Garden Room."

Both Roxanne Pulitzer's boyfriend Count Jean de la Moussaye and her new husband, Harald Dude, were regular customers. Harald is "the nicest guy in the world, but when he was married to his previous wife, he couldn't keep his pants closed," Brown said. One night, Dude was drinking at the bar with a young woman. He told her to meet him at the bar the next night at seven.

"I come in that night, and he's sitting with his then-wife at six," Brown said. "So the girl came in at seven, and he's drinking wine and talking to both of them. The wife is not sure who this other woman is. At eight another girl comes in. Harald said, 'Richard, help me.' I said, 'Harald, you deserve this.' But he got away with it. When he married Roxanne, who is known to have a strong sexual appetite, I thought they were the perfect match."

"I think they had a pretty open relationship, is my guess," Roxanne said of Harald and his previous wife.

At least one in five of the people who come to Chuck & Harold's is a poseur, according to Brown. There was the guy with a brand-new Jaguar. "He told me he was Italian," Brown said. "He hobnobbed with the rich and famous of Palm Beach. He would spend money, bring in pretty girls, talk business deals. One day, I saw his car in Palm Beach. I followed him in my car. I thought I'd have a drink with him. I saw him stop at what is now Galaxy Grille."

Brown asked Brookey, a bartender who is now at the Palm Beach Tavern, where the man went. He said he lived upstairs in apartment 13. Superstitious, the man had covered over the 13 with a 14, Brookey told him.

"You're kidding," Brown said. "Those apartments rent for three hundred fifty or four hundred a month. Look at the jewelry, the suits, the car."

Less than a month later, the man, forty-year-old Louis A. DiCarlo, was arrested for bank fraud in connection with a telemarketing scheme. It turned out he was a Colombian drug dealer who had had extensive plastic surgery to conceal his identity. He pleaded guilty to bank fraud.

Almost five years later, Brown saw DiCarlo at mass at Saint Edward's Church, which Rose Kennedy attended. "I talked to him after mass," Brown said. "He had started a company called Jeins & Company selling jeans packaged in stylish paint cans. He was driving a Bentley. People from Palm Beach invested more than one million in it before it went bust."

16. NAKED IN THE GARDEN

In a banquet room of Bice, an overpriced Northern Italian restaurant on Peruvian Avenue, twenty men sat with Pam and me around a long table as waiters brought plates of pasta and poured great quantities of Merlot and Pinot Grigio.

"Is your husband agog?" one of them asked Pam.

"What?"

"I said, is your husband a GOG? A gentleman of the garden."

"No. Have you been one for long?"

He looked at his watch. "About two hours, twenty minutes."

It was early October, and the men were holding the monthly dinner meeting of the Gentlemen of the Garden. Ostensibly, the organization was founded to contribute to the Ann Norton Sculpture Gardens on Barcelona Road in West Palm Beach. Its real purpose is to give the guys a night out and let them pretend they have their own secret fraternity. It's the male rejoinder to maternal Palm Beach society.

Kirby Kooluris is one of the group's twenty-one founders. So are Robert Eigelberger and Willie DeGray. Until 1997 DeGray had been married to Helen DeGray, an heir to the $2.7 billion Wrigley gum fortune. With an investment of $32, her great-grandfather, William Wrigley, Jr., started a soap company in Chicago in 1891. To lure merchants to order his soap, he began giving out free baking powder. The baking powder became more successful than the soap, so he stopped selling soap. Then, as an incentive to buy the baking powder, he gave out two packs of gum for each can. The gum took off, and Wrigley now dominates the world chewing-gum market.

When DeGray was married to Helen, they had five full-time servants. He bought a Bentley for $180,000. One vacation they stayed for a month at the Hotel Villa d'Este on Lake Como in Italy. The bill, which DeGray put on his American Express platinum card, was $74,000.

"I had two houses, a boat," DeGray told me. "With that much money, the things you worry about are nonexistent. The only hard part is finding the time to schedule vacation trips. My job was to carry expensive luggage on first-class flights to fancy places." After their divorce, Helen married James Rosburg, a sculptor.

Robert Eigelberger, who now heads the Gentlemen of the Garden, is married to Susan Phipps, heir to the $5 billion Phipps family fortune. Henry Phipps, the progenitor of the clan, was a founder of Carnegie Steel Corporation. When he sold his share of the company to J. P. Morgan, he pocketed $50 million. In 1907 he formed Bessemer Trust to serve his family's needs. Through Bessemer, he bought up miles of ocean frontage on Long Island, coastal tracts in the Carolinas, and vast acreage on the Florida Gold Coast. In 1972 Bessemer began offering trust and investment services to non–family members.

Still owned by the family, Bessemer Trust manages $23 billion in assets. Accounts must be $5 million or more. While Bessemer is based in New York, it has an office on Palm Beach's "Bankers Row"—Royal Palm Way—where America's largest banks have branches.

Kirby is a regular at parties given by Eigelberger and Phipps. When Kooluris rented his house to Malcolm Pray, a collector of antique cars, and his girlfriend, a former German flight attendant, Kirby took her best friend's daughter to one of their parties.

"The girl was seventeen," Kirby recalled. "I have never seen a more beautiful girl in my life. They said, 'You dirty dog. Now we know where you've been.' Nothing was happening. I think she had a little crush on me. I wouldn't fool around at home. This person was paying my rent."

An architectural designer, Eigelberger started the trend of restoring Mizner homes instead of tearing them down. He began with the coral-colored Warden House. Built by Addison Mizner in 1922 for Standard Oil partner William Gray Warden, the home is at 200 North Ocean Boulevard. In 1979 Eigelberger rescued the forty-five-room home from demolition (the previous owner was behind on his taxes) and converted it into condominiums, while preserving its original features.

Like almost everyone else who comes to the island, Mizner reinvented himself here. The four-hundred-pound man never received a diploma or license but had served an apprenticeship under San Francisco architect Willis Polk. Suffering from necrosis, lung constrictions, heart palpitations, and a general physical breakdown, Mizner had been given only a few months to live. Moreover, at age forty-five, he was in heavy debt. His friends in New York raised $12,000 to ship him off to the Royal Poinciana Hotel in Palm Beach for his final days.

Meanwhile, Paris Singer—one of eighteen illegitimate children fathered by sewing machine inventor Isaac Singer—had broken off with his mistress, Isadora Duncan, the renowned dancer. Distraught and exhausted, he moved to Palm Beach, where he, too, stayed at the Royal Poinciana. Mizner and Singer spent their days fanning themselves on the porch of the hotel, both bored and expecting to die soon.

According to an account in Murray Weiss and Bill Hoffman's *Palm Beach Babylon*, an authoritative history of Palm Beach scandals, they began musing about what they would do if they lived.

"I'll tell you what I'd do," Mizner said. "I'd build something that wasn't made of wood."

This reminded Singer of his effort, after another crushing romance, to build a hospital for Army veterans. He suggested building another hospital for returning World War I veterans.

Very much alive, the two men found an unobstructed view of the mainland near Joe Frazier's alligator pen. "Alligator Joe" kept the alligators as pets. This is where they would build their hospital, at the foot of Worth Avenue.

A perfectionist, Mizner kept making changes to the plans. As a result, the building was not finished until the veterans had returned home. The hospital never opened. Instead, in 1919, Singer turned it into the first private club in Palm Beach. He named it the Everglades Club.

Soon the Vanderbilts and Drexels were asking for admission. To bolster his own standing, Singer declared that he would decide each year whether to renew memberships. Meanwhile, Mizner, who had collected colorful tiles from ruins along the Mediterranean, began installing them in the new club. If he couldn't find worn tiles, he attacked them with a hammer, breaking them into pieces and cementing them back in place to give them a distressed look.

When Lucretia Stotesbury saw the work, she gushed, "Oh, Addie! It's beautiful!" Her husband, Edward T. Stotesbury, was the Philadelphia financier who chaired Drexel and Company and was an owner of the J. P. Morgan Trust Company. He was worth more than $30 million. Mrs. Stotesbury decreed that Mizner would build a home like the Everglades for them. She wanted the home, on a twenty-three-acre plot spanning the island, to be large enough to hold twelve hundred guests. A display case would hold diamonds, emeralds, and pearls. Her husband merely asked for a zoo stocked with twenty-five monkeys and twenty-five parrots. The home— since demolished—was called El Mirasol.

The estate and her lavish entertaining established Lucretia as the island's first grande dame. Soon every resident wanted a Mizner home. Mizner was swamped with orders for his whimsical designs reminiscent of Spain—pastel villas with red-tiled roofs, crammed with courtyards, balconies, secret walkways, and outside staircases.

To give the wood for the homes an aged look, Mizner had workmen beat the lumber with chains and apply paint and then partially remove it. He spent nearly a year in Europe buying villas and monasteries for their stone and old wood.

Mizner turned to putting his stamp on Worth Avenue, creating two- and three-story apartment buildings with arcades of shops on the first level. As in Europe, along the avenue he interjected inviting "vias" that trail into courtyards and alleys with fountains and bougainvillea. On Via Mizner, Mizner's monkey Johnny Brown is buried with the date April 30, 1927, on the gravestone. The gravestone is behind Johnnie Brown's, the store co-owned by Frank Shields.

Having served as chairman of Palm Beach's Landmark Commission and restored more than forty homes, Eigelberger now devotes himself to creating a magnificent garden on his $4.4 million estate. It's a wonderland with almost seventy varieties of palms; a citrus grove with lemons, oranges, mangoes, and lichees; an orchid garden; an herb garden; a rose garden; and a small tropical rain forest.

To get the proper humidity in the rain forest, he installed sprinklers high in the trees overhead. In the crepuscular light below the canopy are exotic broadleaf plants he brought back from Ecuador. In other parts of the estate, he brought in mature trees to supplement the established banyan, kapok, and sausage trees—whose limbs are accented with lovely flowering bromeliads and Spanish moss.

The roughly thirteen acres are what remains of the Phipps estate, which his wife inherited. The couple sold twelve acres to developer Dan Swanson for an exclusive community of four-thousand-square-foot homes selling for $3 million to $4 million, situated between North County Road and North Lake Way. But you can't see any of the new community from the Eigelberger-Phipps oasis. And all you can hear is the distant trill of music from inside the Spanish-style house, a tinkling fountain at the pool, a gonglike wind chime, and, once in a while, thin reeds of voices from somewhere beyond the sussurating palms.

The tropical villa itself is an eclectic mix of antiques and things South American, walls festooned with bright plates and antlered heads, a house put together by well-traveled and colorful people. Its decor is Suzie Phipps's personal style—she dresses rich Bohemian, in bright-patterned peasant dresses and turquoise necklaces, while everyone else is wearing simple lines and solid colors.

Later in the evening, Suzie Phipps dropped in at Bice. Preserving a ritual, whoever saw her first cried out, "Woman present!" Then all the men stood, as best they could considering the wine, and loudly applauded her.

"She is very rich, very social, and nonconformist," Donald Bruce said of Phipps. "She's pretty and doesn't wear makeup. No one can do her any harm."

On an island of conformity, Eigelberger, like his wife (they are known as the Phippsbergers), does his best not to fit in. Bob is gregarious, lusty, with a broad, easy smile. Chain-smoking, wearing moccasins with no socks, he tells a great story. He would be comfortable anywhere and has continental panache—sporting a red sash with medals at black-tie events. But he seems most at home on his terrace along North Lake Way, looking across a sea of closely cut grass, with two tropical islands of towering palms, spiky agave, and luscious kalanchoe, to a distant shore of hot-weather perennials, accented with purple fronds of Moses-in-a-boat and tiny coral bouquets of ixora. It is the kingdom of small lizards and a jubilant English bull terrier named Bear.

"About four years ago I got a call from a broker in town," Eigelberger told me. "He said he had a client who would like to see my property." At the time, Eigelberger was considering selling his estate. The client turned out to be Michael Jackson. "This turquoise van pulled up. Out jumped Michael Jackson wearing a black fedora, black long-sleeved shirt, a bandage on his nose. He was wearing one red sock and one white sock. He had his bodyguard with him."

Eigelberger walked him around the property for an hour. Meanwhile, Suzie Phipps was giving their two dogs a bath. When she came out to meet Jackson, she took one look at him and said, "If my nanny dressed me the way you're dressed, my mother would have fired her."

Jackson laughed.

When Jackson saw their guest room and the display of magazines, he became animated and asked if he could have some. "He walked out with a stack of magazines," Eigelberger said.

After the visit, as Jackson and his broker were driving past the Breakers Hotel, Jackson commented, "That's more the size of house I'm interested in."

At Bice, James Carmo, an architect sitting to my right, told me he was designing the renovation of a Mizner home for John Kluge as well as a new, twenty-thousand-square-foot home for Bill Koch. Kluge bought two homes and tore them down so he could extend his garden.

"Mizner's Mediterranean style went out after World War II," said Carmo, of Bridges, Marsh & Carmo. "They went to French Regency, then in vogue. In the last ten years, Eigelberger started a new trend with Warden House by saving it from being torn down. He turned it into condos. That started people finding these gems, great Mizner homes and Spanish- and Italian-style homes," preserving Palm Beach's European look. Today "people are looking for more traditional, classical elements in Palm Beach," he said. "The days of doing everything in marble are over. They are trying to get back to where they were—terra-cotta floors, wood floors. Essentially that's the way it was in the twenties."

Sitting across from Eigelberger at Bice, his friend Andrew said, "Do you think Bob should write a book about his garden? No. He does it out of passion, not to write a book about it. Not to make money from a best-seller. That's not important. Passion. That is what is important. Money? Not important. You *have* money, who needs it? You don't need any more. It's not important."

Andrew was attractive and charmingly preppy, straight from one of those Princeton dining clubs, however vague he was about his own curriculum vitae. That goes with the territory. The Gentlemen of the Garden are secretive. Even though the group is a nonprofit organization whose finances are public, the treasurer refused to say how much the club contributes each year.

"They can't say how much they contribute because it's not much," Kooluris observed later. Kirby's mother had just had a car accident, and because he was taking care of her in New Jersey, he was not at the dinner at Bice. "To pay my dues, I let them have my house for meetings," Kooluris explained. "Someone else supplies the food and wine. Then he lets me take the credit so it looks like my party."

Until recently, the group's fund-raising parties featured nude women, a tradition started by the group's first president, the late Jim Butler. At one such party, DeGray said, "they pulled away a curtain. There was a perfect example of each sex, naked. The guy held an index card in front of him. The girl had on nothing. The original girl did not show up. But a secretary at the garden was offered the job and accepted—beautiful breasts. We proceeded to auction them off. We got sixteen hundred dollars for the guy and twelve hundred for the girl. The winners were given finger paint and could go off in the bushes and paint them."

The dinners at various Palm Beach restaurants follow the business meetings. At this one, the group voted to donate $1,500—about what their meal cost—to the Norton. Over time, the group has donated $40,000, according to Eigelberger.

In fact, according to the group's filings with the Internal Revenue Service, the Gentlemen of the Garden recently took in $102,740 in contributions and dues but paid out as donations only $14,477 of its receipts—14 percent. The rest went for "fund-raising," meaning parties and dinners at pricey places like Bice.

"We meet once a month and decide nothing so we can meet again," one of the members at the table said.

A man sitting next to Pam asked her, "Are you going to move down here?"

"No, I don't think so."

"Is your husband writing this book to get into Palm Beach society?" He sounded quite serious.

The question puzzled Eigelberger, who doesn't believe in clubs or society. "There is a benefit to certain clubs—there's a benefit to the Sailfish Club if you have a boat and want to tie up at their dock. If a club discriminates against someone, why would you want to be a member of that club?" he asked rhetorically.

Certainly Eigelberger would not fit into the Everglades Club, which distributes to members fourteen pages of rules, including qualifications for guests: "It shall be the responsibility of members to introduce as registered guests only those individuals who conform to, and whose conduct is consistent with, the standards prevailing for members . . ." Nor would Eigelberger stand for the lengthy dress rules, which sound like a summer camp's instructions on what kids should pack:

> *Ladies and gentlemen are required to wear formal attire on formal evenings in the Orange Garden as indicated in the club calendar. Dress is informal at all other times, however, gentlemen must wear jackets at luncheon, except on the Gold Patio and in the Gold Pavilion between 3 P.M. and 7 P.M. Ladies are permitted to wear slacks, trousers, or pants during the daytime. For gentlemen, jackets and ties are required after 6 P.M. for all regular club events and at the Sunday brunch buffet. For ladies, elegant evening pajamas are permissible in the Gold Terrace and the Cloister Café but skirts or dresses must be worn in the Orange Garden.*

Moreover, members and their guests "will refrain from wearing unacceptable clothing anywhere on the club grounds. Unacceptable types of clothing include: T-shirts, tank tops, numeral or logo sports jerseys, jeans, cut-offs, bathing attire, warm-up suits and shorts, other than Bermuda length."

Staff must warn members or guests if they are not dressed in conformance with the rules. "If the member or guest refuses to comply, that fact shall be reported to the executive committee, which, if it is satisfied that the violation occurred, shall suspend the member for a period of 10 days."

Eigelberger struggled with the question of what attracts people to submit to such regimentation—to pay to give up their freedom. "I guess they want to be accepted by the other people who go to the parties and clubs," Eigelberger said, looking dumbfounded.

17. $100 Million Is for Paupers

"At age three, I would go everywhere in limos with my nanny," said Heather Wyser-Pratte, recalling what it was like to grow up in Palm Beach. "None of the men ever worked. I remember when I first got married and my husband went to work, I thought he didn't love me anymore. 'Where are you going?'"

Heather, fifty-five, is blond and shapely, with a perpetual throaty laugh. She drives a replica of a Bugatti and lives in a home called Le Maroc with a turret that rises from the living room and overlooks the pool. Her home is straight from *Tales of the Arabian Nights*, in white stucco, with gates instead of doors, pointed arches for windows, and graceful Arabic calligraphy scrawled over the walls. The living room is open to cross breezes from the garden and the pool. Family photos crowd the surfaces. A guest house in the back she calls the shit pit, where her daughters used to bring their friends, about ten at a time, where Heather as single mother could keep an eye on them. Amused and philosophical about her admitted lack of organization, she serves drinks with a napkin that says, "The only difference between this place and the Titanic is they had a band."

Heather is going with Allen F. Manning, a bastion of the Old Guard, who lives along Lake Worth. He was married to the late sculptor Diana Henrietta Guest of the Phipps family. Her alabaster figures still decorate Manning's home.

In mid-October, Manning threw a dinner party for Pam and me. Over Thai food, Heather said she had been flipping through the pages of her yearbook from Palm Beach Day School. Her classmates were "coddled, overprotected," she said. "My school yearbook is scary. I was looking at the names and the things that wealth can't cure—illness. One fellow was stoned to death in Spain because he was gay. Freaky, horrible things when they were quite young. You see great unhappiness, fighting over money."

Heather is living it herself. Her mother, Patience Mullendore McNulty Campbell, left tons of money, and now the family is duking it out over the estate.

Palm Beachers don't talk about how much money they have. But taking advantage of an author's prerogative, I asked Heather if she is worth more than $100 million.

"Those categories are for paupers," she deadpanned. "I have the Midas touch." She said she used to tell her then-husband, Guy Wyser-Pratte, a prominent speculator in takeover stocks: "Darling, this stock or geographic area has to be the best investment in the world." Each time, she said, he did the opposite, and he "made a bloody fortune."

As a child Heather played on Via Bellaria off South Ocean Boulevard, where two homes known as the "ham and cheese" houses are located. They are joined by a tunnel so a husband could easily visit his mistress in the matching home he had built for her next door.

"In my class at Palm Beach Day School, there were three to six children," Heather said. "We had four-hour lunch hours and went to the Bath & Tennis Club. We had half a hamburger and ran off and went swimming or played tennis. Then we would get back in the afternoon."

Then as now, the Bath & Tennis Club, which some call "Bitches and Twitches," was, along with the Everglades Club, the inner sanctum of Palm Beach society. "You've really arrived when you die in the reading room of the B&T," Heather joked. Once when she was twelve, she was swimming there, wearing a pink bikini. "I was flat as a board," she said. "A lifeguard covered me with a huge towel and told me it was not a decent swimming suit."

Heather is of the Old Guard, but her membership is fraying. When she went to the Everglades Club under her parents' membership, she had an encounter with the club's dress code. "The Everglades asked me to remove my pants," she said. "I guess you're supposed to go home and change. They were long silky flowing evening pants. I thought they resembled a skirt, so I could get away with it. But they had a sharp eye. I just removed the pants and came out in my tunic top, which equals a mini." Allen Manning's late wife, Diana, resigned over the pants rule, Heather told me.

Without pants, "You get cold knees. You could catch pneumonia," she said, laughing. Worse things happen at the club. "You could get run over by one of the members who can't see," she said. "A member ran over a poor valet one year. It's a very lively place."

Heather finds it amusing that business is not supposed to be discussed at the clubs, yet that is a major reason people join clubs. Certainly George Bissell was discussing business when, over drinks at the Bath & Tennis and Everglades clubs, he persuaded members of the Old Guard to invest nearly $14 million in an orchid nursery. They didn't know until it was too late that he had paid one group of investors with money from another group and pocketed the profit. "If they overhear you discussing business, they can *e-lim-in-ate* you," Heather said, emphasizing each syllable.

Allen Manning heads the Palm Beach chapter of the English-Speaking Union, dedicated to promoting the English language and heritage. He also heads the Pundits, an elite group of a hundred Palm Beach folk who invite people like Gerald Ford and Alexander M. Haig, Jr., a Palm Beach resident who was secretary of state, to speak to them at their luncheons. Finally, Manning is a senior member of the Coconuts, which is so exclusive that new members can join only when one of the existing twenty-two members resigns or dies.

"The Coconuts was formed during the Depression, when bachelors around town accepted invitations during the year and wanted to reciprocate," Manning said. "So they pooled their resources and had this annual New Year's Eve party and invited people who had been hospitable to them. Ambassador Earl Smith was the head of it. Now the former ambassador to Denmark, Guilford Dudley, Jr., is the chief Coconut. It's a very private group."

The fact that someone of Manning's stature had taken me under his wing—and invited me to speak to the Pundits—opened even more doors. I had met Allen through the usual chain of referrals—Kirby introduced me to Judy Schrafft, who introduced me to Heather, who introduced me to Allen.

By now, when I wanted to raise the subject of anti-Semitism, I had taken to saying, "I'm Jewish, but Pam's mother is a member of the DAR, so we balance each other out." Whatever works.

Talk at Manning's dinner party turned to a woman who has a reputation as a hanger-on. Palm Beach is full of them—bottom feeders who live off the nightly functions that don't require invitations. The tradition goes back to the duke and duchess of Windsor, who were known in Palm Beach for never paying their bills. "It was beneath them," said Donald Bruce, the former owner of the Worth Avenue store that bore his name.

The woman mentioned at the Manning dinner party had been a beauty, until a car accident shattered her face. She was still pretty, but the experience also shattered her self-esteem. "If you say you're going out, she'll say, 'Where?'" Heather said. "If you tell her, she'll show up before you, uninvited. I felt sorry for her. I still do."

What makes Palm Beach special is the beaches, but most Palm Beachers never go near them. "One of the few times they go to the beach is when they walk their dogs on the 'doggie beach' at Wells

Road," said Judy Schrafft, another dinner-party guest. Schrafft has two Portuguese water dogs. "There are leash laws and poop laws, but you just dig a hole in the sand with your foot," Schrafft said. "Who has time for the beach? Most don't wake up until ten-thirty or eleven A.M. Most people prefer to go to the pool."

Now that the Kennedys have left the island, "I don't know what we're going to do for excitement," said another guest, Jim Ponce, the unofficial town historian. Ponce said their estate was a disgrace. "Rose never spent a nickel on the home." Ponce was a clerk at the Brazilian Court in the '60s when Rose called to reserve four rooms for younger family members.

"And how much is that going to be?" Rose asked.

"It's thirty-four dollars a night, Mrs. Kennedy."

"It was thirty-two last year."

"Mrs. Kennedy, it's thirty-four."

"Well, why can't I have it at last's year's rate?"

"Mrs. Kennedy, do you want it for thirty-four dollars or not?"

Rose wound up taking the room at the quoted rate.

Heather recalled the time she was having caviar and champagne at The Four Seasons hotel—which was then the Ocean Grand—for one of her mother's birthdays. With her mother were eight of her "old grande dame" girlfriends, who were very used to caviar. The manager came out and said, "Madame, I'm terribly sorry, but Mr. Khashoggi"—who was sitting at a corner table with his children and had rented a floor—"has devoured every gram of caviar at the Ocean Grand."

Palm Beach is "charming like Europe but fifty years behind the times in many ways," she said. "Any night, you can play Cinderella. The police still bring my dogs back. Garbage collection is five days a week. No one will ever starve here, because we have A&P, and Kellogg, and Post," Heather said. Her kids' friends had names like Cinnamon and Celery. "They were a walking deli," she said. When she asked the mother of Celery why she did that to her, the woman replied, "I was pregnant, and a lady asked what I would call her. I looked down at my Bloody Mary and saw the celery stick and said, 'I don't know, Celery.'"

Manning said he knew a woman in Palm Beach who said to him, "You know, my husband and I were not on the best of terms. And," she said, "he detested Maxwell House. You see that can on the mantelpiece?" she asked Manning. "His ashes are in there. Every time I pass it, I say, 'You son of a bitch, that's where you belong.'"

Said Heather, "I know a woman who checks the air conditioning at First National in Palm Beach every day to see that her husband's ashes are okay."

Inevitably, the conversation turned to Roxanne Pulitzer. Heather said her nanny was friends with Roxanne's nanny. "Roxanne is a devoted mother," she said. "Even the old biddies sided with her."

"She always said she played the hand she was dealt," Schrafft remarked.

Explaining that his butler was away in France, Manning scooped ice cream onto pound cake for dessert. Kay Rybovich, another guest, reported that Kirby Kooluris was still in New Jersey taking care of his mother. He called her to let her know his mother is recovering. Kirby told her he bathes and dresses his mother. "He's so real," Rybovich said.

"Header," Schrafft said to Heather ("Judy calls me 'Header' because one of my husbands was Dutch and couldn't pronounce *Heather*," Heather explained), "remember when Kirby had a South African tall ship at his dock? Instead of staying one day, the crew stayed for the summer. We would go over, and the crew would dive for fish for dinner. The owner wanted to sink the boat to get the insurance. He successfully sank it in the Caribbean."

The talk turned to Mayor Paul R. Ilyinsky and his trip to Russia with his wife, Angelica, for the burial of the last czar. Ilyinsky's middle name is Romanoff. "I had a long talk with Angie last week about the Russia trip," Schrafft said. "He was impressed by the outpouring of affection for his family."

In a back room of Ta-boó, Mayor Ilyinsky apologized for wearing sunglasses. He had just had cataract surgery. The chunky dark glasses, with his white hair, gave him the appearance of a tall, good-looking Onassis.

The mayor was sporting the customary blue blazer and, of course, was sockless.

"We have a uniform almost," he said. "I have two blue jackets. I keep one in the trunk of the car at all times. They last about three years, and I get a new one."

Ilyinsky had just returned from a National League of Cities meeting in Miami. He went in proper Palm Beach style, sailing on his yacht, the *Angelique*. Now he was weeks away from announcing his intention to run for a fourth two-year term as mayor. Everyone in Palm Beach was speculating about what he would decide.

When a court struck down the Palm Beach law requiring employees to register with the police, Ilyinsky, who was then town-council president, had been wistful. "It was a nice feature of living in a town like Palm Beach," he was quoted as saying. When Ilyinsky was on the town council, he voted for an ordinance that requires moviemakers to register with the town and present evidence that they have insured the town for $10 million in the event any damage occurs. When an airplane is involved, the amount rises to $100 million. Even then, shooting must be limited to off-season. The ordinance requires payment of $1,000 as well. According to Mary A. Pollitt, the town clerk, no one has ever applied for the permit.

"People don't like to walk out of their houses and see TV cameras sitting in the garden," the seventy-year-old Ilyinsky said over smoked Norwegian salmon with chopped onion, dill sauce, and capers on toast points. "During the William Kennedy Smith trial, the whole square around town hall was full of TV cameras." He added, "I'm sort of antipress. I think they can be liars and exaggerators. Look at what's happened to the president. It's insane."

Ilyinsky may be an aristocrat in a town full of grandees, but he has the common touch. While the movie ordinance clearly exempts videotaping of "news events," a TV crew the mayor knows thought they needed to circumvent it to film the Kennedy home for a documentary. "I'm very careful about these things," Ilyinsky said. "So I talked to my code-enforcement officer right away. He said, 'I'll tell you what you can do. Can they fit in the back of your car?' I said, 'Yes.' So I squeezed them in, and off we went. I drove by the Kennedy estate about eighteen times. You can get around some of these things."

Another example was when a Japanese tractor maker submitted the low bid for two tractors the town needed. "I called my friend at John Deere. He happened to be the president. I said, 'How come your dealers didn't bid to supply tractors for Palm Beach?' He said, 'I'll call and find out.' Of course, we had to advertise for bids. He said they didn't feel like bidding. So by that afternoon, they very much felt like bidding on it. This was real clout. By God, they underbid the Japanese. Now we have four or five tractors—American tractors, by God. They'll probably put me in prison one day for this, and I'll proudly go."

A former Marine colonel and a professional photographer, Ilyinsky has a three-hundred-car model railroad in his home. The set—both O gauge and HO gauge—includes some cars and locomotives left to him by his father, Grand Duke Dimitri of Russia, whose father was the youngest son of Czar Alexander II. As a young man, Dimitri was one of three conspirators who plotted the murder of Grigory Yefimovich Rasputin. Rasputin had acquired influence over Empress Alexandra, the wife of Czar Nicholas II, because of his claim that he could ease her son Alexei's suffering from hemophilia. But Rasputin's debauchery and abuse of power led Dimitri and others to believe he was a cancer on the Romanovs and the Russian people. After the conspirators shot Rasputin and dumped his body in a river, Nicholas II, Russia's last czar, banished his cousin Dimitri from Russia. As it turned out, that saved his life. He would have been executed during the coming revolution.

Ilyinsky was born in England. For unknown reasons, his parents named him for a town in Russia and gave him Romanov as a middle name rather than a last name. In 1935 his mother and stepfather began visiting Palm Beach, eventually moving here.

Growing up in Palm Beach, Ilyinsky was tended to by a nanny and driven to school in what commonly was called an Afromobile, a rickshawlike bicycle pedaled by blacks. His father had no money from Russia, but his mother's family was wealthy. Ilyinsky can understand spoken Russian but can't read it.

As an adult, Ilyinsky went to John F. Kennedy's cookouts. Ilyinsky's mother knew Joseph P. Kennedy, the father of the clan. She considered him "one of the greatest crooks she ever met," Ilyinsky recalled.

Ilyinsky met his wife, Angie, at the bar of the Colony Hotel. She was with a date, but the bartender asked Ilyinsky, who was wearing his Marine uniform, if he knew her. The bartender said Angelica Kauffmann lived on El Vedado Road, the same street where Ilyinsky's mother, Audrey Emery, then lived in the home now owned by Celia Farris.

Ilyinsky didn't know her but said to the bartender, "She's a good-looking girl. Why don't you introduce me?"

When Ilyinsky mentioned the neighborhood connection to her, she said, "I don't think I know your mother, and I don't like Marines." Retelling the story, Ilyinsky paused for effect. He smiled broadly and said, "We've been married forty-six years."

At his wife's insistence, the mayor stopped smoking five years ago.

"I was having lunch yesterday," Ilyinsky told me. "A man was smoking at the bar. He said, 'You don't mind if I smoke, do you?'"

"As a matter of fact, I do," Ilyinsky replied.

"Don't I have any rights?"

"Absolutely not."

The man asked the bartender, "Who is this guy?" The bartender said, "That's the mayor of Palm Beach."

"He put out his cigarette!" the mayor said gleefully.

As Ilyinsky was telling the story, Franklyn de Marco strolled in Ta-boó's back entrance with Betsy Fry. Fry was in town for a black-tie birthday party Franklyn was throwing for himself and his father, Franklyn senior, at the Breakers Hotel that Saturday night. Franklyn was sixty; his father was ninety. Nearly three hundred guests showed up for the champagne buffet dinner of beef tenderloin, shrimps and scallops in a white wine sauce, and sliced-to-order smoked Norwegian salmon. A Chinese table offered spring rolls and *shao mai*.

Ilyinsky told De Marco he understood he was having trouble building a new home because of the town's size restrictions. "What's the matter with the house?" Ilyinsky asked. As De Marco was explaining, the mayor said, "Sydell Miller is building a thirty-seven-thousand-square-foot home in a different area. We've stopped a lot of these towering monsters. We take the attitude, if you want to sue us, get in line."

Ilyinsky decided to try his "Palm Beach is misunderstood" routine with me. "Fifty-one percent of the people in Palm Beach go to work every day," he said.

"In their Rolls-Royces or on their yachts?" I asked.

"No, not in their Rolls-Royces, in their Chevrolets and Buicks. Many residents are lawyers and doctors. This town is not that different."

"There's nothing wrong with rich people, is there?" I asked.

The mayor realized the gambit wasn't working. The rich like having their balloons deflated. A certain amount of irreverence does wonders. Soon the mayor was back on track. "We probably have more millionaires per square foot than anywhere else in the world," he said. "There is no place like Palm Beach."

While that's confirmed by bankers and accountants with access to confidential client financial data, the U.S. Census Bureau puts two other towns—Atherton, California, and Kenilworth, Illinois—ahead of Palm Beach in median household net worth. But the census figures are based on special surveys rather than hard data. Billionaires likely would not respond to such surveys, much less give accurate and complete figures on their assets, including such items as trusts, which they may have set up to hide assets from creditors. What's more, the census results include assets of servants living in their employers' mansions, diminishing still further the apparent wealth of a place like Palm Beach.

"If I received a survey like that, I wouldn't answer it unless I were required to do so," said a wealthy Palm Beach lawyer whose clients include some of the island's billionaires.

Palm Beach may be sinfully rich, but it cares about defenseless creatures. Somehow, a little dog had become caught in a sanitary sewer line, which carries away rainwater. "He had worked his way up three to four hundred feet away from the street," the mayor said. "If the tide had come up, he would have drowned. Someone heard him barking. The fire rescue people dug up the street, literally. They saved that dog and the water was up to here." Ilyinsky pointed to his neck.

Tears welled up in the mayor's eyes as he recalled how the town of millionaires saved the life of a little dog. "She is a beautiful white dog," he said. "The people who heard her cry kept her. We pay a lot of attention to things like that. Whales get washed up on the beach. There is a magnificent kapok tree behind Royal Poinciana Chapel near the Flagler Museum. There is none bigger than that. A property owner wanted to knock it down. The neighbors got excited and said, 'You can't do that.' They saved the tree."

Then there is the problem of sea turtles. People steal their eggs after they are laid in nests in the sand. The hatchlings that survive instinctively head toward light. When they see street lamps or spotlights at night, they waddle off to the west instead of eastward to the ocean. They are eaten by predators or crushed on the road, or they simply die of dehydration. In response to the problem, government officials encourage resorts to turn off nonessential lights at night or to install turtle-friendly red lights.

"We worry about all these things," Ilyinsky said.

Having lived in Palm Beach off and on since he was a kid, Ilyinsky knows almost everyone. When people have problems, they call "Paulie" directly, usually at home. He guesses he works at his unpaid job at least three hours a day, skipping out when he goes for a cruise.

One woman complained to him that she had been given a ticket for parking in a prohibited area on a street. He drove by the location. The curb was plainly painted yellow.

"Did you notice the color of the curb?" he asked her later.

"No," she said. "But I'm not going to pay it."

"Why don't you not pay and see what happens?"

Later, she called Ilyinsky to say she had received a notice requiring her to appear in court or face arrest. By then, the fine had doubled.

"Paulie, what will I do?" she asked.

"Why don't you write me a check for fifty dollars, and I'll pay the ticket for you," he said.

"Would you do that for me?" she asked plaintively. The woman couldn't bring herself to write a check to cover a parking ticket.

"So that's what happened, and I made another friend. You catch a lot more flies with honey than with vinegar."

Some years back, Worth Avenue had to be torn up.

"We had a character, Mrs. Queeney-Helene Marie Shelton Tuchbreiter," Ilyinsky said. "She lived on South Ocean Boulevard and was a member of the Everglades Club. She was a marvelous Southern lady with a Southern accent you could lay moss on. She had a heavy crush on me."

Mrs. Tuchbreiter, in her seventies, was known for her very short skirts with slits. Around town, she was called "Mrs. Touch-Pussy." This was news to the mayor.

Tuchbreiter had an enormous Rolls-Royce touring car. "As they were closing Worth Avenue, she decided to make one last run at Martha Phillips," Ilyinsky said, referring to a top Worth Avenue dress shop. "The crews were stopping cars, but they knew her and let her in. She promised she wouldn't be there more than an hour. She parked her car on the curb, which she always did. Her car was the only one on the avenue."

As she came out of the shop, she saw her car majestically disappear into the ground, swallowed into a crumbling sewer pipe.

"We took her home in a police car and pulled her car out," the mayor said.

That night, she called Paulie. "Paulie, guess where I've been?" she said. "I've been in one of your sewers, and I didn't like it very much."

Two years ago, another woman went out for a morning swim in her pool. "She smelled something," Ilyinsky said. "By God, a contractor had hooked a sewer pipe to the storm sewer, causing a backup of sewer water into her pool. The pool was full of sewage. Can you imagine? We moved her out, we moved her dog. We did everything. That took a big chunk out of our undesignated funds."

That brought to mind Mollie Wilmot's encounter with the Venezuelan tanker *Mercedes I*, which tossed up on her property at 1075 North Ocean Boulevard during a storm on Thanksgiving 1984. Wilmot, known for her short skirts, is heir to a Boston department-store fortune. After she divorced Paul Wilmot, an advertising executive, someone asked her at a dinner party if she had picked out her next husband.

"My next husband hasn't been born yet," she said.

Wilmot has the distinction of owning one of the largest swimming pools on the island. It holds 90,000 gallons, compared with 25,000 for the average home pool. When the tanker beached on her property, it covered the pool. Wilmot's maid woke her at 9:30 A.M. to tell her the news and urge her to see the vessel. Visualizing a small boat, Wilmot said, "I'd like my breakfast first." The maid was so upset that Wilmot put on her robe and took a look. The tanker was so big that Wilmot couldn't see the ocean or the palm trees through her windows overlooking the ocean. The police and Coast Guard were already on the scene. Wilmot told me she ordered food for the crew.

Despite the crises, being mayor has its advantages. As Ilyinsky drives past construction crews, flagmen bow to him, a reminder of his royal lineage. But Ilyinsky hasn't played with his model trains for two years. He's too busy doing the town's business and fending off the hundreds of social invitations he and his wife receive.

"We accepted invitations to three cocktail parties and two dinner parties one night this week," he said. "We forgot to tell each other about them. The left hand didn't know what the right one was doing."

At night, Ilyinsky swims in his pool and talks to his Maluccan pink-crested cockatoo. "Smart. Unbelievable. He has a twenty-word vocabulary," he said. "When I come home, if Angie is playing bridge and I open the back door, he'll say in perfect English, 'Is that you?' If he doesn't hear me answer, he starts to holler."

The other day, Ilyinsky said, Robert J. Doney, the town manager, called. "The bird was on my shoulder. I picked up the phone. The bird said, 'Hello.'"

Doney said, "Mr. Mayor, you're sounding more like that parrot every day."

WINTER / SPRING

finale

18. THE TRUMPSTER

On Worth Avenue, a Christmas tree in the middle of the street in front of Tiffany's marked the beginning of the season. Two stories tall, it sang like Johnny Mathis. Bentleys, Aston Martins, and Rolls-Royces maneuvered their way around the tree and the pedestrians who stopped to admire its gold ornaments. In Palm Beach the ornamentation of choice is gold of course, gold and white balls and stars and snowflakes, the trees wrapped up like gifts with stiff gold ribbon and bows at the top.

But Christmas is at a disadvantage here. Warm tropical breezes wreak havoc on wreaths. Not responding at all well to salt air, cut greens become skeletal. Inside, Christmas trees quickly droop and dry into an unappealing light brown. Still there was rejoicing on Worth Avenue, and nightly, one shop or another had a reception to bring in the crowds, more or less invited, for champagne and a free gift. From Chanel, in small shopping bags, Chanel No. 5 for the lady, body lotion for the gentleman. Through the large shop windows, party goers could be seen laughing and chatting and toasting one another. One night Mary Mahoney's invited 250 select guests to a party to view a collection of shipwreck artifacts being offered for sale, and around the corner, Christian duPont hosted a champagne reception among its fine antiques.

At night the little palms planted along the avenue twinkled with tiny white lights. Garish aqua spotlights that underlit the palms from the ground made the trees look plastic. It's what you do with an embarrassment of riches.

For the ultrarich of Boston, New York, Grosse Pointe, Dallas, Philadelphia, and Washington, the season offers an opportunity to escape the stodgy buttoned-down world of commerce, get away from stuffy old banks and overheated boardrooms, from drying winds that wrinkle, and to dress up and dance all night, to schmooze with other socially minded people.

For some, the socializing can be a strain. Charles H. "Carl" Norris, Jr. blamed commuting to Palm Beach during the season for the breakup of his sixteen-year marriage to Diana Strawbridge Wister. Wister, worth $900 million from Campbell's Soup Company stock, is the granddaughter of John T. Dorrance, Sr., the chemist who built the condensed-soup empire. A lawyer, Carl had met Diana when he worked on her legal affairs when he was with the Philadelphia firm of Morgan, Lewis & Bockius. At the time, she was married to a fox hunter.

Besides a $5 million home on Lake Worth in Palm Beach, the couple had a house worth $2.8 million in Vail, a sprawling $25 million estate called Runneymeade Farm in Coatesville, Pennsylvania, and property in Mount Desert Island, Maine, a summer haunt of blue bloods. In Palm Beach the couple belonged to both the Everglades and the Bath & Tennis.

During the divorce proceeding, Diana testified that each home was staffed at all times with social secretaries and servants in case she dropped by. In some years, she conceded, the couple spent $600,000 on clothing alone. Asked why she failed to answer her door at her Palm Beach home when a deputy sheriff arrived to serve her with divorce papers, Diana was perplexed. Then she smiled as the meaning of the question dawned on her. It would never occur to her to answer a doorbell. "That is the duty of the household staff," she said. "I've never answered a door."

In the end, Carl did not feel the need to tell her he was divorcing her. He simply filed papers, she said. She countered with her own divorce suit. Since they both had signed prenuptial agreements disclaiming rights to each other's assets, Carl was owed nothing, she said. But Carl countered that he had signed the agreement under "duress." His boss at the law firm had pressured him to do it. Since Carl was a lawyer experienced in the practice of marital law, that claim was "nonsense," a spokesman for the man's law firm said.

While Carl blamed the breakup on the demands of the season, Diana had a more prosaic explanation: "Carl left me for another woman."

People descend on the island in yachts, Lear jets, and Rolls-Royces for the season, but few arrive in their own commercial-size jets. For the Trumpster, as he is often called, the season began when he left his black stretch limo on the tarmac at La Guardia Airport a week before Christmas and stepped into his Boeing 727-100. Donald Trump would continue to commute almost every weekend during the season, staying at Mar-a-Lago. Besides Trump, the only other passengers that Friday evening on the flight to Palm Beach were his fifteen-year-old son, Eric, Pam, and me. The cost for jet fuel alone for the flight to Florida and the return on Sunday night would be $40,000—ten thousand dollars per person.

Smiling as if he had just made a few extra billion, Trump stood in the galley of his 727 and offered us pretzels. In person, Trump is younger, thinner, and blonder than in his photos. He likes to wear his hair long at the neck. His typical facial expression is to set his mouth in a moue, somewhere between a pucker and a pout. It says, "I'm a handsome guy. I'm going to WIN."

Sitting at a mahogany table on the plane, he sipped a Diet Coke—the strongest beverage Trump drinks—and told his favorite Palm Beach story. He was at a social gathering in Palm Beach with three of the town's elected officials. "These men were in their sixties, with their wives," he said. "By the way," he had said to them, "I'm having a party tonight at Mar-a-Lago, and the most beautiful women in the world will be there."

The men looked askance. While they were free that evening—their wives were leaving for New York that day—they indignantly said they could hardly attend such a party. Trump returned to Mar-a-Lago. By then, the men's wives had taken off.

"Listen, about that party," one of them called Trump to say. "If the invitation is still open, we'd like to come."

According to Trump, "they came, and they were very happy. They had acted really indignant at the idea of being invited to a party with pretty girls. There is a lot of falsity in Palm Beach."

As Trump's plane taxied down the runway, there were no fussy announcements from the three-man crew, no warnings to fasten seat belts. The plane simply took off. Because of the heavy insulation, the plane was so quiet and vibration-free that it didn't feel like it was flying. The soft beige lounges and carpeting added to the illusion of being on the ground.

"It's the only way to travel," Trump said. "It's the nicest private plane you've ever been on."

Trump offered an array of sandwiches. Eric, who shares his father's calm confidence, pronounced them good.

Mike Donovan, a jovial redhead who is the captain, came back to chat. He had been an Eastern pilot for twenty-seven years. Donovan said the plane carries more fuel than commercial flights. Besides the added safety, that means he can buy jet fuel where it is cheapest.

"We carry enough fuel to take us to Cincinnati," Donovan said. "The fuel in New York is two-fifty a gallon. In West Palm Beach, it's a dollar fifty. We can shop for the lower price. The extra weight uses more fuel, but if the price difference is twenty-five percent or more, it's worth it."

Trump left behind a city howling because he had just announced plans to build the world's tallest residential building across the street from the United Nations. Some of the city's wealthiest and most influential residents protested that the 861-

foot Trump World Tower above First Avenue would block their views. It's the kind of drama Trump loves. Trump against the powerful people, Trump against the establishment. Most of all, Trump in all the papers.

Nowhere is that drama played out more effectively than in Palm Beach. As Donald tells it, he was about to attend a dinner party in Palm Beach in 1982 when he asked his limousine driver about properties for sale. The driver mentioned Mar-a-Lago, the 140-room estate built by Marjorie Merriweather Post. Post had left the property to the federal government, hoping that it would become an outpost for diplomats. The government did not maintain it properly and, in 1980, decided it had no use for it. For one thing, security would be hard to maintain. The deteriorating property reverted to Post's foundation, which had trouble finding a buyer. By all accounts, it was the jewel of Palm Beach. But no one wanted to assume the cost of maintaining the mansion— at least $3 million a year, including taxes.

Trump asked to see the estate and was mesmerized. He arranged to tour it the next day. His first offer of $9 million was rejected. But later in 1985, the foundation reconsidered and suggested he could buy the property for $5 million. He accepted and threw in another $3 million for the furnishings.

Trump used Mar-a-Lago as a winter home for himself and Ivana, his first wife. In 1990, when he was having financial difficulties and had to sell his 282-foot yacht, he decided to add eight homes to the property. The town, which had previously approved a subdivision plan submitted by another would-be buyer, rejected Trump's plan. He sued. Finally, on the suggestion of his Palm Beach lawyer, Paul Rampell, he decided to turn Mar-a-Lago into a club.

The town was horrified. Trump represented everything Palm Beach society claims to hate. Trump was not only nouveau riche, he was aggressive and flamboyant. Instead of driving the conventional Rolls-Royce, he drove a Lamborghini, which can zoom up to 180 miles per hour. (The automaker comps him a new one each year.) Instead of wearing the traditional blue blazer with no tie, he wore nicely tailored suits with white shirts and ties. Instead of maintaining a mistress in a hideaway home, he flaunted dozens of beautiful girlfriends. In contrast to the Old Guard, he enjoyed having money. Most of all, he enjoyed being Donald Trump.

The fact that Trump had sued the town did not help. Moreover, he planned to open the Mar-a-Lago Club to anyone who could pay the fees—$25,000 at first, then later $75,000, plus annual fees of $6,200. Most of the key elected officials of the town belong to the Everglades or Bath & Tennis Club, or both. To this day, neither club accepts Jews as members. Trump rubbed the noses of town officials in the fact that his club would not discriminate.

Discrimination by Palm Beach clubs had come up as an issue before. Richard Rampell, the brother of Trump's lawyer, was incensed when a friend of his son Alex had invited all the kids in their class to a birthday party at the Bath & Tennis Club—all except his three Jewish classmates, including Rampell's son. Rampell's daughter Cathy got her own taste of anti-Semitism when a boy in her class told her, "I'm a member of the Bath & Tennis Club, and you can't come because you're Jewish."

"It was like being beaten up by a bully," Richard, a Palm Beach accountant, said of the snubs and taunts.

Richard had begun to see the club system as a way of poisoning future generations and perpetuating prejudice, not only in Palm Beach society but in corporate America. After all, no other area of the country has such a concentration of families controlling so many companies and so much wealth.

"I hate the fact that I think this way, but every time I meet someone here, I think, 'Are they Jewish or not?'" Richard told me. "It bothers me that this is an issue. It bothers me that I think, 'Is this person a foe or a closet foe?' On the surface, they are very cordial to you, when in reality, they don't want to have dinner with you. You think, 'Are these people really my friends?'"

Richard Rampell wrestled with the question of whether he should go public: He would likely lose some clients, and his kids might suffer even more. Some of his friends who belonged to the WASP clubs said they were trying to change the system quietly. But Rampell was running out of patience. "I believe there is a hard core who believe these bigoted policies are something to fight for," Richard said. "They typically become the most active members of the clubs."

Richard could not live with himself if he remained silent, as did the countries that refused to take on Adolf Hitler when it became clear he was exterminating Jews. "I came to the conclusion that people will not change because you're nice to them," Richard said. "One guy said, 'If Jews behaved themselves, we would realize they're not bad and they would be accepted.' The reason they hate Jews is not because Jews are not nice to them. They hate Jews because *they* are not nice. I decided this is my town. Why do I have to act as if I'm a guest?"

Rampell took on the Sailfish Club. Like the Everglades and Bath & Tennis clubs, the Sailfish Club had no Jewish members. Unlike the other clubs, it leases land from the state—the two acres submerged under its docks. Rampell applied for membership. On the application, the club asked for his "church" affiliation, a reminder that Jews who worship at temples or synagogues were not welcome. In fact, while Richard had been bar mitzvahed, he did not attend services. He considered himself Jewish nonetheless.

Five years later he still had heard nothing about his application. In considering new members, the clubs impose a cloak of secrecy. But in this case, a club official told Rampell confidentially that he would never get in because he was Jewish.

Robert M. Montgomery, Jr., a lawyer who was a member of the Sailfish Club, is a client of both Rampell brothers. Besides having one of the few homes in Palm Beach right on the ocean instead of across the street from it, Montgomery stands out because he has been married to one woman, Mary, for forty-six years. When Montgomery heard from Richard Rampell about the problem at the Sailfish Club, he challenged the club to prove that it did not discriminate. The club brushed him aside.

That was a mistake.

The son of an aggressive Birmingham, Alabama, criminal lawyer, Montgomery began his legal career representing insurance firms, railroads, trucking firms, and banks. In 1975 he represented an insurance company against a five-year-old black girl who suffered severe brain damage after the car in which she was riding hit a barrier put up during road construction. Because the barrier was just over a hill, the driver couldn't see it. Despite his realization that he was representing the wrong side, Montgomery won. The experience changed his life.

"I went home that night and said, 'That's the last time I'll use my talents to keep someone from legitimately recovering what they should,'" Montgomery told me. "About the same time, Travelers Insurance Company called me and griped about a bill. My bill was thirty-four hundred dollars, and they said it was four hundred over what it should be."

Montgomery told the company to shove it. "If I cut bills, it would indicate I had overbilled," he said. "They sent me a check for three thousand dollars. I called up Travelers and said, 'I don't appreciate this. Come out here and pick up your files.' They said, 'You can't do that.' I said, 'I'm going to tell you something. I'll give you twenty-four hours to pick up your goddamn files or you'll find them on my front lawn because I'm going to throw them out my third-floor window.' I had just had it. I just didn't need insurance companies. So I told them all to take their files— Aetna, Hartford, all of them."

Montgomery turned to personal-injury work, suing the same companies he had represented. He represented Kimberly Bergalis, a virgin who said her dentist had given her AIDS. All the medical associations said such a transmission was impossible, but Montgomery eventually proved through DNA analysis that she was right. More recently, he was one of eleven lawyers to win a $13 billion settlement against the tobacco companies on behalf of the state of Florida. It was the biggest liability award ever. In the process, Montgomery made more than $200 million in legal fees. He donates millions to charities each year.

Montgomery knew Robert Butterworth, Florida's attorney general, and in 1992 he told Butterworth about the Sailfish Club's membership policies. The state ordered the club to stop discriminating or lose the lease for its docks. Suddenly, the club—which had denied it discriminated—accepted one Jewish member. By then, Montgomery had resigned from the club.

Five years earlier, Montgomery had sued the Beach Club, claiming that when he joined, he had been misled about its discriminatory policies. Reluctantly, the club admitted a Jewish member or two. While Montgomery continues to be a member of the Beach Club ("to keep them honest"), he usually goes to Mar-a-Lago or to the Palm Beach Country Club, where he is one of a handful of non-Jewish members. "That's where all my friends are," Montgomery explained.

The Palm Beach Country Club is the wealthiest club of all. It charges $150,000 to join, plus $14,000 a year in fees. Before accepting a member, the club reviews his tax returns to see if he has contributed a sufficient portion of his income to charity. Each year members are required to turn over to the club checks made out to the United Way, Good Samaritan Hospital, and Saint Mary's Medical Center.

"Gene Isenberg, who is enormously wealthy, said when he joined the Palm Beach Country Club, 'I thought I was rich and old. Now that I'm in, I find out that I'm young and poor,'" Montgomery said, referring to the chairman of Nabors Industries, a Houston oil-drilling company.

To be sure, the Palm Beach Country Club is snobbish. But when members of the Old Guard told me it's the most picky club of all, I began to realize that that was a ruse to hide their own prejudices. The fact is they would not be interested in joining the Jewish club. In America, it is the WASP clubs that are the most desirable. Moreover, if the Palm Beach Country Club is selective, it is not discriminatory—a crucial difference.

"The judgment is on whether the guy is charitable, whether some people like him, whether he has friends there, whether the wife picks up the fork with her left hand or eats with her mouth open," a prominent member of the club said. "Who knows? Maybe someone didn't like him in business and influences others not to have him in. Purely subjective."

Paradoxically, Joseph P. Kennedy, the father of the clan, joined the Palm Beach Country Club because the Everglades Club would not take him. Yet Kennedy railed against "kikes" and admired Hitler. He told the German ambassador in London that Hitler had done "great things" for his country. However, Joe confided, no European leader spoke well of the Germans because most of them were "afraid of the Jews." The Jews had "brought it on themselves." Anti-Semitic though he was, Joe had several close Jewish friends. No one ever said prejudice is rational.

Montgomery, who once represented the Everglades Club, now refuses to go there. When Montgomery's friend, developer E. Llwyd Ecclestone, Jr., invited him to his wedding at the Everglades, Montgomery told him he would not attend, and he told him why.

"There are buccaneers and people of a rebellious nature like me, and then there are others who go with the herd," Montgomery said. "They're so damned afraid that they're going to be cut off by these blatant bigots, that they won't be invited to their parties."

Montgomery was surprised that Alexander Haig joined the Everglades Club. "That lowered my esteem for him," he said. "The clubs are discriminatory. They know it. Why the hell don't they change? What's wrong with these people? Do we live in a fascistic damn country? Don't they know anything about history? It's crazy. I truly get angry about it."

Since the state has no leverage over the Everglades or Bath & Tennis clubs, as it does with the Sailfish Club because of the state lease, those clubs can legally discriminate as much as they like. Members of the two clubs occasionally claim that they know of one or two Jewish members. But invariably, upon investigation, the information turns out to be spurious: The members had Jewish ancestors and a Jewish name but either disavow being Jewish or were brought up as Christians.

Just recently, both clubs began claiming they allow members to bring Jewish guests, but I learned that was another subterfuge. The Everglades' rules provide that members may only bring guests who "conform to . . . the standards prevailing for members." In practice, Jewish guests are accepted only if the other members know and like them, according to Robert P. Leidy, a stockbroker who belongs to both clubs.

"If I invited a [Jewish] client of mine for lunch, that might be risky on my part, but if it's a Jewish client who is also a buddy of ours, that would be okay," Leidy said.

"In Richard Adams's *Watership Down*," said the member of the Old Guard who did not want to be quoted about prejudice on the island, "the rabbit had an underground labyrinth of tunnels. He ran around keeping check on his little empire under the ground. It was all very secretive. He died finally because an empire like that is founded on fear. That's why it was underground and compartmentalized. He died from the sound of the beating of his own heart. He scared himself to death. It's a parallel to what goes on here."

As if to underscore her own point, the member of the Old Guard later did the Palm Beach Shuffle, clamming up and refusing to discuss anti-Semitism on the island with me any further. The friend who had introduced me to her explained that she wanted to rise in an Old Guard organization. Even though she knew she would not be quoted, perhaps she feared that somehow word would get out that she had told on her brethren.

The fear that pervades Palm Beach is no different from the dread that kept people from standing up to Senator Joseph McCarthy when he conducted witch hunts for imagined Communists in the early 1950s. Back then reprisals could mean losing a government job or being blacklisted by the film industry. On the island, it's a matter of being dropped from a party list.

Asked about the policy on Jews, William G. Pannill, president of the Everglades Club, said, "We don't have any comment on that."

Fitz Eugene Dixon, Jr., president of the Bath & Tennis Club and former owner of the Philadelphia 76ers and Philadelphia

Phillies, said, "I don't think it's anybody's business except the club's business."

So entrenched is prejudice in Palm Beach that the *Palm Beach Post* recently ran the headline "A Palm Beach Happy Meal: Catholics, Jews Break Bread" over a story about a dinner given by the Palm Beach Fellowship of Christians and Jews. "The miracle was in the meal," the story said. "Wonders will not soon cease when nearly 400 Jews and Christians gather for a festive banquet at the Breakers."

What still troubles Richard Rampell is that members of the Bath & Tennis and Everglades clubs list their memberships publicly, as badges of honor. They should be considered badges of shame, he said.

At first, Richard's unexpectedly aggressive stance caused tension with his brother Paul. Richard is taller and more intense than Paul, who has a wry wit. "We barely talked for a long time because he thought he was losing clients, and his son was losing friends because of me," Richard said. "My wife was mad at me because my daughter was upset. My daughter felt she was being excluded from parties."

Paul Rampell denies that he worried about losing clients. But he says he was used to dealing with such issues in a less confrontational manner. In any case, he has since overcome his reservations and is proud of his brother's stance.

While the town council agreed to allow Mar-a-Lago to become a club in 1995, in the name of avoiding traffic congestion on South Ocean Boulevard, it imposed restrictions on membership, parking, and traffic. Only 500 people could join, and only 313 car trips were allowed each day to the mansion. Because of the restrictions on daily trips, Trump had to limit memberships to 350. No such restrictions applied to the clubs that discriminated.

Trump and Paul Rampell thought the town had more in mind than controlling traffic. As Trump's lawyer, Rampell sent copies of the movie *Gentleman's Agreement* to each elected official, suggesting that the town's opposition to the club was based on the kind of anti-Semitism portrayed in the movie. That enraged town officials, already gloomy because Donald had refused to allow the Preservation Foundation of Palm Beach to continue its fund-raising events at Mar-a-Lago.

As a preserve of the Old Guard, the Preservation Foundation ranks with Bethesda by-the-Sea Episcopal Church, a Gothic edifice with stained-glass windows, and the Garden Club. Besides contributing small sums to beautify the town, the Garden Club pats its own members on the back for gardens that their landscapers plant. "I'm surprised they mix species of flowers," a member of the Old Guard drily remarked. But the Preservation Foundation performs a real service by running Pan's Garden. An oasis on Hibiscus Avenue halfway between the Chesterfield and Worth Avenue, Pan's Garden grows only the local flora, including some endangered species.

Trump said he kicked out the Preservation Foundation because its members failed to clean up properly after a previous event and had not even bothered to thank him that evening. In fact, at the function, they thanked everyone but the person who had made it possible. But kicking out the Preservation Foundation piqued the Old Guard.

Comparing him to Madonna, Paul Rampell told me Trump alternates between conventional conduct and behavior that people consider outrageous. "He can be intentionally provocative," Rampell said. "He is like that."

To be sure, Trump knows how to woo influential people he likes: Barton Gubelmann, for example. When Trump married Marla Maples, he threw a dinner party at Mar-a-Lago and invited Barton and her husband, Walter. Barton recalled Trump railing that the flight path for the West Palm Beach International Airport passed over Mar-a-Lago. Walter was about to point out that no one could do anything about the airplanes. "Shut up and let him talk," Barton whispered to her husband.

As it turned out, after he sued Palm Beach County, Trump was able to get the airport to move the flight path one road north—on the grounds that residue from jet fuel was damaging a national historic site.

After Trump married Maples, the couple visited Barton at her Newport home. "Barton is the salt of the earth," Trump told me. "She's the queen of society, and yet she's a pretty tough, street-wise woman. She is exactly the opposite of what I had thought she would be like."

While Trump charmed the queen, he also publicly referred to the trust-fund babies who opposed his plans for Mar-a-Lago as the "lucky sperm club." Sending *Gentleman's Agreement* to town officials was the last straw. "It's like saying the emperor has no clothes," Paul Rampell said. "Discrimination by clubs was an unmentionable. The mayor belongs to Bath & Tennis. Lesly Smith [the town-council president] belongs to the Everglades and Bath & Tennis clubs. They expected him to bow to them. Donald was the extreme in the other direction."

When the issue of allowing Mar-a-Lago to become a club came before the town council, one council member became so agitated he had to take nitroglycerin for his heart. A woman in the audience stared at Paul Rampell, all the while holding up her middle finger. In its newsletter, the eighteen-hundred-member Palm Beach Civic Association referred to Trump as "the notorious New York developer and part-time Palm Beacher."

Paul Rampell, who specializes in trust, estate, and marital law, has lived in Palm Beach all his life. He has never seen anyone threaten the status quo as Donald has. "This town has incredible pressures to conform, to dress a certain way, to go to polo and wear Gucci loafers and blazers and to vote Republican," he said. "It's the perfect setting for Donald to tweak the noses of conformists."

Town-council president Lesly Smith called Donald's injection of the issue of discrimination into the controversy a "diversionary tactic." But Hermine Wiener, a Jewish member of the five-member town council at the time, told me the town's motives were not altruistic. "Probably ninety-five percent of [the regulations imposed on Mar-a-Lago] had to do with the fact they didn't like Donald," she said.

Jealousy was behind it all, Robert Montgomery suggested.

As Trump's plane climbed to 37,000 feet, Trump—a Presbyterian of German descent—imitated the constricted, nasal tones of blue bloods condemning his club. Gleefully, he recounted how Sean "Puff Daddy" Combs, a black rap star, shook up the Bath & Tennis Club one weekend when visiting Mar-a-Lago. Walking along the beach, Combs and his sexy Hispanic girlfriend thought the Bath & Tennis Club, originally built by Marjorie Merriweather Post and adjoining Mar-a-Lago, was just part of Donald's club.

"So Puffy hangs a right to the Bath & Tennis," Trump said. As Shannon Donnelly put it in her society column in the Shiny Sheet, they began doing the "Horizontal Rhumba, if you know what we mean," on a lounge. A guard from Bath & Tennis kicked them out.

"My German manager, Bernd Lembcke, and their German manager are friends," Trump said. "So in German, Bernd says, 'Hans, what's going on here? This is terrible.' The other guy says, 'Bernd, they were fucking on the beach.'"

Trump said, "There's nothing like the Everglades Club anywhere in the country. If you're Jewish and marry a gentile member, forget it. You can only be a guest. They wouldn't let Estée Lauder come in with C. Z. Guest."

If the prejudice is out of the forties, so are the customs. Every three or four years, Trump attends the International Red Cross Ball, which is the highlight of the season. "It's amazing," he said. "It's from a hundred years ago. It's like a religion to them. They worry about this three hundred sixty-five days a year. It's incredible. Only in Palm Beach."

Trump kept walking back to the 727's galley for another hard pretzel. Then he broke out the Pringles. He seemed to need constant refueling.

Trump was thinking about watching a movie from the plane's videotape collection, and Eric said, "Let me guess which one." But instead of selecting his current favorite, *Blood Sport*, Trump picked out *Breakfast at Tiffany's*. "No one was more beautiful than she was in that movie," he said, feeling no need to mention Audrey Hepburn's name. Later he would preview a short film starring his friend, Czech model Eva Herzigova. Throughout, he kept saying how beautiful she is.

"I'm going to make a prediction," Trump said to Pam. "Your husband is going to screw me. Now, you I wouldn't mind."

My friend Edward Klein, author of *Just Jackie: Her Private Years*, a contributing editor of *Vanity Fair*, and a former editor of the *New York Times Magazine*, had vouched for me with Trump. I still had to sell myself. One morning, Donald's secretary phoned. "Donald Trump is calling," she said. She put him on. For twenty minutes, we discussed Palm Beach and the project. The rich have a way of engaging in monologues. They have no need to hear what anyone else is saying. I was impressed that Donald listened carefully to my every word. He made no promises, but a few weeks later, his assistant, Norma I. Foerderer, began making arrangements.

Trump's plane landed at the West Palm Beach airport at 7:15 P.M. The flight had taken slightly more than two hours, about what a commercial plane requires to fly from Washington to West Palm Beach. Joe Cannizzaro, the flight engineer and second officer, explained that the captain charts more direct flight paths.

Trump pointed out a jet owned by Nelson Peltz, the Palm Beach resident who does leveraged buyouts. "I've been to many airports all over the world," Donald said. "I've never seen so many private planes. Next weekend, there will be thousands of private jets."

The hyperbole goes with the territory. By definition, everything that Donald touches is the biggest and the best.

On the tarmac, Howard Willson, the operations manager of Mar-a-Lago, opened the door to Donald's black stretch limo.

"Howard, how is everything at the house?" Trump asked. "How many do we have for New Year's Eve?"

Told that the club could not accommodate all the requests, Trump said, "Everyone wants to come to Mar-a-Lago. For New

Year's Eve, we have hundreds of requests for reservations. We can't get them in. Rod Stewart took a table, Ron Perelman took four tables. We've had Whitney Houston, Celine Dion, Diana Ross, Jay Leno, Julio Iglesias, Tony Bennett, the Beach Boys, Tom Jones. It's the hot place."

In ten minutes, the limo pulled through the gates of Mar-a-Lago. Spanish for "sea to lake," Mar-a-Lago stretches from the Atlantic to Lake Worth. Unique even to Palm Beach, the mansion brings to mind Coleridge's lines: "In Xanadu did Kubla Khan/a stately pleasure dome decree. . . ."

The house is of Dorian stone from Italy, surrounded by a manicured lawn to the lake in back and to South Ocean Boulevard in front. A private tunnel under the road leads to the beach. Trump bought the beach, which was originally part of the estate, for another $2 million. The estate covers nearly 18 acres.

At the front entrance, a dozen of the two-hundred-member staff (sixty off-season) lined up to greet Trump, Eric, Pam, and me. The mansion is a club, but it is also Trump's home. In Trump's mind, the club's members are his guests. All new money, they range from golf pro Gary Player to Lowell Paxson, founder of the Home Shopping Network and PAX-TV; Ronald Perelman, the Revlon chief; George L. Lindemann, who owns $1.3 billion in cable and cellular-phone companies; Nelson Peltz, the Royal Crown Cola and Snapple man; Carl Icahn, a corporate raider; Abe Gosman, who runs health-care companies; tobacco-settlement lawyer Robert Montgomery; and the Fisher brothers, who own $1.3 billion in real estate, mostly in New York. Celebrities like Rod Stewart, Charlton Heston, Sylvester Stallone, Steven Spielberg, and Denzel Washington are considered honorary members and regularly show up as guests.

If admitting Jews was a shocker, admitting blacks was enough to make the Old Guard tremble. Other than servants, black residents are virtually unheard-of in Palm Beach, where a black family might move in and, after a few years of being ignored, move out. Besides Denzel Washington, baseball star "Sweet" Lou Whitaker of the Detroit Tigers is a member.

The week before Trump's trip, Mar-a-Lago workers erected a twenty-four-foot Christmas tree in the grand salon, which both the former and the current owner have called their living room. The room has clear panoramas of both sea and lake. Under its thirty-two-foot coffered ceiling are symbols of old-world luxury—tapestries, frescoes, marble-topped tables, oriental rugs, and gilt plasterwork. Despite the morning blaze of sun in the front windows, Post thought the grand salon too dark. In the sixties she had Bristol crystal chandeliers installed.

The living room has a raised platform where club members can have intimate dinners at center stage or in one of two corner nooks. Pam and I would later dine in the nook at stage right. For an intimate five-course dinner in the left nook, one couple paid $3,000. The price included caviar, a bottle of Lafite Rothschild, and use of Marjorie Merriweather Post's gold service.

Over the enormous fireplace, the gold-leaf family crest changed with Post's husbands. Post's natal family crests line the walls of the entrance hall, along with two lavish Dresden urns and a collection of tiles dating to the fifteenth century. Tiles in bands along the wall bear the Latin phrase *plus ultra*. This, Anthony P. Senecal, Trump's butler, only half joked, is synonymous with Donald Trump.

Senecal is a former mayor of Martinsburg, West Virginia. He came to national attention when the *Washington Post* accompanied a front-page feature story about changes in West Virginia with a photo of Senecal sitting with his cat Morris on the shoeshine stand of his tobacco shop.

"When I first started, I wasn't the servant type," Senecal told me. "It was touch-and-go, until Mr. Trump found out I was a former mayor. That made me a cut above. Then," Tony said wryly, "I became the mayor of the wealthiest and largest town in West Virginia.' In fact, Martinsburg is neither. "Mr. Trump said, 'What's your title going to be?' I said, 'Personal butler to Donald J. Trump of Palm Beach.' He said, 'Here's a man who has a bigger ego than I do, and yet he wants to be called a butler.'" .

Trump said of Senecal, "He treats the members as equals. In fact, I think he might think he is above them. Every great place needs a Tony."

Mar-a-Lago has ten suites where members may stay for up to $1,500 a night. The Spanish suite, where Pam and I stayed, overlooks the ocean and is attached to a series of sitting rooms. The centerpiece is a large convex fireplace covered with a mosaic of colorful shards of tile. Mrs. Post filled a series of niches over the hearth with porcelain figurines representing sixteenth-century European ladies of court. Over the bed, a crystal chandelier hangs from the coffered wooden ceiling, which is stenciled with lions, falcons, and coats of arms. Even the bathroom has its chandelier and basket balcony.

Trump retreated to his wing of Mar-a-Lago, where he ordered his favorite dish—meatloaf. It resides on the club's menu next to the prime strip steak and the swordfish.

Eric disappeared, but at around 10:00 P.M., he was spotted carrying a fishing pole. He said he had been fishing off the wall along the lake in back. Nothing was biting that night.

19. COME PLAY WITH ME

At breakfast time the next day, Trump strode across the terrace between the pool and the mansion, a piece of thick-cut, apple-smoked bacon in hand, and went off to parts unknown. Soon he returned for another foray to the kitchen. He strode across the terrace again, another piece of bacon in hand.

As I sunned myself at the ninety-degree pool, Trump introduced Angelia Savage, the manager of the spa. "She was the 1996 Miss Florida USA," he said. "Then she was in the Miss USA pageant. I own Miss USA. She won the bathing-suit contest. She came in third in the contest itself. I watched her and saw she had a lot of talent and beauty. I hired her as an assistant. I made her the head of the spa this year after she had worked there two years."

Once a car garage and staff quarters, the spa has a fitness center (classes include Hot Hot Hot Yoga), a beauty salon (with vibrating pedicure chair), a staff of aestheticians and massage therapists (offering simultaneous massage for two on the Couples Day of Delight), and a copper Japanese steeping tub.

Trump called a 10:00 A.M. meeting of his staff in the living room. On a coffee table were architectural drawings. Trump and his people were figuring out how to present to the town a plan to build fourteen cabanas, along with a 100-foot-long saltwater pool and a snack bar, on Mar-a-Lago's 360 feet of beachfront. To make the plan more palatable, Raymond W. Royce, another local Trump lawyer, said Trump should attach self-imposed restrictions. One by one, Trump dissected the restrictions and discarded them.

"Okay, first of all, 'Cabanas are not to be used for sleeping,'" he said, looking at the list of suggested restrictions. "I don't like to put that in because the zoning already covers that." Trump asked if the Bath & Tennis Club had asked for the restriction. "Have they reared their heads on the application? Because if they fight us, we fight them."

Trump moved to the next restriction: no cooking in the snack bar. He said, "You have to be able to cook in a snack bar. Bath & Tennis does it."

Bernd Lembcke, a former food-and-beverage director of the Breakers Hotel who is managing director of Mar-a-Lago, said the Bath & Tennis Club does not cook on the beach. "They have a main kitchen," he said.

"What about hot dogs?" Trump asked.

"Hot dogs we'll have in a warmer," Lembcke said. "But once we start cooking steaks, the town becomes concerned."

Royce proposed a conciliatory approach. "We can either negotiate this out with Bath & Tennis and resolve it with them, or they are going to come to the meeting and raise hell," Royce said. "Then we'll have to negotiate it with the town."

Trump disagreed. "I think you're better off letting them come to the meeting, but here's the problem," he said. "Any agreement you make now, they're going to come to you later and want more. You're better off getting everything at one time. I've done this shit all my life. You'll make a deal and think you have support, and they'll still be knocking you behind your back."

Warming to his own idea, Trump said, "In fact, I wouldn't do any negotiating with Bath & Tennis. I think you're wasting your time, and I'm wasting lawyer fees. I think you go in, and either get what's fair or fight it out later."

Royce said Bath & Tennis would comment on the plan regardless.

"You better let them know not to fuck around with me," Trump said. "Tell them."

"They know that. They know that," Lembcke said.

"You'll send Puff Daddy back over there," I interjected.

"We'll send in Puff Daddy," Royce confirmed. "If he's not available, we'll send somebody else."

Trump was going to play golf but canceled the game to hold a second meeting at eleven-thirty. This time, the problem was how to present to the town a plan to build a ballroom to replace the tent used for large social events. Because Mar-a-Lago has been designated a historic site, the town has to approve every detail of the construction.

Trump objected to calling the ballroom a ballroom.

"The word *ballroom* is a hard word to get approved," Trump said. "*Pavilion* is a softer word. Use *pavilion*."

Trump looked at the architectural drawings. He asked for a black felt-tipped pen.

"Here's what I would do," he said, drawing on the plans. "I would add this—another bay," meaning an alcove. "I think actually it makes it look better. It has more definition. It will look even more beautiful." Then he looked at the plans for the existing tent. "The workmanship on the tent is terrible," he said. "Do me a favor. Put doors in here. Build a frame, put in the special hardware."

He asked how large the new ballroom would be. He said he wanted it to be even bigger than originally planned—17,500 square feet. "It will be the best in Palm Beach," he said. "Do it." (Trump later scaled back the project to 13,500 square feet.)

Eric walked into the meeting to say he was going out. Calling him "honey," Trump kissed him on the cheek.

Next, Trump wanted to inspect the $40 million, 215-acre golf course he was building near the airport. In the airport in West Palm, an illuminated sign advertising Trump International Golf Course says, AN INVITATION FROM DONALD TRUMP: COME

PLAY WITH ME. The pitch sums up Trump's appeal: Belong to his club, play at one of his casinos, or buy an apartment in one of his buildings, and you get a piece of the action and become a partner in the glamorous empire of the man whose name is synonymous with wealth and an opulent lifestyle.

The same synergy can be seen in Trump's use of his home as a profit-making club and his attacks on discrimination as a way of calling attention to his club, attracting new members. He genuinely abhors prejudice, just as he genuinely loves having people around him. If those tendencies promote his enterprises, so much the better.

Trump jumped into a black Durango SLT four-wheel-drive vehicle with Royce, the lawyer, and Bruce Zabriski, the golf pro at both Mar-a-Lago and the new golf course in West Palm Beach. "Bruce is one of the best players in the country," Trump said. "He's the only four-time PGA Club Professional Player of the Year."

At the golf course, Trump talked about the course, tuned in to conversations in the vehicle, and cracked jokes while driving and turning his head to look at his passengers behind him. More than 3 million square yards of earth were being moved to create the course, including 58 acres of lakes. As he drove onto the dirt, he said, "I spent a million dollars to plant these trees, eight hundred ninety royal palms, to outline the course. They're forty feet high. They'll grow to eighty-five feet."

Trump stopped at the construction trailer and picked up Jim Fazio, Sr., the golf course architect. "You've got to finish that area," he said, pointing to one corner of the course that looked forlorn. In that area, he said, "the ficus will be twenty-five feet high."

Bumping up and down the terrain at the unfinished golf course was like Mr. Toad's Wild Ride at Disney World. Trump made sudden turns, and the passengers—slightly nauseated and glad they hadn't eaten lunch first—couldn't brace themselves in time.

Trump drove to the site of a thirty-five-foot waterfall being built for $2.5 million. On the ground were samples of rocks ranging in color from white to red.

"I like the lighter color," Trump said. "I don't like the red. To me, a red rock is more like granite from New England."

He asked the construction crew which color they liked, then he asked his staff, Pam, and me. He seemed genuinely interested in everyone's opinions, and when most said they preferred the reddish samples, he decided to go with them.

That night, acting like a maître d', Trump went around to diners at Mar-a-Lago, introducing them to me. Trump takes pride in the fact that he is a successful draw. Club members call to see if he's coming down for the weekend, and they're far more likely to make reservations for dinner when he's there. He works the room and never tires of it.

"This is Zachary Fisher," Trump said. "The Fisher brothers own tremendous real estate. He builds homes near military bases so families of servicemen who are hospitalized can stay nearby. Anytime a serviceman is killed in the line of duty, Fisher gives the family twenty-five thousand dollars." Fisher has since died.

For fear he will pick up germs, Trump is leery of shaking hands before eating. But he shook hands with guests like Ray Perelman, Ron's father. Brashly, he even sipped from one guest's glass of red wine as he toasted the family.

When Trump bought Mar-a-Lago, he retained several seventy-year-old gardeners who could barely pull weeds but had worked loyally for Mrs. Post. When butler Tony Senecal's home air-conditioning system gave out, Trump had it replaced. When Senecal had heart problems a few years back, Trump insisted he stay at Mar-a-Lago to recuperate. Alain Cohen, the Palm Beach antiques dealer, recalled that when Trump looked at furniture for Mar-a-Lago at Cohen's warehouse, he gave a hundred-dollar tip to the worker who moved the items around for him.

"The man was so overjoyed," Cohen told me. "It was half his weekly salary."

After introducing diners at the club, Trump inspected the kitchen. Trump called each worker by name and gave cigars to two chefs. He asked Senecal to open a walk-in vault, and he led us inside. It had a musty smell.

"This is Marjorie Merriweather Post's safe with original twenty-four-carat solid-gold place settings," Trump said. "The whole room is worth tens of millions of dollars. I bought the house for five million and the furnishings for three million. They had no idea of the values."

The next afternoon, Donald filled his plate with roast turkey, gravy, and hash browns at Mar-a-Lago's buffet brunch. He passed up the American sturgeon caviar, smoked salmon, mammoth cold shrimp with cocktail sauce, blintzes, eggs Benedict, ham, prime rib, poached salmon with lobster, pies and cakes.

Trump gave a tour of his suite, the same one Marjorie Merriweather Post used. A guard is always posted outside, part of an elaborate security system supervised by Franklin J. Logalbo, a former liaison officer between the New York State courts and the probation department.

Trump opened a door to a small stairway. "This is a secret passageway that goes up and down all over the house," he said. "So if I want to visit someone in another room, I can do it without five hundred security people watching me."

Trump is proud of the restoration work he has done. He employs Richard Haynes, whose father originally gilded Mar-a-Lago, to do nothing but replicate and restore Mrs. Post's work. Haynes was preparing to regild the forty rams that jut from the roofline. He would be using $10,000 worth of gold leaf, thinner than tissue paper. "We kept it exactly as it was," Trump said. "Central air conditioning has been put in. I've spent many millions to restore Mar-a-Lago."

As the place is largely unchanged, the ghost of Marjorie Post seems to walk here, and if she and the Donald commune on some level, they have a lot in common, each in their own way having taken Palm Beach by storm.

For the trip back to New York, Trump suggested leaving at 3:00 P.M. Pam would still be at the spa, I said.

No need to check airline schedules.

"Then let's leave at five," Trump said.

On his plane, Trump picked up the current issue of *New York* magazine and read the cover-story headline aloud: "Who Will Be the New Trump? I love this," he said.

20. ROMAN ORGIES

For months, impresario Bruce Sutka had been orchestrating the black-tie New Year's Eve celebration given by the Young Friends of the Red Cross at the Breakers. Sutka, a party organizer, was known for giving good theater. In years past he had staged Roman orgies complete with topless women and drag queens. For a James Bond party, he featured a gold-painted nude girl reclining in a gold bathtub.

At one of the dances, a guest offered a Rolex watch to one of Sutka's blond dancers if she would perform oral sex on his twenty-one-year-old son in the men's room. She not only took him up on it, she performed the service on the dance floor.

H. Loy Anderson, Jr., now president of Palm Beach National Bank & Trust Company, started the Young Friends twenty-two years ago. The idea was to give the younger crowd a New Year's party that made money for charity while grooming them for the big time, the International Red Cross Ball. In fact, revelers of any age show up. In the past, the party has been held at the Flagler Museum. This season it took place in an air-conditioned tent at the Breakers.

Palatial is the word for the Breakers, with its towering ceilings and glittering decor. It is so sumptuous that you forget it's a hotel. At one end of the lush central courtyard is a ballroom; at the other, the lobby. Along the length of the courtyard are marble passageways lined with restaurants and other ballrooms and meeting rooms. A seafood restaurant with aquariums for tabletops looks out on the ocean.

Under garlands left over from Christmas, young friends and heirs apparent paraded from one end of the main lobby to the other and back again, waiting for the New Year's Eve party to start at ten o'clock. Wearing black velvet gowns, the young women clomped in clunky heels. The young men stuck their hands comfortably into the pockets of the tuxedos they sported with red, green, or plaid bow ties and cummerbunds.

Bernard Nicole, the concierge who presides over the Flagler Club on the Breakers' top two floors, where rooms are $560 a night, was standing by for emergency requests. Nicole, fifty-one, was born on the Riviera and speaks French, Spanish, Italian, Portuguese, and English. He previously worked for Marta Batista, the widow of former Cuban dictator Fulgencio Batista. She lives in Palm Beach, Paris, London, and Lausanne.

In his seventeen years at the Breakers, Nicole has attended to such guests as Bette Davis, Elizabeth Taylor, Dolly Parton, Ava Gardner, Zsa Zsa Gabor, Sean Connery, and Elizabeth Hurley, not to mention former presidents Nixon, Carter, Ford, Bush, and Reagan. Many guests stay year-round, renting suites at $650 to $2,400 a day.

The needs of the wealthy range from the mundane—a bow tie for a ball—to the bizarre. "For one family, I booked twenty-seven seats from here to New York and back, including space in the luggage section for a dressed Christmas tree," Nicole told me. When a guest's Cadillac broke down, he found her a new one for $35,000.

"A gentleman from England was here," Nicole said. "He invented a device that brought him a lot of money. He came here with his wife. He said, 'Bernard, we've heard of the Hatteras boat. Could you help us look at one?'"

Nicole put him in touch with the boatyard, and the man bought one.

"Could you ship the boat to London for us?" the man then asked. "I said, 'Certainly.' I had no idea how to do that. I got on the phone and found out how. It was enormous. We're not speaking about a rowboat. It had to be sent in seawater in a bigger boat. The cost was more than a hundred thousand dollars."

The Breakers does not allow pets, so some guests keep their dogs in recreational vehicles with the engines and air conditioning running twenty-four hours a day. "I had a guest who has a dog, and she bought a Volkswagen diesel for the dog so she can run into stores and keep the air conditioning going," Nicole said. "When she goes out without the dog, she uses another car."

One man took two rooms at the hotel and asked that no one go into one of them. But one day a maid entered the forbidden room—to discover a rabbit. The guest had covered the carpet with plastic sheeting shipped in earlier.

When a woman about to attend the Red Cross Ball found the gown she had brought no longer fit, Nicole bought her four gowns at Daniel Foxx so she could try them on in her room. She paid him for three and sent the other one back.

Nicole has spotted women wearing two different shoes. When he tells them, they are suitably grateful.

"A lady was going to the Red Cross Ball," Nicole said. "She had on a beautiful dress. Ten minutes later, I saw another lady wearing the same dress."

"Are you going to the Red Cross Ball?" Nicole asked her.

"Yes," she said.

"I just saw the same dress going down."

"I love you," she said.

As many women do, she had packed more than one gown and was able to run back to her room and change.

Despite its special cachet, not every member of the rich and powerful set stays at the Breakers. When Adnan Khashoggi (down to one commercial-size jet from three) attends the Young Friends and the Red Cross Ball, he usually stays at the Ritz-Carlton Palm Beach, taking an entire floor. The hotel is down-island in neighboring Manalapan, but calling it "Ritz-Carlton Manalapan" or "Ritz-Carlton Palm Beach County" would never do.

On occasion, Khashoggi rents a home on the ocean. One year he rented 780 South Ocean Boulevard, a sixteen-thousand-square-foot home that had been owned by Mary Hartline Donahue, the widow of Woolworth Donahue, whose grandfather founded the chain of dime stores. Mizner designed the home for himself in 1925, but National Tea Company founder George Rasmussen bought it before Mizner moved in. The home is now owned by Lowell W. "Bud" Paxson, cofounder of the Home Shopping Network and creator of PAX-TV. Paxson bought the home for $12 million in 1994.

The sultan of Brunei stays at The Four Seasons, formerly the Ocean Grand, ten minutes south of the center of town. To accommodate himself and his entourage, the sultan rents an entire wing—a third of the hotel.

The night before one of his stays, "All their luggage was delivered to us," a former concierge told me. "Just for his party, we had six rooms of luggage. That didn't include the luggage of his security and office staff. They wanted every piece of his clothing ironed before he arrived the next day. So, four of us were up the entire night, ironing. I was paid overtime, and they charged him big time."

One night during the sultan's visit, the concierge got an urgent call from the sultan's secretary. He said the younger prince, who was twelve, had a splinter in his foot.

"We have to get a doctor," the sultan's secretary said.

"It's almost midnight," the concierge said. "We can take him to the emergency room. We can call paramedics. But no doctor is going to come here at midnight."

"No, we have to have a doctor right now," the secretary insisted.

"I thought of my periodontist, Dr. Marvin Rosenberg, who is a friend," the concierge said. She called him. "Marvin, I have not been drinking," she said. "I need you to come over here and fix the foot of this twelve-year-old prince."

"I'm a periodontist," Rosenberg said. "I treat gum disease."

The concierge asked him to come as a favor to her: "They said you'll be well compensated."

Fifteen minutes later Rosenberg drove up the circular drive-way in his white BMW. The concierge gave him bandages and rubber surgical gloves from a first-aid kit. A few minutes later, the periodontist came back from the prince's room, laughing.

"I went in that room, and there was a huge banquet table with sandwiches and cakes and pies—enough for a hundred people," he said. "The prince was sitting on this enormous bed, watching a basketball game. By then, the splinter had come out by itself."

The secretary paid Rosenberg $800 in cash.

"Call me anytime," Rosenberg said to the concierge, and he bought her a glass of wine at the hotel bar.

The tunnellike entrance to the Young Friends' tent set the mood for the Russian Winter Ball theme. Strobe lighting against mid-night blue gave the effect of a soft snowfall. But the larger tent where the ball began had a circus atmosphere. A team of acrobats dressed like cossacks went about the room piling on each other's shoulders and leaping off. Guests would immediately clear a path or suffer the consequences. Then the acrobats applauded one another profusely. Rasputin-like men wandered the room offer-ing riddles and folklore to whoever would listen. To underscore the Russian theme, images of onion domes and icons were pro-jected on the tent ceiling.

The expectation was that guests would dress like characters from *Doctor Zhivago* or *Anna Karenina,* but it was the usual black tie, a little more risqué and festive because it was New Year's Eve. At the door the women were crowned with faux-pearl tiaras and the men were honored with neck ribbons that held a pendant of red or green glass. In other words, the Royal Order of Nothing.

Meanwhile, everyone was getting drunker and quickly tiring of the cheap appetizers. If a customer pays enough, the food at Breakers' functions (as opposed to its restaurants) can be superb.

It also helps to know the chefs, as Franklyn de Marco did when he threw a birthday party for himself and his father at the Breakers. But tonight the food was barely worthy of a frayed bar.

The guests wanted to dance, but the dance floor wouldn't open until after eleven. Later, Homer Marshman, who was on the planning committee, agreed that was a problem.

Marshman was still raving about a dinner party thrown by Angela and William Koch, who is worth $650 million. Their rented home, down the street from Barton Gubelmann's house, has a wine cellar the size of a two-car garage. The collection includes an 1870 Château Latour Bordeaux worth $6,000. Meanwhile, the Kochs are building a huge new home on South Ocean Boulevard.

"That was the wine experience of a lifetime for me," Marshman told me. "We had a 1982 Château Lafitte Rothschild, a 1982 Montrachet, one of the best whites I've ever had. We had ports and a 1959 red. Bill ran it through a machine to take out the sediment. His cellar is just unbelievable."

A few days later, Marshman made the *Palm Beach Post* after he and Cheryl attended a performance by the Marvelettes at the Kravis Center in West Palm Beach. The performers wanted a member of the audience as a foil.

"They were trying to get the older fellow in front of me," Marshman recounted. "He didn't want to go. An older man next to me didn't want to go, either. His wife pointed to me. I'm not sure they wanted me as the clown. They wanted someone older and more conservative-looking. But they grabbed me and pulled me up onstage. The lights are in your eyes, and you can't see a thing."

Joking, one of the singers said, "You must think you're quite a man with the ladies."

"I not only think I am, I know I am," Marshman said.

The singer decided to see if Marshman could dance. "Do you have any moves?" she asked.

As the Marvelettes sang "Don't Mess with Bill," Marshman did one of the Temptations' steps. He grabbed the singer. He was rolling, his hips swaying.

"We were jiving to the music," Marshman said. "She was going, 'Oh, no. This was not the way I expected it to play out.'"

"Have you ever seen this move?" Marshman asked. He dropped to a split, then got back up.

"You're not going to do that again," she said.

"This?" he said, and he did it again.

The crowd was hysterical. As Marshman returned to his seat, the singer said, "If you ever come to my show again, don't you ever come up on my stage."

Before the next act, someone in the audience started chanting, "Homer, Homer!" Soon, the entire crowd was chanting: "We want Homer!"

With the season here, Marshman was preparing to stop drinking. He does it every year, from January 1 until the day before his birthday, March 12. Since he's a real-estate lawyer, the season is his busiest time.

"In high season, we're going to two or three parties a night almost every night," he said. "When I have to be at work the next morning and people are paying me pretty good money to do a really good job, I think it helps to abstain completely. As a byproduct, I lose ten to twelve pounds. It's also when there are tennis and golf tournaments. So it helps with that."

A mile to the south of the Breakers, the Coconuts of the Old Guard were holding their sedate New Year's celebration at the Colony Hotel. The Everglades Club came alive, and limos and town cars in somber hue, black and off-black, discharged their bespangled passengers. On Worth Avenue, refined hubbub.

At the municipal dock two blocks north of Worth Avenue, parties were being held on multimillion-dollar yachts. Ta-boó and Club Colette had parties as well. But the most spectacular party was the black-tie affair Trump was throwing at Mar-a-Lago, where Donna Summer sang.

Back at the Breakers, a sparkling woman named Stephanie, who with her willowy stature and raven hair makes a statement when she walks into Ta-boó, was at the Young Friends and asked us, "If you're going over to Mar-a-Lago, what are you doing *here*?"

At around eleven, while the crowd of six hundred at the Young Friends was still waiting for dinner and recorded dance music, eating fried appetizers and watching bad acrobats, paid for with $275 tickets, the exclusive crowd at Trump's Mar-a-Lago had finished a meal of surf and turf with Möet & Chandon White Star and was rearranging chairs for a better view.

As colorful strobes and searchlights illuminated the stage, Donna Summer belted out the familiar tunes of the disco era. "Hot Stuff," "Dim All the Lights," "MacArthur Park," "Last Dance." She had the audience on its feet. It was a remarkable sight, billionaires with their hands in the air, gyrating to a disco beat, clapping and singing along at the diva's command. As Summer, shimmery in a silver sheath, sang "On the Radio," they responded lustily: "Oh ohhhhhhh oh oh."

On a raised platform, I danced with Gianna Lahainer, the woman who had stored her husband at the funeral home for forty days until the season was over. The first member of Mar-a-Lago, she was at the party with Guido Lombardi, a business-administration expert from Italy. Two days earlier, she had given Pam and me a tour of her apartment at the Biltmore.

The Biltmore was once owned by John D. MacArthur, whose foundation funds the genius grants that bear his name. A penny-pinching billionaire, MacArthur lived in nearby Palm Beach Gardens but spent much of his time in Palm Beach, where he attended parties given by Mary Sanford. While her husband, Laddie, was alive, Sanford entertained lavishly and became the queen of Palm Beach. According to Sherman Adler, MacArthur's executive assistant, after Laddie died the money from his trust fund stopped. In return for throwing parties that raised money for charities, Mary arranged to receive consulting fees from the charities. "She would say, 'I need twenty thousand dollars,' and she would host a lovely party to introduce someone to society," Adler said.

Meanwhile, Laddie was otherwise occupied. "Mary always wanted to keep Laddie happy," said Tanya Brooks, a friend of hers. "She thought having pretty girls around would make him happy. Unfortunately, one became his mistress. He bought her a home on North Lake Way. By that time, he was in a wheelchair. He had a ramp built into her home."

At the Biltmore, Gianna led Pam and me past her home's antique furnishings from all over Europe. Clearly, they were collected by someone with an appreciation for detail and craft, that very Italian refined aesthetic sense—from the red chinoiserie chest, to the English silver chandelier, to the wall sconces with silver cherubs seeming to crawl out of them, to the sensual still-life of a cornucopia of figs. In her bedroom, the Baroque headboard—ornate scrollwork, gold leaf—once framed a mirror over a mantelpiece.

"Faboolus," Gianna said with her usual enthusiasm.

Hostess at her own perpetual party, she bubbles like the cuvée imperial champagne she serves in chilled gold goblets to her visitors. With green eyes and red hair in a bouffant style, she has giant breasts. Like many other Palm Beach women, her daytime earrings are pavé—a rich field of diamonds. At night, she often wears a necklace of white South Sea pearls as big as grapes.

Guido, fifty, is protective, reminding her of English words and interpreting her meaning. When she is outspoken, he tones down her phrases. Sitting back to listen, he smiles easily as she speaks. He clearly admires her through and through. And he is having the time of his life.

I met Gianna through Jason Cimino, manager of Dempsey's. Cimino had previously been a lifeguard at the Biltmore, where Gianna told him the story of putting her husband "on ice," as she put it.

Over smoked salmon in her apartment at the Biltmore, Gianna listed all the parties she attended before she had her husband buried. As for the forty-day delay, the Quattlebaum funeral home was happy to oblige her. Once embalmed, Frank Lahainer did not have to be refrigerated.

"I called the funeral home and said, 'How is my husband?'" Lahainer said, laughing. "They said, 'He's in good company with a famous writer.'"

At Mar-a-Lago, Trump's table was off in a bay where Ron Perelman also had tables. Perelman, fifty-five, sat with director Penny Marshall and TV gossip commentator Claudia Cohen, a former wife—his second.

People are always claiming to know Perelman or to be related to him to try to get something for nothing. In June 1995, Kevin P. Eckenrod checked into The Four Seasons claiming to be Perelman's son. After he walked out on a $700 bill, Palm Beach police arrested him at the Colony Hotel, where he was staying under the same fictitious name.

As an Orthodox Jew, Perelman keeps kosher, so at the buffet dinner he had just thrown earlier on New Year's Eve, there was no caviar. Sturgeon have no scales, so their eggs are verboten.

In New York, the tabloids were beating up on Perelman, suggesting that the billionaire was miserly. Besides his $16 million home in Palm Beach, he owns three Manhattan townhouses valued at $3 million to $15 million, and a fifty-seven-acre estate in East Hampton worth $15 million.

During a court hearing on child-support requests from forty-four-year-old Patricia Duff, his third wife, Perelman said he had made $170 million over the last three years. But the tabloids quoted him as saying of his four-year-old daughter, "When Caleigh eats with me, she eats three dollars' worth of food a day. She eats chicken fingers, hot dogs, cereal for breakfast, hamburgers, and some pasta."

Ron's parents, Ray and Ruth Perelman, who were at one of Ron's tables at Mar-a-Lago, were not pleased. A few days later, they would grimace as the subject came up over dinner at Club Colette.

Club Colette is one of the island's most exclusive dining clubs. Elegant with its dark wood bar and a grand piano, it was started by Colette Henry, a French freedom fighter who always wore pink, as an adjunct to her beauty salon. After Aldo Gucci bought the building on Peruvian Avenue, Daniel Ponton took over the club in 1982.

Beyond the price of the food, members pay $2,500 to join, plus $1,000 a year. It is nondiscriminatory and counts the Perelmans, John Kluge, Jimmy Buffett, and Abe Gosman as members. While the cuisine is better than at Café L'Europe, it is inferior to Chez Jean-Pierre, owned by Jean-Pierre Leverrier, who grew up in Normandy, France. What sells the club is its exclusivity. Each year several hundred people apply for membership. Dan Ponton takes only about ten. "Being rich and powerful is not necessarily important," Ponton said. "Are they interesting and stimulating?"

At the club, Ray Perelman was saying that of course kids don't eat much. Ron testified that he was paying $12,000 a month for his daughter's support, plus school, medical, and nanny expenses—in all, $360,000 a year or $1,000 a day. That in addition to payments to Duff of $30 million in cash, real estate, and jewelry, plus $1.5 million a year in alimony. The tabloids' focus on New York's richest man paying $3 a day for his daughter's food was unfair, Ray said.

Then there was a foolish story saying Ron, at the last minute, had invited a model on a cruise on his yacht to Saint Martin and other Caribbean islands. She had turned him down. Not true, Ray Perelman told me. He himself went on the cruise, and Ron had not invited any model.

Ray looks very healthy, which he attributes to riding his bike two hours a day, seven days a week. Ruth seems to have an animal brooch for every occasion: frog, lizard, cat, and so forth, exquisitely detailed in enamel, gold, and precious jewels. This night she wore a perfect pavé bow.

The conversation turned to discrimination by the other clubs.

"We can't get into the Everglades or Bath & Tennis," Ray Perelman said. "There are a handful of Jewish people at the Sailfish Club. If the Beach Club has any, it's only a handful. It's mind-boggling, in this day and age."

This year, Ray said, Ruth is vice chairman of the Red Cross Ball. "They would never have a Jewish chairman," Ray said.

A kindly zephyr passed over the lake from the mainland and bathed the terrace at Mar-a-Lago with warmth late into the night. The New Year's Eve moon was full, the temperature 70 degrees. Outside on Donald's golf course, the tall trunks of the royal palms glowed festively fuchsia, purple, green, and blue.

After the Donna Summer concert, a champagne breakfast was served in the cloister. As Donald walked past a group of five standing at the buffet, one young man called out to him, "See? We're eating the bacon!" The group ingratiatingly munched on.

The dancing that had started in the tent flowed with the crowd into the small ballroom and out around the illuminated Olympic-size pool. If Donald is self-conscious about dancing in front of strangers, aware of Who He Is, it doesn't stop him. And while his dancing is reserved, his rhythmic shuffle is right on the beat.

"Donald likes disco," club manager Bernd Lembcke said. Was there a trace of a shrug? Probably not, probably imagined. Polished and urbane, Bernd has a sophisticated understanding of How Things Work. Next year, he said, the price for New Year's will be $2,000 per person.

"That's the theme, 2000," Lembcke said, smiling.

With his sexy girlfriend, model Melania Knauss, Trump greeted the guests. "Melania for the millennium," Pam remarked to no one in particular.

Trump loves being with beautiful women. After midnight during the season, some of the most stunning women in the world flock to the private disco at Mar-a-Lago. Or Trump will make a foray to 251, where he dances with spectacular blondes with impossibly tight behinds or schmoozes with the owners in the private bar upstairs.

Like most attractive, successful men, Trump knows how to use his eyes with women. As Pam said later, he directs a look. He holds the look just a little longer than expected. No hidden message. Just open and interested.

But for all the gossip-column hype, Trump is cautious about having sex. He spends most of his time working, making calls, and doting on his kids—Eric, Donny, and Ivanka from his first marriage, and Tiffany from his second. He completely loves what he is doing, and he said his energy comes from that. When asked if it is true he only sleeps four hours a night, he said, "Who told you that? Actually, it's three."

"Donald doesn't fool around much because he's so scared of diseases," Vera Swift, a Palm Beach real-estate agent who is a friend of his and of Ivana's, told me. Swift had just returned from a cruise to Italy on Ivana's yacht. "He may be seen with pretty girls in public, but trust me, unless he knows them well, nothing usually happens. He's happiest when he makes a deal."

As Donald and Melania, holding hands, gazed at the lake at 2:00 A.M., Stephen Fagan, who had been on front pages for allegedly kidnapping his daughters, could be seen sitting at one of the tables around the pool. At another, Lesley Friedman with a date. A story about Friedman had just appeared in *The Wall Street Journal*. It seems Friedman had sold her company, which supplied temporary lawyers, for $21 million. Just over forty, she had never been married. She decided to apply the business techniques that had made her so successful to finding an appropriate husband. Her second career would be "dating."

Having settled in Palm Beach, Friedman hired a consultant at $100 an hour to advise her on clothes. Over the course of a year, she had seventy-three blind dates. When an eligible man wanted to sleep with her, she agreed, but only if he promised to stay monogamous for twelve weeks. "She has a fallback position: She's actually willing to settle for six weeks of monogamy," the story said. The man accompanied her home, gave her a peck on the cheek, and said, "I've heard your terms." They went out a few more times, but the sizzle was gone.

For want of a real scandal, Friedman replaced Fagan as the hot topic of conversation on the island. Why would an accomplished businesswoman become involved in a front-page story that made her look so foolish? Doesn't she get it? What was she really after? Most important, how attractive is she? Opinions were mixed.

The letters to the editor following the story hardly helped. One of Friedman's former employees wrote, "On the outside, she's a self-made woman with a law degree. But on the inside, Lesley Friedman is a whiny adolescent girl pinned down by the trappings of the Cinderella Complex. All the designer ballgowns and frequent-flyer pumpkins from Palm Beach won't help her locate Prince Charming."

Unbowed, she unburdened herself to the *Palm Beach Post*, just as she previously had to the *Wall Street Journal*. The local story revealed that she is "hippy," meaning she has broad hips, but is learning "the art of being a woman." Palm Beachers thought it was about time. After the stories appeared, Friedman told Ray Perelman she received two hundred proposals from men, along with a book deal.

When I asked if he would like to meet her, Trump—about to be divorced from Marla—said, "I have enough problems."

21.   A PALM BEACH PARTY

After New Year's, the island became frenetic. Every night there were balls and other charity events—sometimes as many as three to five a night—not to mention private parties. Jell-O heir Orator Woodward hosted one, as did Betty Scripps Harvey and designer Ann Downey, whose late husband, singer Morton Downey, had been a close friend of Joseph P. Kennedy. In the middle of it all, three hundred Ferraris descended on the island, part of a car show sponsored by the Boca Raton–based *Cavallino* magazine.

For months, Kevin O'Dea had been preparing for the season, hiring and training more employees at Ta-boó. In the season, the total complement of chefs, servers, and bartenders goes from forty to eighty. Compared with the previous season, business was up 15 percent. The restaurant was doing five hundred dinners a night and weekly selling one hundred pounds of shrimp, three hundred pounds of strip steak, and six hundred pounds of chicken. Kevin was working sixty hours a week.

"In the season, I can't read," he told me. "I don't have the concentration. During the day, I don't want to see anybody. I can judge my stress level by my sweet tooth. I go eat a chocolate brownie with hot-fudge sauce on top of it. But I love the action. It's exciting. You get keyed up, you're on. It's fun. The trick is to keep up your stamina. You can't get sick."

Customers were jammed four deep at the bar almost every night, and reservations between seven and nine o'clock were impossible without at least a week's notice. One night a party of three women came in. Kevin had a table for them, but they said they had asked for the table next to the fireplace. O'Dea was holding that table for a sweet woman who almost always sits there. While usually punctual, this time she was fifteen minutes late.

"I'm sorry, I can't give you that table tonight," O'Dea said to the party of three.

"I booked this reservation before Thanksgiving, and I was told I could have this table," one of the women said. The reservation book gave no indication of her request.

"Well, you can't have it," O'Dea said.

"Who are you?" one of the women asked.

"I'm the manager."

"Well, if you can't handle this, sonny, you should be in an old folks home taking care of them."

Kevin gave in. The other woman would have to sit elsewhere.

O'Dea needed a break. In the season, he usually gets off work at 3:00 A.M. or later. On New Year's Eve, he left at 6:30 A.M. He wakes up at ten. Kevin dotes on his cats, Squish and Leon. He dates, but his hours make a long-term relationship difficult. In the morning, he swims at the Scuba Club six blocks from his house in West Palm Beach. "I cleanse myself, making sure I'm right with my Maker, right with myself. I go home, suit up, and face the crowds."

O'Dea smoked a cigarette outside and did some deep breathing. Then he came back in, feeling guilty. He went up to the server who was asking the party of three if they wanted drinks.

"David, I've been very mean to these people," O'Dea said. "Buy them a drink on me. My apologies, folks."

"We accept your apology, young man," one of them said.

With a grin on his face, David said, "Now you've humbled Kevin."

Everyone laughed.

"There's almost no tactful way to say, 'Sorry, we need the table,'" O'Dea said. "I have my tricks. Sometimes I'll have Armando the busboy clear the table of plates. He'll say we need the table. He can get away with it. If someone has paid the bill and has been sitting there for forty-five minutes, I might say, 'Can I buy you a cocktail at the bar?' Some people will go. Others will say, 'No, I'm sitting here as long as I want.' One lady sat for three and a half hours. I offered her a cocktail at the bar. Now she challenges me. When she sees me, she says, 'Is Kevin going to make us move?' Eventually, I won her over, and we're great buddies."

When a customer complained about not getting a table, Betsy Fry, Franklyn de Marco's sassy girlfriend, sympathized. "I sleep with the owner, and I can't get a table," she said.

In fact, when De Marco gave his mother a party at the restaurant for her eighty-eighth birthday, the lines were getting longer, and Franklyn said, "Happy birthday, Mom. You can have your cake tomorrow."

"You need the table, son?" she asked. The party was over.

Three days after New Year's, Manfredo Horowitz and his wife, Jasmine, gave their annual black-tie party to celebrate his birthday. Formerly Harry Winston's overseas emissary, Manfredo counted the sultan of Brunei among his clients. He is still in the business, quietly supplying only the most important gems to select members of royalty, movie stars, and members of the Forbes 400.

When it comes to parties, if an individual has enough cachet, Palm Beach society is more than happy to overlook the fact that he is Jewish. In that case, the Old Guard will say, "He's Jewish, but . . ." Horowitz, who is of Jewish descent, has unique access to the wealthiest people in the world—including members of the

Saudi royal family. That means he transcends the caste system on the island. To be invited to his parties is a status symbol: for the lucky few, a crowning achievement of the season.

Over the years, such A-list members of the Old Guard as former ambassador to Denmark Guilford Dudley, Jr.; Orty Woodward; and Robert and Eunice Gardiner, owners of Gardiners Island off New York, have attended the soirées, not to mention Ivana Trump, George Hamilton, Adnan Khashoggi, and Henry Ford II's widow, Cathy Ford.

Jasmine and Manfredo met in Monte Carlo and have been married twelve years. She is his fourth wife—a low number in Palm Beach. He is in his eighties; she is in her forties. Despite the age difference, Jasmine and Manfredo are obviously devoted to each other.

Born in Poland and brought up in Switzerland, Jasmine has the ageless beauty of some European women, with a kittenish face and high cheekbones. Her voice is a softer version of Zsa Zsa Gabor's. With delicate grace, she greeted everyone enthusiastically at the door with a perfect open smile. Her long brown hair was streaked vermilion and swept back from her face in a futuristic style. Her dress, celadon green with a bodice of glistening pink and green flowers, seemed daring with her darker green emeralds.

Among other things, she pays the bills, makes sure they go to all the social events, and supervises the maintenance of their homes—besides La Perla on Dunbar Road in Palm Beach, one in Lugano, Switzerland, and one in Sardinia. Until recently, they owned a ninety-eight-foot yacht as well—the *Why Not*—staffed by a crew of six.

It was at a dinner party in their Sardinia home where Baron Hans Heinrich Thyssen-Bornemisza, one of Europe's richest aristocrats, met his future fifth wife, Carmen, a former Miss Spain. The Thyssen family made its money in shipping and steel in Germany. The baron has eight homes, including one in Lugano, called Villa Favorita, where Jasmine and Manfredo were married. Heini was Manfredo's best man; Tita, as she is called, was Jasmine's matron of honor.

Jasmine does everything, including invitations and thank-you notes, by computer—a rarity in Palm Beach. In fact, telephone-answering machines have yet to reach the island. When they are away, residents either allow their phones to ring or rely on servants to take messages, which means callers can't leave any information beyond a name and a number. Because of their poor English, some of the servants have trouble understanding the messages, requiring lengthy calls as each number and letter is repeated over and over. Then the messages often come out wrong. But having the servants take the calls—or simply allowing their phones to ring—projects the correct image: Islanders have no need to hear from anyone; the world comes to them.

"The moral of the story is we have to learn Spanish," Heather Wyser-Pratte joked.

As valets parked the $300,000 Bentleys, guests sipped Mumm Cordon Rouge Brut Millesime champagne in the Horowitzes' French Regency–style home, designed with the swimming pool as its focal point. As wine is to France and beer is to Germany, champagne is to Palm Beach. At the parties and charity balls, it is as expected as hot dogs at a ball game. At restaurants, Palm Beachers commonly order it with lunch as well as dinner. They call it "shampoo."

Jasmine looked worried and asked Pam, "Where's your drink? Don't you have a drink?" Pam explained sheepishly that she had put it down. Several waiters had tried to serve her more drinks. During the season, it's nearly impossible to take a night off from drinking. At Orty Woodward's party, however, Pam noticed that one woman had the solution. She asked for ginger ale served in a wineglass.

Kirby Kooluris came with Helen Boehm, one of the two women he escorts most frequently. Since her husband, Edward Marshall Boehm, died in 1969, Boehm (pronounced "beam") has carried on as chairman of Boehm Porcelain Studio, which makes porcelain animals, flowers, and figurines that grace the White House, the Vatican, and Buckingham Palace. Douglas Lorie, Helen Boehm's shop on Worth Avenue, sells Waterford and Baccarat crystal, Lladro figurines, and so forth, besides Boehm porcelain flowers, animals, and figurines. One Boehm centerpiece is priced at $150,000.

One afternoon a balding man in shirtsleeves was walking with a couple past the shop. Looking in the window and seeing a self-draining fish platter, he said to his friends, "You kidding me? The one time you cook fish in there, is it worth six hundred dollars?" Then he pointed to the name of the store on the window. "Oh, look, 'A Boehm Company,'" he said, mispronouncing it "bome." "Oh, my God, that's top of the line." The name has cachet no matter how it's pronounced.

Boehm has impeccably coiffed dark honey-blond hair and carefully dresses in brightly colored suits and two-piece dresses that suit her effervescent personality, her ready laugh and sense of humor. She is in her late seventies but still walks comfortably in high heels. She is her own best press agent.

"Who needs a public relations person when you have this?" she said to us in her apartment, where she was showing photos taken of herself with the British royal family, Sophia Loren, Pope John Paul II, and Barbara Bush. Boehm had just sold her Breakers Two condominium on the grounds of the hotel for $4.2 million and moved to Trump Plaza in West Palm Beach. Her 19½-carat diamond ring, she says, is "thanks to a four-letter word, w-o-r-k."

Boehm devotes herself to charity work, always making sure to include Boehm porcelain in the items auctioned off to raise money. If she hobnobs with kings and princes and has private audiences with Pope John Paul II, she also tells it like it is.

"There are a lot of wild marriages here, trophy wives," she told me. "The man is sixty-three, the wife is twenty-seven. That's the magic number. Then the beautiful young women have boyfriends on the side."

Everything has its story: her presentations to royalty, her trips around the world with millions in merchandise, her polo team, which beat Prince Charles's. Once, she gave Prince Charles a tour of her studio in London and presented him with a figure called the Fallow Deer, valued at $3,000. She gave a dinner party that night, and he said, "Do you mind if I exchange that?"

Boehm asked what he would like instead.

"The black rhino."

"One was three thousand dollars, the other was fourteen thousand," she said. "What do you say? They don't have cash in their pockets. So I didn't say anything."

Then the prince added, "And when you deliver it, Buckingham Palace would like to have a tea for you."

"As I drank the tea later, I thought, 'This is costing me eleven thousand dollars,'" Boehm said.

Kirby met Boehm through his friend Monica von Hapsburg, an archduchess from Austria. That's the right way. In Palm Beach it's easy to become classified as part of the help. To relate to someone on the same level, one must move in the same circles, or at least act that way.

Boehm is one of the few people in Palm Beach who know that Kirby is half White Russian Jewish, half Greek. In his forgiving way, Kirby blames people who are not at the "top echelons" of society and have never been exposed to Jews in those circles for their "bigoted" views. If they had been, they would be "ashamed" of themselves. But Boehm sees no excuse.

"There's a lot of anti-Semitism here," Boehm said. "I don't know how the place gets away with it."

Boehm lectures Kirby about his boyfriend, Bill, calling him "a very dangerous young man." Helen first met Bill when Kirby brought him to a fund-raising cocktail party at the home of Mary and Robert Montgomery, the tobacco-settlement lawyer. Later, she told Kirby that Bill seemed to lack confidence—he wouldn't hold his head up and look her in the eye. Despite her misgivings, she let Kirby bring Bill to brunch at Mar-a-Lago one afternoon. Bill began ordering one beer after another.

"I'm sorry, cancel that order," Boehm said to the waitress after Bill ordered his fifth beer. To Bill, she said, "It's not because it costs five dollars. It's something called w-o-r-k." Gesturing toward the magnificent pool at Mar-a-Lago, Boehm said, "You see this around you? It costs money. I get up every morning and go to work. That's what it takes. You have to get your act together."

Afterward, Bill said to Kirby, "Jeez, what's with her?"

By now, Kirby had rented his house to Marion "Kippy" Boulton Stroud Swingle, the philanthropist behind the Fabric Workshop/Museum in Philadelphia. The workshop is the MacArthur Foundation for sculptors, architects, and painters like Roy Lichtenstein and Red Grooms, who want to channel their creativity into fabric.

With part of the rent, Kirby paid off $25,000 in back property taxes. Kirby considers Kippy a friend, and she let Bill and Kirby stay free temporarily in the guest house at another home she rented for her guests. Bill and Kirby were supposed to move out of Kippy's guest house by New Year's Day. Bill took his time moving, and Kippy had her caretaker, Randy, come collect the keys. Bill became violent and pounded his fists on Kirby's BMW, denting it. The car looks as if coconuts fell on it. Randy called the police, who found an X-Acto knife in Bill's belongings.

By way of explanation, Bill said, "How will I protect myself if I have to live in West Palm Beach?"

Characteristically, Kirby was sympathetic to Bill. The move was causing stress, he said. Perhaps it was his fault, Kirby thought. Maybe he should have made arrangements for a new place sooner. "Bill didn't understand," Kirby said as he and Helen sat with Pam and me near the buffet of poached salmon and chicken at the Horowitz party.

"Kirby," Boehm said, "he damaged your car. He really wanted to damage you."

"Well, that was a huge frustration he felt," Kirby said. "He said I was the one that didn't want to leave. In a crazy way, I understand his point of view. I can be the biggest procrastinator in the world. Maybe it was a two-way street."

Kirby said he knows a body shop that will charge him just $350 to restore the car. "I'll just deduct it from the salary I paid him for work done," Kirby said. "I gave him money to help him. I owe him seven hundred dollars for preparing the house for Kippy. I'll deduct the three-fifty. I feel I did all I could for him. But I feel sad that one person had a glorious party the next day with billionaires, and another person whom God created was wondering what was going on."

"I have seen Kirby take the last dollar in his pocket and give it to someone," Boehm said.

When I mentioned Kirby's temporary lack of a residence to Kay Rybovich, one of the women he escorts, she offered to have him stay with her.

Jesse D. Newman, who has been president of the Palm Beach Chamber of Commerce for twenty-eight years, took Kirby aside at the Horowitz party. "That young man is writing a book," Newman said, referring to me. "We don't know Ron, so be careful what you say. We love our town."

"Yes, we do, Jesse," Kirby said.

"He was giving me a clue: Watch it," Kirby said later.

Palm Beach may be populated by some of the most sophisticated people in the world, but it is still a small town. Jesse Newman epitomizes the mentality. Witty and well-tanned, Newman—who is Jewish—has long aspired to be mayor of Palm Beach but never developed enough support. By all accounts, he runs the chamber efficiently. But as both a public relations consultant and president of the chamber, Newman automatically places himself in a conflict of interest. He seems to feel no discomfort. During an interview months before the party, Newman told me he could introduce me "to people like Jimmy Buffett, for example, someone who might not otherwise talk to you. I can arrange book parties, open doors." The implication was he wanted to be paid. Then he began knocking the Chesterfield Hotel, where I was staying, recommending the Brazilian Court instead. He never mentioned that he represented Abe Gosman, owner of the Brazilian Court.

In 1992, Anna Raphael, a London producer, encountered a similar pitch when she filmed a piece in Palm Beach for Channel 4.

"We needed some location permissions for exterior shooting," she told me. "I had met Jesse. He started by being quite helpful. And then he as good as asked us for quite a lot of money to smooth the way, and he implied that if he didn't get it, we would find that our way was made next to impossible. I frankly just ignored him."

Raphael said the money—in the thousands—was separate from fees the town charges for permits to film. "It was clear it would go directly into his pocket," she said.

Asked about this, Newman said he doesn't recall Raphael. As for knocking one hotel while representing the owner of the other, he said he was merely expressing his personal opinion—notwithstanding the fact that he is president of the chamber and represents the owner of the Brazilian Court.

"I don't have to say I represent anybody," Newman said. He would never say he should be hired to open doors, he asserted. "I don't look for customers or clients. People know me, and they hire me."

But Hermine Wiener, the former member of the town council, said that Newman "uses his position at the chamber to get the clients."

Adair Chew, formerly manager of the Colony Hotel, said that when he took over, "Jesse tried to get our business, but he is president of the Chamber of Commerce, so I felt it was a conflict of interest. . . . How can he be president of the chamber? Is he going to promote everybody?"

After I ignored Newman's implicit request that he be hired, I began hearing that he was advising people not to talk with me. From writing my book on the FBI and interviewing 350 of its agents, I learned never to be intimidated, never to bow to threats. With Newman, I took the position that anyone who listened to his advice was not worth interviewing anyway. While Newman may have contributed to some folks' engaging in the Palm Beach Shuffle, my access to the top people in Palm Beach remained unimpaired.

The ultimate irony was that, after years of touting Palm Beach, Newman, who likes to be called Mr. Palm Beach, sold his home here and moved to Breakers West, homes developed by the Breakers Hotel in West Palm Beach. The Shiny Sheet broke the news with a banner headline and a story that took up most of the front page.

Decorated in the neoclassical and Empire styles, the Horowitz home makes a tasteful artistic statement, with white marble everywhere and a collection of cubist paintings in the living room. A musical trio in Andean costume performed pop standards. One of them played the harp. Two illuminated bedrooms with king-sized beds are on either side of the terrace, which had been enclosed with clear plastic drapes that were dropped to keep out the rain. It was unseasonably cold and damp.

"We get one week of this weather every year, and this is it," someone said hopefully.

This was an evening for the women to delight in trotting out their furs. Helen Boehm lent her white mink jacket to a shivering woman in a backless dress. Cheryl Marshman was delighted to be able to wear her mahogany mink for once, but someone remarked she was too young to be wearing it.

Artist Ralph W. Cowan and his aide were trying to hustle Helen Boehm, but she would have none of it. Palm Beachers pay Cowan $15,000 and more to paint embarrassingly flattering portraits of them. Cowan did one of Trump from photos and gave it to him free of charge. Cowan insisted the unfinished hand was part of his art, but Donald paid him $1,000 to finish the hand. Donald hung the portrait in the bar at Mar-a-Lago, facing a portrait of Marjorie Merriweather Post. When the Old Guard heard he'd done this, they had a fit.

"It's because he was in his tennis clothes, for one thing," explained Heather Wyser-Pratte.

At the Horowitz party, Cowan's aide wanted to add the Boehm porcelains to Cowan's catalog. Trying to stimulate her interest, he talked about selling to the sultan of Brunei. But she has already made millions of dollars in sales to the sultan. "I don't need those two," she said. "I took their cards and put them in my handbag."

Some of Palm Beach's finest jewelry was on display. It was the night of the emeralds, a soirée for pearls. It was hard to tell which pair of emerald teardrop earrings was bigger, Jasmine's or Helen's. Helen wore a starburst emerald-and-diamond brooch to match her earrings. A large woman sailed majestically past wearing four very long strands of pearls that cascaded over her matronly chest and down past her waist. "As long as she doesn't trip over them," one wag whispered. His date was wearing a tastefully short strand of even larger South Sea pearls. Another woman wore a string of white and a string of Tahitian black. Jasmine's jewelry included a thirty-carat emerald ring and emerald drop earrings. Her diamond ring is twenty-eight carats, D color—meaning colorless—and flawless.

"Manfredo was one of the first jewelers to sell to the sultan of Brunei at the end of the seventies and the beginning of the eighties," Jasmine told me. "Then a lot of people followed. Now the sultan has stopped buying because he got it all. But he made fabulous profits for all the jewelers of the world. He made a million dollars every second. Now he makes a little less. He has to spend that money some way. He bought the Beverly Hills Hotel, the Dorchester in London, the Palace Hotel in New York, the Plaza Athénée in Paris. He had to buy the most beautiful pieces in the world. He bought ten *billion* dollars' worth of jewelry. A jeweler would not walk out of his palace with a check of less than ten or fifteen million dollars.

"Jewels have always been an expression of love, but they also show a man's influence and position in society," she continued. "He cannot show it himself. Very important people with the means can show on their wives their wealth. Your wife is your calling card. I saw Lamia [one of Adnan Khashoggi's two wives] at a party last year, and she had fabulous jewels. So AK is not where he once was, but he has enough for the two million dollars' worth of jewelry she was wearing that day at a private house."

Sometimes, she said, a man with a beautiful house, car, and wife has bought her "little pieces" of jewelry. "This is very bad," Jasmine said. "Just as you have to educate your taste in antiques, in cuisine, you have to educate your taste in jewelry. I have taken good lessons from my husband. He will see me before I am going to a tea or a party. He says, 'Is that all you're going to wear today?'"

The guests at the party included Ray and Ruth Perelman; Cathleen McFarlane, who chairs Palm Beach charity balls; marquis and marquise Carlos San Damian of the jet set; Hunter Marston of the Old Guard; John Revson, son of Charles Revson of Revlon; and Ann Fisher, whose husband, Jerome, is cofounder of Nine West, the biggest U.S. maker of women's dress shoes. The Fishers just built a 35,000-square-foot mansion on Lake Worth.

Also at the party that night were Jay Rossbach, the chairman of the Palm Beach County Chapter of the American Red Cross, with his wife, Linda; Allen Manning, with Heather Wyser-Pratte; Robert W. Gottfried and Pamela Hoffpauer, top real-estate agents on the island; and Gianna Lahainer, who had introduced me to Jasmine and Manfredo.

When asked how his lifestyle, as a widower of a Phipps heir, differed from that of an heir, Allen Manning replied, "Live well with budgeting, versus live well without budgeting. You downscale. You go coach or economy class instead of flying in your own private jet."

People with little historical perspective think the biggest change in Palm Beach in recent years has been the large houses or the new wealth. They forget that old wealth was once new, and that large houses are not exactly novel—witness Marjorie Merriweather Post's Mar-a-Lago. In Cleveland Amory's 1960 book *Who Killed Society?* agitated socialites lament that the nouveau riche have destroyed the proper society they once knew. Now those parvenus are considered old wealth. The real change has been Donald Trump's impact on the town and its clubs, Manning said.

To the Horowitzes' party, Mort Kaye, the society photographer, brought along Lorraine Hillman, a thirty-six-year-old knockout blonde. Hillman explained to Pam that Kaye was just a friend. "The hostess is lovely, she greeted me so nicely, but what does she really think?" Hillman wondered aloud.

Hillman has shoulder-length straight blond hair. She nearly sparkles. "Women don't like me because of my looks," she said. "That is, until they get to know me and find out I'm not after their husbands."

Originally from London, Hillman has a slight Cockney accent. She worked for Time Warner and Columbia Pictures before going out on her own. She became successful in a niche of real estate, finding locations for specialty retailers like Publix, Sports Authority, and Staples. "I've arranged over a million square feet of retail space," she told me. "Everyone I deal with makes money."

Hillman bought a house a year and a half ago from Patricia Dixson, a legendary Palm Beach and Washington real-estate broker. Besides her half-million-dollar house with a pool, Lorraine has a black Mercedes convertible.

For all her success and good looks, Lorraine confided that she has a problem: "I can't find a guy in Palm Beach."

22. GETTING ONE'S AFFAIRS
IN ORDER

🌴

"I'm a very open-minded individual," Lorraine Hillman told me over drinks at the Chesterfield's Leopard Lounge. "Having been in entertainment, real estate, and marketing, I get to meet a lot of people. But there's such a thing as getting your issues in order. Eligible men that you think are eligible don't know their issues, by which I mean their sexual issues. They don't have their affairs in order. I'm not sure what they are. I don't think they know what they are. I mean they are bisexual or homosexual. I think many of them haven't done anything with men but don't know who they actually are."

Since coming to the island, the blond bombshell has dated several men and slept with one of them. That man "doesn't have his affairs in order," she said. The term says it all. "I don't know where the phrase came from. Have you ever heard it?" Then she acknowledged that she had coined it. "I said to some friends, 'I'm going to start getting my affairs in order.' One said, 'Are you dying?' I said, 'I fucking hope not.' But it's a good way of putting it. It came into my head. A sexual affair is in your head. You have to get them in order."

Certainly, Hillman is a catch. With an impressive body, big blue eyes, and a deep, ready laugh, she is the stuff of men's wet dreams. Smart, witty, and prosperous, Lorraine says what she thinks, sometimes so loudly that she drowns out her own thoughts. When she has a problem, she works it out in public. You hope she's not being her own worst enemy. She punctuates her assertions with "yeah, yeah," or "no, no." Lorraine is perversely delightful, lovable, and loud—and eccentric, which means she fits right in.

Michelle Gagnon, the cocktail waitress at the Leopard Lounge, told me Hillman once gave her a $500 tip for a glass of wine. Hillman denied it: "If she's getting five-hundred-dollar tips, I'll take the job." But when Gagnon reminded her that she had said to split the tip with several others at the Chesterfield, Hillman recalled that she had tipped $500. More commonly, she tips $100.

"These people work hard," she said. "They deserve it."

Patricia Dixson, who sold her home to Lorraine, introduced her to the Rotary Club. Lorraine faithfully attends the 7:45 A.M. breakfast at the Brazilian Court every Tuesday. Few people in Palm Beach are up at that hour, but before the breakfast, Lorraine gets in a 6:00 A.M. run on the beach two blocks from her house. She takes the club very seriously and tried to interest me in some of its activities. "This is Rotary material," she said, proffering a set of documents. "These are the leadership awards. This is all we do there. I'm an absolute Rotarian."

The club has named her to several committees, and she helps arrange charitable events and attends its lectures on subjects like orchid growing. In the dating arena, her efforts have met with less success.

"When I first came here," she said, "I went to the docks and went out on a large boat. The person who took me was born in Palm Beach and went to the best parties. He said, 'Have you ever been with any beasts?' This was the first indication I was in a bizarre environment. I assumed he was referring to animals. I said, 'No, actually, no, I've never been with any *beasts*,'" drawing out the word.

Men are constantly asking her out and claiming they slept with her, Hillman said. "When I go to the post office. If I go to the bank, yeah. They say, 'Hi, I haven't seen you before. You're English. Would you like tea?'"

A real-estate agent asked her out. "He said, 'I'm one of the six straight men on the island in your category,'" meaning he buys and sells homes of $12 million and up.

When Lorraine met Kevin O'Dea at Ta-boó, she told him he could be "number 12." She said, "I've danced with him, and he's the best dancer." At the time, "I was probably up to ten—no, eleven guys I had slept with in my life. That's right, eleven. I probably slipped one in. I may go to bed with Kevin, if I know what his affairs are. Kevin, you can put me at the worst table, but I can't go out with anyone unless I know that their affairs are in order."

She continued, "Women claim they've slept with three, four, or five. That's what they claim. I don't know if I believe it. I don't think eleven is a bloody lot of men. Not really. If you live in a small town, it is." Asked if she had had any additional one-night stands, she said, "Not that I recall."

Lorraine was married once for seven years. "He thought I didn't have enough education for him," she said. "They say the brilliant don't finish college." A count asked her to marry him. "'The count of no account,' I called him."

Lorraine's seventh was Peter Nygard, a Canadian fashion designer who owns a $12 million home in the Bahamas. "Peter was great," she said. "It was in and out, but it was great. A one-afternoon stand." Then she said cryptically, "I have to breed in my own dimension."

She corrected herself. "I can remember every one night-stand, unfortunately. A few in my life, one back when. Not on this island. No. It would be lethal to have a one-night stand on this island. They don't have their affairs in order. Or they would be married and their wives would cut my throat."

Because she doesn't like men to drive drunk, she'll invite them to sleep it off in her home. Hillman has three bedrooms and three bathrooms, "so they can stay." She said, "I'm unbounded. A lot of people are unbounded."

"People assume because guys come to my house and swim in the pool that I'm sleeping with them," she told me. "Or they knock on the door at all hours of the night. I must live in a retail store here. It's another watering hole. It's impossible to be alone here when you want to be alone," she said. In Palm Beach, "You have friendships with the landscaper or the valet or the captain of the boat and they say I'm fucking the help. If I invited a respectable man into my home for dinner, I'd be afraid because the next thing you know I'd be sleeping with him. If you go out with someone to a restaurant or dance with someone, everyone automatically thinks you've slept with him. You're not allowed to have friends."

Of course, she said, "a lot of them would like to go to bed with me. A lot would like to say that. I've been around the block. I'm not old-fashioned. But for the last five or six years, I've been working."

Lorraine sometimes goes topless in her pool, generating more talk in the small town. "I'm European, for chrissakes. Tits are tits," she observed. "I'm unbounded. You can't go topless in Palm Beach on the beach. You'd get arrested. Not that I'd like to see any breasts here," she said. "They're siliconed up. They wouldn't look normal. They would look like two Mount Everests. In the blazing sun, they'd melt. They don't slide down by the armpit. They bounce up. Who do these women think they're kidding?"

Walking into a restaurant or a party can be scary. The facial surgery in Palm Beach makes everyone look like "Muppets," she said. "A lot of my friends have surgery and look different from month to month."

The masks come off in a place like Razook's Beach Shop, which sells bathing suits of every description, around the corner from Worth Avenue. Saleswoman Diane Diorio says they have a model working for them who has had so much plastic surgery she can no longer close her mouth. Another problem with cosmetic surgery is the face doesn't match the body. "You have a fifty-year-old face on an eighty-year-old body," she said. "It's freaky." With the aging process, the skin thins and sags, becoming like parchment. Sadly, this means for the elderly ladies who have had breast enhancement during their lives, you can see the breast implants through their skin. "I feel sorry for them," she said. "I am so glad I started working here, because now I know I will never get plastic surgery."

Lorraine told me she has had no surgery, no silicone implants. "My breasts are big enough," she said. "I don't need any silicone, not yet. It's all real. I'm an original." Besides, "Beauty comes from inside. It creates an illusion. I think we're spirits. We're not real bodies anyway. We're bundles of energy."

Lorraine's effervescence has spawned nicknames like "Champagne Lorraine" and "Hurricane Lorraine." Her e-mail address—rainpb@aol.com—is based on "Rainy," another nickname.

Even though they are practically illegal, Hillman occasionally wears jeans to run errands. "You get dirty looks," she said. "They think, 'What are you, an urchin?' If you wear them, nobody will invite you anywhere."

Despite the island's ban on jeans, Lorraine attended the opening of the Louis DiCarlo jeans store on Worth Avenue a few months earlier and bought a pair. DiCarlo, whose name appears on the jeans, was the man who turned out to be a Colombian drug dealer and had had extensive plastic surgery to conceal his identity. In Palm Beach style, he kept reinventing himself, starting the company called Jeins & Co., which sold jeans packaged in stylish paint cans. In February 1997 DiCarlo filed for protection under the bankruptcy laws, citing more than a million in debts.

In his new incarnation, DiCarlo convinced Anna Veksler, originally from Maryland, to open a jeans store using his name. Who in Palm Beach would buy jeans anyway? Most likely the tourists who descend on Worth Avenue during the season. Almost invariably, they wear shorts. Licking ice cream cones, they meander in front of the windows of designer shops. They don't go in.

While they seem to islanders thick as flies on honey, the number of tourists is quite low compared with Rodeo Drive. Ever polite, when they see them, islanders look away, hiding their disdain.

When DiCarlo showed Veksler his impressive office and convinced her to go into business with him, Veksler knew nothing of DiCarlo's background, she said. In fact, she said, he never showed up for work. She is now suing him.

"Somebody faxed me the articles [about DiCarlo's past]," Veksler told me. She had one thought: "Oh, my God." When Veksler tells people she is from the DiCarlo store, "No one wants to hear from me," she said. "I tried to put an ad in the paper. They wouldn't take my check. I have to pay everyone in advance, and they have to wait for the funds to come in before they can cash the checks."

In April 1999 DiCarlo filed a second time for protection under the bankruptcy laws. When I called him, he had no comment.

Lorraine Hillman attended the DiCarlo opening with Susan Potter, a fresh-faced Miss Congeniality. Franklyn de Marco had introduced them. Just friends, Lorraine and Franklyn go to parties together and have lunch at Ta-boó. Lorraine insists on calling him Frankie, which he hates. Besides her Mercedes, Lorraine had a black Lincoln Town Car, which she kept in front of her house "for security." The car bothered Franklyn almost as much as panty hose does. Having spent more than $600,000 for his red Corniche convertible and silver Wraith, Franklyn firmly believes in projecting the right image through one's vehicles. He called the Lincoln a "Mafia hearse." He finally offered to buy it from Lorraine just so he could dispose of it. He never wanted to see it again. She agreed to put the car on the market.

Lorraine said Susan Potter dates what Lorraine calls "fly-by-nights." These are men who "come in here with their jet planes and convertible Bentleys," Lorraine said. "They are players. I meet them at private parties. They fly into town and fly out. They are rarely here for more than three or four days." But, to quote the song, she added, "Players only love you when they're playing."

Potter began dating a fly-by-night who is one of Palm Beach's most powerful men, someone whose business is in New York and who flies into town on his own plane on weekends. He would send a chauffeured car to pick her up in Boca. Only one problem: He's married, a fact he concealed from her.

At Ta-boó Franklyn told Susan the man was married. She couldn't believe it. "You can tell if another person lives in the house," Franklyn told her. "Run upstairs and look."

"How can I do that without going to bed with him?" she asked.

"You can go to the ladies' room," he said. "You can look at the toiletries."

De Marco thought Susan was purposely being dense. "She doesn't want to know," he said one night as he served limitless beluga caviar with champagne at his home. "If she can get an audition and maybe get the part," he said facetiously, "she's willing to try it."

But more likely, Potter was being naïve. After several other people told her the man was married, she broke off with him.

Meeting Lorraine, Pam, and me at the Leopard Lounge, Susan related her other experiences dating Palm Beach men. She said she went out with one man who had a beautiful home on the island and a Rolls. After a black-tie affair, they went back to his house. He excused himself.

"He came back with his shirt and bow tie still on and no pants or underwear," Susan said. "He said very casually, 'Would you like a glass of champagne?' I said, 'Oh, that would be wonderful.' A housekeeper handed it to him. I said, 'Wow, it is late. I had so much fun.' He followed me and said, 'If you have to go, don't come back.' I was laughing my head off."

Another night, Potter was dining at Chez Jean-Pierre, the outstanding French restaurant.

"Are your parts working?" a wealthy older man asked her as she ate her Dover sole.

"Excuse me?" she said. "What are you talking about?"

"All of your parts," he said.

"Parts of what?" she asked.

Then it dawned on her. He was talking about her reproductive organs.

Potter said the man was about seventy years old and worth at least $20 million. "Now you know why I stopped dating older men in Palm Beach," she said. "Young men don't worry about that. They're worried about *not* getting you pregnant."

Lorraine interjected, "People want to know if Susan slept with someone. Is she a slut? I've never heard anybody say anything good about anybody else. I've never heard anybody say, 'That's a nice girl.' It's almost like they want to torture you."

Lorraine said many of the men she has taken home have a "masculine side to them. They want to screw me. They do. But then some of them want to look in my closets. They like to look at my outfits and the hair products and toiletries I use—something bizarre I've never experienced before."

Beyond those who are gay or don't know what they are, many men on the island have drinking problems, she said. They need psychiatric help. Or they are inbred trust-fund babies, their brains withered from disuse.

"If anybody thinks they should get married to a man for money, they'll have a very unhappy life," Lorraine said. "A lot of these older men go out with these young women to get energy. But they suck the life out of these women. That was before Viagra. Now we have Viagra. A lot of times you see younger women thinking twice about going out with older men because they'll have to perform with them."

Lorraine once asked an heir to a beer distributorship, "Don't you work?"

"Every time someone drinks a beer, I get a cent," he said. "So why should I go out to work?"

Another trust-fund baby is "waiting for his mother to croak so he'll inherit another two hundred million," she said. "They have no substance. When you meet a guy who has been totally mollycoddled, he is not able to do anything for himself. Everybody here has baggage. It's like finding a needle in a haystack. I've never met such bizarre people in all my life."

In fact, the man she slept with in Palm Beach turned out to be more interested in masturbating in front of her than in having intercourse. "He didn't know what he was," she said. "He wasn't interested in sex. He was into masturbation. They say some men don't want to have intercourse with you because they want to have power over you. The ultimate power is actually having intercourse with you so that they control you that way. I found out people knew about him because people here know everything. Former girlfriends reported the same thing. You never really know for sure what they are. He might not know himself," she said. "Talk about safe sex. On the island, you're lucky if you get that."

"When you go out with someone whose affairs are not in order, you think it's you," she said. "There's nothing worse than that. But there's nothing wrong with me. No. Absolutely nothing."

Whether marriage would help is an open question. According to Dino Laudati, who has been doing Palm Beach women's hair for twenty-three years, "A lot of married women complain they don't get enough sex. Whether they're young or old, they complain that it's either too quick or not enough."

Now at the Brazilian Court, Laudati hears about women's divorces and affairs before their husbands do. "I hear about women who go on trips and tell their husbands one thing and go with another guy," he told me. "Or have affairs while the husband is playing golf. A lot of people are not happy in their marriages."

A handsome man of forty-six, Laudati often becomes the object of their affections. In fact, two pretty wives who are married to older husbands have insisted that Laudati come to their homes, where they answered the door—"totally naked," he said. Laudati is devoted to his wife, Maryanne. "I am always professional," he said. "I ask them to put a robe on. Then I cut their hair."

For all its bizarre features, Lorraine said she loves the excitement and beauty of Palm Beach. "People here make me laugh," she said. "It's a different level of people. You have mental stimulation the minute you walk out the door. They have all succeeded at something. You cannot be on this island unless you had some success story in your life." But, she said, "You can't believe all you hear. There's a lot of hogwash, too. The owners start looking like their dogs, and the dogs start looking like their owners.

"People say they come here to relax," she continued. "I don't see anybody relaxing in this town. Everyone here is doing business. It's one big networking place. They're all strung out like rubber bands."

Many of the women in town are lonely. "They want to go out with people and have company," she said. "That's why people who don't have their affairs in order flock to this town. They can hide here." Meanwhile, some enterprising young men become gigolos. "There's a lot of that going on here," Lorraine said. "They're carrying the women's shopping bags. Yet the women are often married to other men. It's amazing that the women keep their wedding rings on. Can you imagine what it's like in their homes? 'Here honey, give me some money. I'll fuck you if you give me some money.' Can you imagine it? Men who don't have their affairs in order prey on the weak and the old."

After a while, the money, the Rolls-Royces, the champagne all become a blur. What puts everything in perspective is illness. A billionaire's child contracted cancer and has only months to live. All the hundreds of millions of dollars the father transferred to his offspring are now of no consequence.

"I think God gets you back," Lorraine said. "You shouldn't be too greedy. People here want it all. They've taken it from the rest of society. They're going to get punished. What goes around, comes around. In smaller towns in middle America, the people are happier."

Lorraine's needs are simple. She wants a soul mate, someone with high intellect whose affairs are in order. "I don't want to end up with a walker, and I don't mean the aluminum kind," she said. "Is there any hope for me?"

Then she said, "I will find the right one here somehow, someday. It will come." In the meantime, she said, "the only penis I've seen is on the ceiling of the Chesterfield."

23.   A RECKONING

At the bar at Ta-boó, Bill ordered a Budweiser. Tanned, of medium height, Bill is a "handsome animal," as Kirby put it. This evening Bill was behaving himself, ordering only one more beer. But he was having trouble following the conversation. When asked a question, he seemed relieved to be included. Trying to sound profound, he turned to me and said, "The only difference between Trump and me is zeros."

"Bill has a big court case coming up that will determine his future," Kirby said. "Either he'll be a free man and will be able to enjoy himself in a place like this, or he'll have a couple of years to answer for what happened. It all depends on how he sells himself as a human being."

Kirby said both sides had subpoenaed him as a witness. "This was when the police tried to . . . you tell the story," he said to Bill. "It happened to you. What happened that night?"

"I was out on the streets in West Palm Beach," Bill said. "I had nobody to turn to. The cops came because a known prostitute said I had a gun. I didn't have a gun. That started the whole thing. I had been drinking. I never attacked them. I just resisted. I said, 'I don't have a gun.' Their adrenaline was flowing. They said on the police radio that a suspect was resisting and supposedly had a gun."

"I'm trying to determine if he's telling the truth," Kirby said, overlooking the fact that Bill was admitting he resisted arrest. "I'm willing to testify about the productive side of him that I know. I think they're getting the drift that he's crying for help."

In the meantime, Kirby said, people hesitate to invite him to parties because they know he would want to bring Bill. Ever sensitive to others's sensibilities, Kirby said, "Nobody wants Bill with me, so it hurts his feelings."

At the same time, Kirby insisted Bill is not his lover.

"I've never had a lover," he said. "Lover to me means a life companion." Bill is someone with whom he has had sex. "I got involved. I had sex with him. It was action. He turned out to be a fine friend."

To me, Bill described himself as being "ninety percent straight and the rest bisexual, with Kirby." But he complained, "I haven't gotten much action lately."

Kirby said his tenant, Kippy, was insisting he install a new air-conditioning system in his home. "They aren't patient enough to wait until the air conditioner defrosts itself, so I have to spend four thousand dollars. I have to get a whole new system." But the next day, he said, "It needed to be done, and I need pushes. The system is seventeen years old."

Julia Clark, a fresh-looking young woman at the bar, was talking with her friend Jennifer McGarry about the hypocrisy of Palm Beachers who attend charity balls. "Their own families are falling apart at the seams," Clark told me. "There is drug abuse, and there are volatile relationships and domestic problems. Then they tell us we should support homeless children and charities that help victims of domestic violence. Their own children are victims of these things."

At the end of the bar, Franklyn de Marco was on another thigh-high jag. His girlfriend, Betsy, was swearing by them—Victoria's Secret has them, Hanes is good—when Monica, a large blond woman of a certain age with a German accent walked in with Robert Eaton, a Hollywood producer who was once married to Lana Turner. Eaton remarked that Palm Beach parties are far classier than those in Hollywood. And what did the woman he brought think about this idiotic panty hose controversy? Her answer was to lift her skirt and show the black-lace tops of her thigh-highs. Everyone around her laughed.

Earlier, at a cocktail party at Franklyn's, over beluga caviar and a side of smoked North Atlantic salmon that I had supplied from New York's Oyster Bar, two women who had been his house guests had a different take. At first, on his recommendation, they bought thigh-highs and put them on. Then, Maryann said, "We found ourselves driving down Worth Avenue, asking each other, 'What are we doing?' These are the most uncomfortable things we have ever worn. They are thick, you're always afraid they are falling down, they make you lumpy, they make you hang over where they aren't."

Sipping his champagne, Franklyn turned to me and said, "Betsy moved into my house."

"I have not moved into his house," Betsy protested. Turning to Franklyn, she said, "When I move in, you'll know it."

Franklyn told me he was on a flight to Morocco arranged by Brownie McLean. "Behind me, I heard a commotion," Franklyn said. "A woman had died. I said to Brownie, 'I don't want to give you any bad news, but a lady has died.' Without missing a beat, Brownie said, 'Was it one of ours?' The plane was full. No one wanted the dead woman next to them for the flight over. I said, 'Let's prop her up in the galley.' The next morning, they couldn't serve breakfast because she had become stiff."

Near Franklyn sat Patricia Dixson, who had sold her house in Palm Beach to Lorraine Hillman. At a side table sat Nancy Sharigan, co-owner of Ta-boó, with her husband, Robert Simmons. As Nancy was explaining to me how the restaurant makes its succulent mahogany duck (marinate fresh duck overnight in ginger, teriyaki sauce, and fresh oranges, and roast for two and a half hours), Robert said he had rented a condo in Boca to Lorraine before she bought her house in Palm Beach. A former savings and loan executive who had had dinner with Lorraine at Ta-boó the previous night came by. He bragged that he spent the night with her and was exhausted from the experience. But Lorraine and witnesses would later say he only had dinner with her that night.

If Palm Beach were any smaller, it would fit in someone's bathroom.

A few days later Kirby had dinner at Ta-boó with Trisha Pelham. With resignation, he reported that Bill had been sentenced to nine months in jail. Before his trial, Bill had told the people he was staying with in West Palm that he wanted to bring a cooler of beer to court when he faced charges.

"Obviously, his judgment is impaired," Kirby said. "That's what we're trying to establish so he'll get help. They should have let him do it. That would have said it all." The jury had a choice of three counts of battery and one charge of resisting arrest. "They came back the next day," he said. "They found him not guilty on battery and guilty on resisting arrest. But they wanted to give a speech. They recommended he not be punished and receive treatment instead."

The judge asked Bill why he wouldn't stop drinking. "What do you suggest we do with you?" the judge asked.

"I think you should build bars on the bridges because when I leave Palm Beach and drink in West Palm Beach, I get in trouble," Bill said.

There was silence in the courtroom. The judge asked Bill what he does to help himself.

"I run on the beach with my Walkman," Bill said.

More silence.

"The judge thought he was being a smart-ass," Kirby said. "But Helen Boehm's friend, who is a psychiatrist, said that's what a manic person with his illness should do. The Walkman drowns out the voices. He was doing exactly what he should do."

The judge asked how the problem with the police came about.

"I don't really know," Bill said. "I guess it was an escalation of emotions on both sides."

That was the last straw. An escalation of emotions, as if Bill and the police had equal authority.

"I'm not going to have you out endangering the police," the judge said. He sentenced Bill to nine months in jail and five years' probation.

"If he breaks parole, he gets a full year instead of nine months," Kirby said. "He has no motivation to get well."

In a way, Kirby said, he agreed with the judge's decision. "But I feel sorry for Bill." He said the sentence will allow him to break away from him. Kirby was not accepting his collect calls from jail. But he did visit him. "I wanted to make sure that he wasn't suicidal. I think he was shocked by the sentence. His exit was bad. In the courtroom they put chains on him. That wasn't necessary."

"It's not your responsibility," Trisha said. To Pam and me, she said, "He doesn't get that visiting him is an open invitation for Bill to come back."

"He bashed your car," I reminded him.

"I know," Kirby said.

The previous night, Bill had been the main topic of conversation when Kay Rybovich took Kirby, former JFK lover Gunilla von Post, and Dr. Arthur Avella to the Palm Beach Yacht Club. At the entrance to the club, on Lake Worth in West Palm Beach, a pristine '75 Chevy Caprice red convertible with white interior was parked next to a '63 pale yellow Cadillac convertible.

A former Park Avenue psychiatrist, Avella is a friend of Kirby's who was clinical director of the psychiatry department at Roosevelt Hospital in New York. When the subject of Bill came up, Avella asked Kirby, "Why do you have empathy for somebody like Bill? What is the basis for your empathy?"

"I can relate to him," Kirby said.

"Exactly," the psychiatrist said. "In what way do you relate to him?"

"I think he's a little lost."

"In his craziness, he does things that you wish you could do, so you identify with him."

"Ohhhh," Kirby said. "In other words, he'll say something I wouldn't dare say."

"Right."

"Like when he said to Kippy, 'We're not leaving.'"

"And you feel you owe him something."

"I think he believes in me."

"Oh, how idealistic."

"He acts like a teenager and can drive you crazy."

"You encourage him to have a totally dependent relationship. Why?" Avella asked.

"To feel useful, I don't know," Kirby said.

Grasping for something positive to say about Bill, Kirby said Bill went to Gunilla's fifty-ninth birthday party at the Beach Club and was "accepted."

"I would use the word *polite*," Avella said. "People were polite to him."

Kirby distracted Avella from the subject by recalling what happened at Green's Pharmacy when Avella came in and saw Kirby sitting with two very attractive young women. Kirby ignored him. The psychiatrist—who calls himself Kirby's counselor—was miffed.

Kirby later told his friend that he didn't invite him over because the two women were undercover officers from the Palm Beach Police Department. They were asking Kirby if they might use his house as part of an undercover operation to thwart thieves peddling stolen handbags. The officers—who knew Kirby because of his repeated calls for help with Bill—did not want to be introduced.

"They look like glamorous tourists," Kirby said. "They ride their bikes up and down the path along Lake Worth and catch people doing things."

The next night at Ta-boó, Kirby said that just after he visited him in jail, Bill sent him a form requesting clothes with no pockets. "Everything must be white or gray," Kirby said. Helen Boehm told him to throw away the request. He promised he would.

"Where do you get clothes without pockets?" Kirby asked. "I've spent all day running to Kmart, Target, Wal-Mart. I finally had to have a seamstress sew up the pockets."

But didn't Kirby tell Helen he would throw the request away? I asked.

"I had to tell Helen that, because she's such a disciplinarian," Kirby said. "You have to say, 'Yes, sir.' But I just don't leave somebody at the bottom of a tunnel."

As the prime rib arrived, Pelham said she had some good news. Her autistic son, Dorian, had had to be hospitalized after a small seizure. He had turned out to be fine, but since he was in the hospital anyway, she persuaded a doctor to try a new treatment on him. Featured on *Dateline NBC* and other shows, it consisted of giving him an infusion of secretin, a hormone secreted by cells in the digestive system when the stomach empties. While secretin is approved for diagnosing digestive problems, it is not approved for treating the 400,000 Americans with autism. As part of a nationwide test of 2,500 children with the disorder, Saint Mary's Medical Center administered it to Dorian.

"There's been a difference," Pelham said. "It's amazing. His attention span is now appropriate for an eight-year-old. He's stopped screaming an autistic scream. They put their hand over their ears a lot to block out sound. He's stopped doing that. He looks you in the eye now. He's actually able to put thoughts together and think things out, which he wasn't able to do before. Now Dorian says, 'I want to go to Burger King.' Before, he said, 'Burger King.' I e-mail the doctor every night and tell him what I'm seeing. It's really exciting. It's a wonderful Christmas present."

The bad news is that Dorian is making up for lost time, engaging in pranks younger kids might engage in. "On Saturday morning, I found he opened a chair filled with Styrofoam pellets, tipped it upside down, and spread the pellets all over the room," Trisha said. "It took two of us three hours to clean it up."

That brought to Kirby's mind an incident with Helen Boehm. "About five years ago, I was left in charge of a white collie," Kirby said. "I had smashed my car and was renting one. The collie shed on the velour front seat. I picked up Helen for a party at the Breakers. She had on a black velvet dress. To my surprise, when she got out of the car, the whole back of her dress was white.

"I couldn't tell her," he said.

Kirby said Helen and Kay Rybovich are keeping him busy, filling up his calendar. "I can't even find a night to go to the movies," he said. Although he would never accept money from either woman, Helen "underwrote" a new bow tie, since she thought the one he had was too small.

Trisha said she spent Christmas Eve at Al Taubman's of Sotheby's. "At each place setting, there were gifts of gold compacts, gold bottle openers, or gold card holders," she said. At another dinner party, she was sitting next to a man just back from Hong Kong, where he had met a feng shui master, whose calling is to bring the material objects of everyday life into harmony with the natural world. The master had bought two houses in Palm Beach because, he said, Palm Beach has the best feng shui in the world. Among other things, it has to do with the sunrise—directly on the town, with nothing obstructing it. So, everything turns to gold.

More recently, Kirby fixed Trisha up with a very wealthy Palm Beach man. He took her to Renato's for lunch. "He was screaming and yelling about Madeleine Albright being Jewish and about Zionists," Trisha said. "Everyone could hear him. I made sure he had a very big bill. It was a good three hundred dollars. I'm real good at that when I want to be. I ordered a final glass of champagne. Then I said, 'You're an oversized man, but from the way you behave, you can tell you are physically small.'"

The restaurant became silent. Then several women applauded. Trisha finished her champagne and left.

Trisha said she was happy to be getting out for the evening at Ta-boó. Because of Dorian's condition, she usually has trouble finding sitters. This evening, the man who rents her guest house had agreed to take care of him.

Later, the inevitable Palm Beach encounter: a bartender at the Chesterfield's Leopard Lounge said she heard I was having dinner with Pelham that night.

"I'm a friend of the man who sat for her," the bartender said.

24.   TIARAS

In late January the palms along the entrance road to the Breakers were underlit with colored spotlights, and the illuminated twin towers, with pennants flapping, made the already regal hotel look like a castle. Inside, more dressed-up than they would be for the rest of the year, the guests stood in a receiving line at the International Red Cross Ball, the number-one social event of the season.

Women wearing tiaras they inherited, bought, or borrowed from Van Cleef & Arpels and men in neck badges and sashes, if they had them, were waiting to shake hands with the honored guests, the ambassadors and their wives, along with the Honorable Marion H. Smoak, the State Department's former chief of protocol, who was chairman of protocol for the ball. He wore the optional tails.

The actual receiving line—through which the guests, when it came their turn, would be hustled by a tuxedoed crowd-tender as impatient as a bad maître d'—was anticlimactic. This was the evening's first opportunity to see and be seen, to gossip and to admire one another's clothes.

Outside the reception room, Kay Rybovich, hurrying down the hall in a little black dress, stopped to greet some friends. She wasn't going to the ball, she said, but was on her way up to a suite rented year-round by a friend. They were going to have an evening of bridge, a way of life for the Old Guard. Rybovich is a bridge life master, a designation based on the number of points acquired at national championships

After a champagne reception, about six hundred Red Cross Ball guests found their places at tables. More money has been raised in the Breakers' Venetian Ballroom than in any other room in America, or so the locals claim. The ceiling is painted with white clouds against a blue ground, and its windows face on the ocean, though this night, no one was looking outside.

On the stage was Neal Smith's twenty-piece orchestra, which has been playing at the ball since 1957, when Marjorie Merriweather Post started the event—along with its tradition of wearing tiaras and importing ambassadors. On the wall above the orchestra stretched a thirty-foot-wide red cross surrounded by white "diamonds." From every table, a string of tiny white lights stretched to the ceiling from the centerpiece of red roses, white lilies, and stephanotis in a tall vase like a large champagne glass. Floating vertically in the stem was a single perfect white tulip.

As the orchestra played "Ruffles and Flourishes," the Marine color guard appeared and the traditional grand march began. The ambassadors and their wives, from Sweden, Spain, Bosnia, Afghanistan, and Rumania, filed in, along with the diminutive young Colombian ambassador and his tiny wife, and the ambassador of Slovenia and his wife. The Slovenian couple was staying with Ruth and Ray Perelman for the weekend.

The orchestra played "Pomp and Circumstance." Some of the grande dames of Palm Beach made their majestic entrance, escorted by the Marines. First, the chairman (Palm Beach has yet to recognize the terms *chair* or *chairwoman*) of the ball, Candace Van Alen, dignified and cheery in bright red. She wore a silver, ruby, and diamond tiara, a gift from Napoleon I to Empress Josephine.

Then a surprise: Honorary chairman, Betty Scripps Harvey, who had chaired the ball to some controversy the previous three years, made her entrance. In a diamond tiara and a low-cut petal-pink ball gown with full skirt, she looked like a princess. Her stunning necklace was three strands of diamonds joined by a diamond floral cluster.

Finally, Barton Gubelmann, the honorary vice chairman, in an off-the-shoulder black Arnold Scaasi gown with a full skirt—the color preferences for the night being black, red, and white and combinations of the three.

Earlier that month, Van Alen had invited Gubelmann to lunch and convinced her that she was doing a good job as general chairman. She told Barton it was important to attend the International Red Cross Ball and be honorary vice chairman, lending her prestige to the event. Barton accepted.

"I came to the Red Cross Ball out of friendship," Barton said as she sat at Van Alen's table, front and center of the ballroom. "I give them a lot of money every year. So I don't have to go to the ball. I can't stand going to all these parties. The only reason I'm here is because I've known Candy Van Alen since 1938."

Barton's escort was Bruce D. Bent, the chairman of the men's committee. Bent's home was previously owned by Franklyn L. Hutton, brother of E. F. Hutton and father of the much-married multimillionairess Barbara Hutton. To Barton's left sat Candy Van Alen's brother, Wallace Alig, who escorted his sister.

Barton had just given a party at the Everglades Club and was planning another at her home. The guests illustrated why she is the island's number-one socialite. There was Lord Charles Hindlip, chairman of Christie's International, and his wife; Dysie Davie, a Standard Oil of New Jersey heir, and her husband, Bedford (Buddy); Princess Ghislane de Poliagnac of France; and William Pannill, president of the Everglades Club, with his wife, Kitt.

For her birthday party at Club Colette in December, Barton's guests included Doris Magowan, whose husband, Robert, founded Safeway Stores, and Cathy Barrett. In Palm Beach, everyone has a colorful history, a success in life, and a story to tell. Barrett is an example. A former runway model for Emilio Pucci, Bill Blass, and Christian Dior, Barrett later became fashion

editor of *Town & Country*. Barrett's family are collateral descen-
dants of Sir Thomas More; the Reverend John Moore, a founder
of Southampton, Long Island; Clement Clark Moore, who wrote
"A Visit From St. Nicholas"; and Marianne Moore, the American
poet. Now married to investment banker Robert J. Barrett III,
Cathy is the widow of S. Joseph Tankoos, Jr., who owned the
Colony Hotel. When Cathy, wearing a red Herrera wedding
gown, married Barrett at the Everglades Club in April 1995,
Barton was her flower girl. The queen of Palm Beach society
wore a petal skirt and carried a basket of flowers.

Just after Ivana Trump confronted Marla Maples on the ski
slopes of Aspen in 1989, Cathy made her own statement about
the Donald by dressing up as Donald Duck for a weekend spa
party Ivana held at Mar-a-Lago.

"The ladies, in chiffon and pearls, gasped," Cathy told me.
"Ivana's secretary thought, 'Who is this? A process server?' The
kids there thought Ivana had arranged this treat for them,
because it was Easter. They started dancing around me, saying,
'Donald Duck, Donald Duck. We love Donald Duck.' Ivana got
up, sort of ashen, and said, 'Oh, hello, Mr. Duck.'"

Cathy took the duck head off, and everyone sighed with relief.

The orchestra at the Red Cross Ball played "Everything's Comin'
Up Roses" as the guests started in on the poached salmon with
crème fraîche and caviar, followed by filet mignon with truffle
demi-glace and Giandika chocolate cake with fresh raspberries.
For once, the Breakers came through. The magnificent meal was
accompanied by Pouilly-Fuissé, Brouilly, and Taittinger champagne. So that I would have no qualms about later looking into
how much money this ball and the Young Friends of the Red
Cross New Year's Eve party actually made, I had chosen to pay
$1,550 to attend both events as a contributor, rather than go free
as a member of the press.

Accompanied by Kirby, Helen Boehm looked almost bridal in
a floor-length white sheath her dressmaker had put together

from exquisite handmade Philippine lace. And when a guest suggested that the huge stone dangling on her diamond necklace was a topaz, she quickly corrected her: "No, it's a golden sapphire." It weighed seventy-five carats. The matching golden chunk on her finger was a gift from her friend Gabrielle, a baroness, to thank her for finding a good doctor for a friend with back problems.

Helen and Kirby sat with Smoak; Braddock Alexander from Washington, heir to an auto-parts fortune that now includes Spaulding Sporting Goods, and his wife, Denise; and baroness Garnett von Stackelberg. Originally from Estonia, the baroness writes a column about Washington society in the Shiny Sheet. In the old days, she complained, "People were better dressed . . . they behaved better."

Kirby was talking with Wrigley's heir Helen Rosburg. It seems Rosburg is an expert at identifying her great-grandfather's brands. In one blind test administered by the *Palm Beach Post*, she correctly guessed that she had been given Winterfresh, Spearmint, and Juicy Fruit to chew. She also identified Warner-Lambert's Dentyne and Topps' Bazooka.

Apparently, the woman sitting next to Helen Boehm thought Kirby wasn't paying enough attention to his date. "You can be replaced," she said to him.

Ever unflappable in his element, Kirby said, "I've been replaced before."

A woman named Marie talked about how tacky the shopping crowd downtown looks nowadays, not like it used to be: "You always got dressed up to go to Worth Avenue. Nice slacks, dresses. You never saw shorts on Worth."

There was talk of the latest scandal within the Old Guard—one of its most venerable married members, a member of Everglades and Bath & Tennis, shacking up at the Ritz-Carlton with a woman in her twenties. Soon the man's wife started an affair with another member of the blue-blood set who is also a member of Everglades and Bath & Tennis. Eventually, the first man decided he wanted his wife back. It was too late.

Ruth Perelman, in blue satin, was on a roll about Trump's bringing in young people, mostly from Miami, to Mar-a-Lago's disco on weekends. "A lot of club members are upset about this," she told Pam.

As the orchestra played, the dance floor filled with couples, and the Marines took up the slack by dancing with any unescorted young women. Jasmine and Manfredo Horowitz sat holding hands under the table. Jasmine wore a gorgeous pink-and-green dress, short in front, showing her legs, with a long tail in back, Guy Laroche haute couture. She had on a sapphire-and-diamond necklace, drop earrings, and minimal tiara.

When Pam stopped by their table to chat, Jasmine expressed pleasure and relief that the Red Cross Ball entertainment had reverted to the tried-and-true. She recalled with horror a previous experiment in livening things up, bringing in someone to perform rather than sticking with the dance band. "Julio Iglesias was here a few years ago, making off-color jokes," she said. "Like, 'Now it is time for you all to go home and make babies. . . .' When so many of the men are seventy to eighty years old!"

"Beloved" Brownie McLean was there. Everyone gives her the title, and they're not being ironic. Everybody likes her. Unmistakable in her signature platinum pageboy and penciled raccoon eyes, with a delightful Diane Keaton face, she gushed about her "jewels": "They're F-F-F-F . . . ! They're fake, phony, fabulous, fun." She sported a chest full of rhinestone and red plastic necklaces with her basic black.

If Betty Scripps Harvey's presence at the ball surprised everyone, she was clearly above it all, dancing up a storm with her husband. Stopping briefly to introduce him, she exclaimed, "Only married a year!" So then your wedding band is still shiny? Gleefully, she held up her hand to show off a wide diamond-and-platinum band.

Still, one male chauvinist criticized her performance: "She came in with the Marine Guard and danced with the mayor! Ignoring her husband! I would have killed her!"

Looking radiant, she had on several million dollars in jewels, according to Laurence Graff, owner of Graff jewelers of London, who was visiting her. Graff's beautiful French wife, Anne-Marie, had on jewels worth a like amount.

"The amount would depend on the insurance coverage they wanted for the evening," Jasmine, whose husband, Manfredo, is a friend of Graff, would explain a few evenings later over dinner at Club Colette with the Graffs, their son and daughter-in-law, and Pam and me. "Graff is one of the few people in today's business who owns all his merchandise," she said.

Graff said Mort Kaye had just photographed Ingrid Tremain, whose husband is president of Hotels of Distinction, trying on $40 million of his jewels, including a fifty-carat, emerald-cut diamond and earrings with a pair of pear-shaped D (colorless), flawless diamonds weighing ninety-five carats.

At the ball, Edward J. Van Kloberg III, a lobbyist for foreign countries, explained the esoterica of his neck badge, sash, and breast stars. "I call it hardware," Van Kloberg said. "You can only wear four stars at a time, you can't repeat the same country, and you wear a star low on your jacket," he said. He pointed to a young man at the next table sporting a large star over his heart. "That gigolo over there with the old babe is wearing it as a pin."

Back in Washington, Van Kloberg is known for representing clients no one else will touch—among them, Saddam Hussein's Iraq. When a *Spy* magazine reporter posed as "Sabina Hofer" of the German People's Alliance, Van Kloberg told her he was willing to represent neo-Nazi–sounding German interests trying to stop immigration and reclaim Poland for Germany. The defeat of former Ku Klux Klan leader David Duke in Louisiana "was a pity." He agreed that Germany never should have lost Poland in the first place. Van Kloberg later claimed the conversation was taken out of context and that he never would have represented the bogus group.

For the past twenty-three years, Richard C. Cowell has attended the Red Cross Ball, always weighed down by impressive medals. Born in Palm Beach, Cowell is a competitive water-skier and a member of the International Water Skiing Hall of Fame. In Palm Beach he water-skis daily with his wife, Jacqueline. In 1994 they cochaired the Red Cross Ball.

For years, Cowell lived on El Bravo Way. The "Three Els"— El Bravo, El Brillo, and El Vedado—are the domain of the bluest of the blue bloods. Over the years, the Astors, Rockefellers, Huttons, Wideners, and Phippses have lived on the three streets, which run parallel from South Ocean Boulevard to Lake Worth.

Around 5:00 P.M. one day in 1993, Cowell's new neighbor, John Kluge, knocked on his door.

"Will you sell me your house?" Kluge asked.

"John, if I do that, I'll just have to buy another one," Cowell said.

"You must have a price," Kluge said.

Cowell threw out a figure of $4.5 million, almost double what he thought the house would fetch. The next day, Kluge delivered a certified check for $4.5 million.

Kluge tore down the home and used the land to expand his garden. In all, he bought four homes, keeping one and using a second as a guest house. Cowell bought a new home on El Vedado Road, two streets to the south. Cowell was born in another house on the same street.

As a former board member of the Bath & Tennis Club whose father was a board member of the Everglades Club, Cowell knows how members are chosen. "The ideal club member is thirty-five to fifty-five years old, is married, and has a house here," Cowell told me in his airy new home that surrounds his pool. "He graduated from New England prep schools, such as Andover or Exeter, and from Harvard, Yale, or Princeton."

Of course, there are exceptions. "Even though you went to Harvard or Yale, it doesn't mean you're a gentleman," Cowell said. The fact that the two clubs now allow Jewish guests won't change things much, he said, since members only bring Jews who are "gentlemen." According to Cowell, "Most of the real gentlemen Jews wouldn't want to go to the Everglades or B&T. It's the wrong type that wants to go."

As a Harvard graduate himself, Cowell fits right in, or so he claims. Under "Colleges" in the *Social Index-Directory*, he lists himself as "Harvard '52," while his wife is listed as "Sorbonne, Florida Southern," indicating she did not graduate. Cowell confirmed that he graduated from Harvard in 1952.

In fact, while Cowell was in the class of 1952, the Harvard registrar's office says he attended only two semesters and never graduated.

When Cowell attends the Red Cross Ball, he wears the Silver Cross, Bronze Star, and Purple Heart, he said. Cowell said he won them while serving in the Marines during World War II. "The Silver Cross is the biggest," Cowell said. "I got it on June 15, 1945."

But, based on a tip, I asked the Marine Corps about Cowell. A spokeswoman said he won "no medals, ribbons, decorations, or awards." When told the news, Cowell said, "I don't want any controversy with the corps or anything else." He later conceded, "Your comments [about the medals] are fairly accurate. . . . I don't have any objection to that."

As for claiming he graduated from Harvard, Cowell said that listing himself as "Harvard '52" did not mean he graduated. In fact, he said he won a diploma through a correspondence school. If he said he did graduate from Harvard, "It might have been a slip."

Welcome to Palm Beach.

Just before midnight, as Mayor Ilyinsky and his wife were giving Barton a ride home, Donald Trump was hosting a disco party at Mar-a-Lago for contestants of the regional Hawaiian Tropic beauty pageant held earlier that day in Miami. An obvious superstar was a tanned blond beauty in a baby-blue bandeau top and miniskirt, and the other of course was the contest winner, a brunette in a black dress with a very low back crisscrossed by spaghetti straps.

An otherwise sane-looking young man blathered hopelessly when the winner departed his table by the pool: "She was talking to me! She was talking to me so intimately. . . . "

Donald was in top form, dancing to the Bee Gees with the young ladies and strutting around the far side of the pool. Donald said with a chuckle, "Listen to this noise. The neighbors don't say anything anymore because they love the sound of the music."

At 1:30 A.M., standing next to the most seductive, freshest-looking blonde at the party, Trump said good night to the guests.

"You're going to sleep?" I asked Donald.

"No, to bed," Trump said, cocking his head toward the young woman. With his arm around her, he went off toward the owner's suite.

25. BRUNCH AT MAR-A-LAGO

The Sunday after the Red Cross Ball, Kirby had brunch at Mar-a-Lago with Helen Boehm, Pam, and me. The brunch gives islanders yet another chance to socialize and relive the previous evening, as they discuss the dessert offerings—triple chocolate mousse cake, raspberry walnut tart, apricot custard torte, caramel chocolate-chunk cheesecake, chocolate pistachio orange cake, blueberry nectarine cheesecake, double pecan chocolate cookies, tropical fruit tartlets, white-chocolate raspberry pie, key lime pie, banana toffee crunch tarts, and homemade chocolate truffles.

A man in the living room was raving to Pam about how wonderful Betty Scripps Harvey had looked at the Red Cross Ball. "And no plastic surgery!" he said.

"Good for her!" Pam said.

"Don't say that," admonished the man, Dr. Luiz DeMoura. "I'm a plastic surgeon."

Dr. DeMoura's wife, Gloria, expounded on the virtues of having their Rolls-Royce shipped from Michigan when they stay at the Breakers during the season. No need to worry about airlines' restrictions on luggage. "We put the luggage in the trunk," she said.

With us at the brunch was Helen's friend Jill Curcio, an alluring blend of sophisticate and girl-next-door with frosted hair, sparkling light green eyes, and perfect teeth. After her divorce from Tire King owner Chuck Curcio, Jill put her Jupiter Island home up for sale. It had just sold for $16.9 million, but Jill still lived in it while looking for a new home in Palm Beach. Kirby had been staying with Kay Rybovich. Now he was staying in Jill's guest house.

At their table in the tearoom, Kirby and Helen debated why he and Joan had divorced. Helen said it was because Joan couldn't stand their gravelly driveway, which was ruining her shoes. Kirby refused to get it paved. Kirby said the problems were a lot deeper. "That was the icing on the cake," he said.

Kirby mentioned that he saw Bill again in jail. "He doesn't want to get help," Kirby said.

Helen didn't hear the full sentence. "Who's this?" she asked.

"Bill," Kirby said.

"Honey, wait a minute," she said. "You should have dropped him after three hours. I picked it up right away." She recounted the brunch with Bill at Mar-a-Lago. She had brought him only because Kirby said the surroundings might inspire Bill to make something of himself.

"It was one beer after another," she recalled. "I told the waiter, 'That's his last beer.'"

"I can't have it?" Bill asked rhetorically.

"No, you can't have it," she said. "You can have it after you leave me or I leave you."

Kirby said the jail doesn't give inmates clothes.

"Kirby did give Bill the clothes," I told Helen.

"No!" Helen exclaimed. "You know, you're a mess," she said to Kirby. "You're not a man of your word." To Pam and me she reported, "He said, 'Helen, I'll throw out his request.'" She looked back at Kirby. "How could you do that?"

"But sweetheart," Kirby said to Helen, "I wouldn't do something to hurt someone."

"You're fooling around," she said. "I'd rather see you work for the kids who need help through the Make-a-Wish Foundation," one of the charities Boehm supports. "There's a little group here. They have seventy kids. They keep begging for money. But feeling sorry for that jailbird who is rude, crude, and takes advantage of you? The kids need you over there." To Pam and me she continued, "He's had a lot of Bills in his life. I know. What about that captain of the boat from South Africa? I wouldn't let him in my house. Kirby collects eclectic people."

Once in a while Helen tells Kirby he should get a job. Now she suggested he go back to real estate. "I don't have that ability you have to close a deal," Kirby said. He said he wonders what drives the tycoons he knows to make so much money. "I happen to like all these tycoons, but when I hear how some of them got there, it's frightening."

For example, Richard M. Schlesinger, who lives in a $9 million home on South County Road, has been fined $1.5 million for hundreds of housing-code violations at his Riverdale apartment complex in Baltimore. When the project defaulted on one federally guaranteed mortgage, an estimated $8 million loss fell on taxpayers. And when Schlesinger failed to pay $600,000 in utility bills, the four hundred residents, lacking heat and electricity, were driven from their apartments. The Baltimore County executive charged Schlesinger was motivated by "pure greed."

That did not deter Schlesinger—whose fleet of cars includes a Cadillac, a Porsche, and a red Ferrari—from throwing a bar mitzvah for his son Bobby that cost $100,000. Catered by Galaxy Grille, the party was orchestrated by Bruce Sutka.

Now the U.S. attorney's office in Baltimore is suing Schlesinger for $1 million, alleging that he improperly used funds from a $5.6 million federally insured mortgage. Asked for comment, Schlesinger wrote, "You should be aware that the U.S. Attorney's office, after an 18-month investigation, discontinued all inquiries regarding my involvement with this project."

While a criminal probe recently stopped, the civil suit is "proceeding," according to Perry F. Sekus of the U.S. attorney's office. Contrary to Schlesinger's claim that "all inquiries" stopped eighteen months earlier, "We're in discovery," Sekus said.

At Mar-a-Lago, Kirby said that Gabrielle, a rich baroness, gave him $1,000 for Valentine's Day. He told her he used the money to buy new railings around his porch.

"I named them after you," he said.

"Oh, I've had many things named for me, but never a railing," the baroness said.

Helen corrected him. She said the money was to thank him for helping to arrange a purchase of two hundred one-year-old cars. "It wasn't a Valentine's Day present," Helen said.

She said a friend, a former treasurer of the Vatican, came to visit, and Kirby gave him a tour of his house. Kirby hoped to turn it into a money-making opportunity.

"Do you think some of your friends might want to buy or rent my house?" Kirby had asked. "I'll give you the brochure."

"Kirby, Kirby," Helen said. "What you need to do is go to that little place that needs you. Take this very serious, you hear? Don't go around with that Bill, sending him stuff. Seventy children. They need food, clothes. They need somebody to love them and be friends with them instead of fooling around with that jerk. Kirby shirks from work. This is your opportunity."

Helen said Kirby told her he wanted to buy her a present, an alligator belt. "He took it out of my gift to him."

"No, it was two for one," Kirby said, meaning he paid for one belt and got the second one—which he gave to Helen—free.

"I let him charge the bow tie. It cost thirty-five dollars. You should go after those children."

"Into the briar patch," Kirby said. "I'm not going to jail for you."

We broke out laughing.

"I said to help them, not sleep with them," Helen said.

The day after the brunch, Nancy Walsh gave a tea in her home on the north end of the island. It was one of those affairs where the hosts throw a party to pay homage to themselves—in this case, the planners of the Red Cross polo luncheon, particularly Helen Boehm. Walsh herself had given $10,000 to the Red Cross and $100,000 to the American Cancer Society. But beyond providing another opportunity to socialize and write it off, the tea served no ostensible fund-raising purpose.

The afternoon was filled with sweet-flowing piano music, tea sandwiches and cookies, and gossip. An annoying magician went around interrupting lively conversations—such as a shapely brunette describing her ultimatum to her wayward, prominent husband. It only made it worse that, after politely tolerating the magician's tricks, no one could figure out how he did them. Meanwhile, I poured tea for Princess Sybil de Bourbon-Parme, who traces her lineage to Louis XVI.

An affable woman, Walsh told me her father had owned a company that supplied many of the leading hotel chains in the country with plumbing fixtures—including toilets. "I was queen of the throne," she said.

The tea included a fashion show put on by Lynn Manulis of Martha Phillips. Fashion shows are a staple of Palm Beach life, as common as church suppers in other towns.

At an Oscar de la Renta ready-to-wear fashion show at Saks, Helen had been sitting with Jill Curcio, Kay Rybovich, and Franny Purnell. Purnell and her husband, George, live in the Seminole Golf Course development. They own Goose Island, six acres connected to the eastern shore of Maryland by a bridge. Jasmine Horowitz sat with Arlette Gordon, whose family owns the black book. To the saleswoman helping run the show, Boehm had said, "Last time [at an Oscar de la Renta show] I spent thirty-five hundred dollars for three dresses."

The saleswoman said, "This time you can buy the whole collection for that," because the dresses were ready-to-wear.

Asked later what she had bought at Nancy Walsh's, Jasmine said with a smile, "Nothing! I told my husband, 'I saved you so much money today!' I was sitting there watching it and counting off how much I was saving."

Sipping champagne and watching the fashion show at Walsh's tea, Kirby observed that one model reminded him of a German shepherd with hip dysplasia. Manulis wouldn't give the prices for the dresses until asked by Helen, who was in charge, and some of the women complained about the lack of a price list. There was a buzz about taking up too much time with speeches. To smooth things over, Helen and Bunnie Stevens, a former professional singer who lives on the island, did a fine duet of "Embraceable You."

Now on a roll, Kirby wondered aloud how he could get a cut of some of the charitable gifts. "Couldn't I make the phone call for the charity and get ten percent?" Then he had a better idea. For a new, lucrative career, he could become an "embarrassment insurance salesman." As he saw it, every time a policyholder experienced an embarrassing moment, he or she would receive a cash payment and feel instantly better. "Let's try it," Kirby said to me.

To Karl Rost, a guest who had just arrived in one of his two Rolls-Royces, Kirby explained that his pants weren't really clean when they came back from the dry cleaners. "So I washed them," Kirby told Rost, who came over from Germany twenty years ago and formerly owned plants that made textile machinery. "I was at a neighbor's house. The water was black. I couldn't put them in a dryer because they would shrink. So I put them on spin. The doorbell rang, and I was in my underpants. I said, 'I hope they dry in time for me to put them on and answer the door.'"

Rost smiled patiently.

26. THE *TAIPAN*

With a sudden spray, schools of small silvery mullet in Lake Worth jumped into the air as if in a water ballet and fell evenly in a circle like water drops in a splash pattern. Minutes later, they leaped again. It was early February—high season—and guests in black tie and evening gowns were making their way to the Australian Avenue dock, where the 157-foot *Taipan* was moored. The yacht was the site of another satellite event of the Red Cross Ball.

The docks at the western end of Australian, Brazilian, and Peruvian Avenues are where Mayor Ilyinsky's *Angelique* ties up, along with yachts owned by Jimmy Buffett, Roger Penske (of racing-car and truck-rental fame), Richard DeVos, who founded Amway Corporation and is worth $1.5 billion, and Thomas A. Kershaw, the owner of Boston's Bull & Finch, which inspired the television series *Cheers*. His boat is *Cheers IV*.

Until it sank, Philip J. Romano's 106-foot yacht tied up here as well. Romano is not a household name, but many of the restaurant chains he started are. Fuddruckers, Romano's Macaroni Grill, and Rudy's Country Store and BBQ were conceived by Romano. He typically owns half of his ventures, then sells his stake to his partners after the restaurant chains become successful.

Romano's grandparents on both sides came over from Italy. They dug ditches and swept streets. Romano's father was an electrician who serviced many of the homes in Palm Beach. After dropping out of Florida Atlantic University in 1968, Romano opened a karate school, then a succession of restaurants, including Romano's 300 on Royal Palm Way in Palm Beach, where the Palm Beach Tavern is now.

One time Adnan Khashoggi dropped in. He wanted Romano to throw a party with Middle Eastern food for King Hussein. "I don't care what it costs," Khashoggi told Romano. "I want the best."

Romano knew nothing about Middle Eastern food, so he consulted his Lebanese barber. The barber said the women from his church could do the cooking. So for four days, Romano turned the restaurant's kitchen over to four Lebanese women.

Khashoggi specified that no pictures were to be taken at the party. Romano called the food editor of the *Palm Beach Post*. "How would you like to do a story about cooking a meal for a king?" he asked her. The editor watched the women cook, and the paper took photos of the scene.

"I made up two bills," Romano said. "One was for three thousand dollars and another was for six thousand." At the end of the meal, Romano asked how everything was.

"Great," Khashoggi said.

"So I gave him the six-thousand-dollar bill," Romano said. "He put on the tip. And I got a great article in the paper."

As owner of Romano's 300, catering to the rich and famous, Romano fantasized about becoming one of them. He moved to San Antonio and started Fuddruckers, an upscale hamburger chain that displays its hamburger patties in refrigerated cases and allows customers to see them being grilled. When salad bars were innovative, it offered a lavish fixings bar.

Romano insisted that each Fuddruckers grind its own hamburger meat and bake buns on the premises. This met with skepticism from experts in the restaurant field.

"They told me I can't grind my own meat at Fuddruckers," Romano said. "They said nobody's done it before at that price level. The same with baking my own buns. They said the numbers don't work out. They said customers would steal from the fixings bar. But if I grind my meat myself, I know what I have. I'm protecting my customers. The same with the buns. I wanted buns that are hot. You can't do that if they're baked somewhere else."

The "point of difference," as Romano calls it, is exactly what makes him successful. "My life has been based on doing things differently," he said. "The reason my concepts have been successful is because they are different. I go against the sacred cows. I break these rules. I call it the 'wow' factor. Customers have to say 'wow' when they walk in the door. Otherwise, they won't come back. You don't become a brand through advertising. You do it through publicity. The way to get publicity is to do something different."

Romano's latest concept is Eatzi's Market & Bakery, a take-out chain that offers everything from sushi and custom-made sandwiches to lasagna, pizza, and mouthwatering brownies—all without the excessive salt, spice, and pepper that many grocery chains insist on using, covering up the natural flavors. Entering the stores through the bakery, customers encounter bags of flour piled on pallets in the window, a baker calling "Fresh bread!" and the scent of yeast and cinnamon. The condiments for sandwiches—including sweet red peppers and three kinds of mustard—are arrayed in front of customers watching their sandwiches being made.

Like the previous ideas, this one took off, and each Eatzi's is doing $250,000 in business a week. The other half of the partnership is Brinker International, which owns Chili's restaurants. In all, Romano's brainchildren generate $800 million in sales a year.

When Romano turned fifty, he contracted cancer near his appendix. He underwent chemotherapy and is now cancer-free. But deciding his marriage was empty, he divorced his wife of twenty-six years. They split everything fifty-fifty. The legal fees were $10,000 for both of them. They threw a black-tie party to celebrate "the dissolution of our marriage."

Two years later, Romano fell in love with Lillie, the dazzling manager of a Fuddruckers in Newport Beach. At sixty, Romano is twenty-one years her senior. Having made more than $100 million, Romano was ready to live the life he had only dreamed about. Four years ago, he moved back to Palm Beach and bought a home in the prized Estate Section. With Lillie and their four-year-old son, Sam, he lives in a sprawling home complete with the requisite pool, two Rolls-Royces, and a chef. The bedroom is dominated by a series of six paintings of Lillie running naked—paintings Romano proudly showed me.

Romano fits right into Palm Beach. As chairman of Fuddruckers, he attended board meetings in a suit and tie but no socks. When his attorney pointed out the incongruity, Romano held out his bare hands and claimed he was wearing hosiery to match his gloves.

Romano joined the Mar-a-Lago Club and flew in twenty people for its New Year's celebration. "You can't beat Donald's parties," he said. But he wishes he could tinker with the menu. "I have some ideas," he said. "Why doesn't Donald invite five of the finest chefs in the world there for a vacation for a week? They would devise a menu. On the menu, he would describe how they did it."

As for his yacht, Romano decided it was not worth the expense. "The yacht cost me fifteen hundred dollars a day, whether I used it or not," he said. When it sank in five feet of water at another port, he decided to sell it.

"Structurally, Romano's boat did not have a good reputation," Karen Lane, the municipal dockmaster, told me. "It had been redone and redone. It sank one night at Palm Harbor in Florida right after they left here. It was sad."

Lane has been dockmaster for ten years. Savvy and sophisticated, she stands up to the billionaires whose yachts tie up at the docks and makes sure regulations are obeyed. Under her direction, Palm Beach just completed an expansion of its docks, allowing larger boats to tie up. The three docks now have eighty-four slips.

"I wanted to expand our capacity," Lane said. "I knew there was a demand for bigger boats. By the year 2000, the average boat will be a hundred fifty feet long." The construction cost for the expansion was almost $1.2 million for the Brazilian dock, $1.2 million for the dock at Peruvian, and $1.9 million at Australian.

"The town looks at this as their little jewel," she said. "They're protective of it."

As Lane was speaking, Alvan Hirshberg, her assistant, told her the crew of the *Crili*, owned by sugar baron Alfie Fanjul, was performing construction work on the boat. Walking purposefully, Lane went to talk to the captain.

"They're doing minor shipyard work on the yacht, and I had to tell them they couldn't do it," Lane told me when she returned. "People are not allowed to do that during the season. That can wait. It's not an emergency repair. It's not like a boat is sinking. This is high season. People are looking to see what everyone else is doing. They'll say, 'He's doing that, so why can't we?' They're like little children. I told them they were making me look bad by doing it."

Despite the occasional need for discipline—unknown in Palm Beach—Lane is appreciated. Owners invite her for drinks or parties on their boats, and she picks up the latest lore.

A prominent Palm Beacher keeps his mistress on his yacht, she said. "He won't get divorced," Lane said. "He has a beautiful wife. He takes his girlfriend all over the world. The girlfriend is gorgeous."

Lane said one Palm Beacher, in his late sixties and arthritic, commissioned a boat that had a see-through, cylindrical glass shower. "That was so he could watch young ladies taking their showers," she said. "The guy would lie on the bed and look at the women. They knew it. He particularly liked women in their twenties. I don't think he could do anything. He was a voyeur."

Jimmy Buffett, who lives in a $4.4 million, fourteen-bedroom home on South Ocean Boulevard, just sold his boat and is buying another. "Buffett comes in with his Land Rover," Lane said. "He has no crew. His houseman washes the boat. Buffett is an exception in Palm Beach. He makes small talk. He's genuine."

Buffett is also a regular at nearby Hamburger Heaven at 314 South County Road. Jackie Kennedy used to bring John junior and Caroline to the restaurant, which answers the phone, "Heaven."

At the pier, the largest yacht is the 143-foot *Octopussy* owned by health-care operator Abe Gosman. The boat has no propellers or rudder—just three jets—and cruises at a maximum speed of forty-three knots. Gosman and his wife, Lyn, go to Europe on it, stopping at Saint-Tropez, Capri, and Portofino.

Until three years ago, developer Edward A. Cantor's 192-foot, $31 million boat, the *Other Woman,* tied up at the pier. The largest motor-sailing water-jet yacht in the world, it was built in Australia and has a twelve-member crew. Decorated with $4 million in Matisses, Chagalls, and Picassos, the yacht has a Steinway grand piano topped by a bar. It has a heated pool that fills with fresh water or seawater, an elevator, five bars, more than a thousand books, a thousand videos, and a medical room with oxygen supplies and X-ray and EKG machines. It comes with two twenty-nine-foot fishing boats, a Plymouth, and a minivan. Usually, a Volkswagen convertible and two motor scooters are on board as well. A landing craft lowers from the boat and shuttles the vehicles to shore.

Weighing more than 550 tons, the boat, like Gosman's, is powered by jet propulsion. In addition, it can hoist sail along twin 150-foot masts. Under motor power, it does twenty knots; under sail, sixteen knots. It carries three thousand gallons of fuel.

"It's treated like another woman—all the attention and the money," the seventy-one-year-old Cantor, a Linden, New Jersey, developer and owner of industrial buildings, once said.

A lesser, 125-foot yacht could cost $500,000 a year to maintain, including $65,000 for docking.

Karen Lane introduced Cantor to his wife, Jane, who is forty-nine.

"The captain and the boat crew were very unhappy with the person he was seeing," Lane said. "They didn't think she suited him, didn't think there was enough class. So the captain and I got together, and we ended up arranging a date with Jane. I went out on the first date with them. He had a Rolls-Royce. We went to Café L'Europe, and they hit it off because she was an interior decorator, and he was really into art. Midpoint during the dinner, I felt like a third wheel."

Two years later, Cantor and Jane were married on the yacht as it sailed up the Hudson River. Lane was among the guests. Recently, the couple sailed to Russia, Sweden, Norway, Finland, Holland, London, France, Belgium, Portugal, and Gibraltar. Cantor charters the boat for $139,500 a week in the Caribbean and $155,000 elsewhere, plus expenses. Among his customers: Oprah Winfrey.

One night winds whipped the boat around and the vessel, while undamaged, made a huge gash in the dock. Beyond his paying for the damage, the town wanted Cantor to build additional support for the dock. After Cantor hired an engineering firm to draw up a plan, he decided to take his yacht to other ports.

Having built a new home at the southern tip of the island in Manalapan, the Cantors show up at all the major Palm Beach events, including the International Red Cross Ball and the Cancer Ball. Cantor allows the yacht to be used for charity events as well.

Helen Boehm had arranged the party on the *Taipan*, owned by a couple who did not want their names revealed—"security," the wife explained—but left brochures about their company on the coffee table.

The yacht had a living room with a wall-sized saltwater aquarium, a baby grand, ten staterooms, a top-deck Jacuzzi-cum-bar, a small gym with weight machines, a formal dining room, and a huge galley where the yacht's chef oversees the preparation of everything served onboard, including this night's buffet, featuring some of the best food in Palm Beach.

Not all the guests ventured from the main bar in the stern, up a winding staircase with a neon rail pulsing with color, to view the ship's pièce de résistance, an intimate bar that is an astronomer's dream: a black glass ceiling of pinpoint stars—constellations and even a shooting star, if you didn't blink. Around the room, neon moldings changed color gradually from green to blue to rose and back again.

A favorite topic on the *Taipan* was shoes—wearing the proper footwear to protect the deck's finish. Standing at the circular mahogany bar, Bunnie Stevens looked at a woman's hemline and asked, "Do you have wide heels on?" The woman lifted her gown a trifle. "Oh, good. They're so hard to find." Some men sported sneakers or boat shoes with their tuxedos, some women wore moccasins. When a woman wearing spike heels walked past Kirby, he muttered, "Such arrogance!"

There was talk of the latest cat poisonings. Catherine Bradley, a former real-estate broker, insists on feeding homeless cats, which she says are often left by residents when they fly off to their other homes. Others think her program—which includes nightly feedings of three hundred cats from a Volvo station wagon—attracts feral cats from all over. Someone decided to take matters into their own hands by lacing the cat food with antifreeze. Eleven cats were found dead.

Kirby introduced Tony Smith and his wife, Lore. Smith's grandfather, Sir Alexander Roland Smith, headed Ford Motor Company U.K. and arranged to make Rolls-Royce plane engines in a Ford plant, helping the British win the war. The Smiths live across the street from Kirby on North Lake Way.

Lore told me the infamous Bill came over one afternoon and asked if he could "have" their telephone.

"What?" Lore said.

"Can I have your telephone?" Bill repeated.

"You can use my phone, but you can't take it," Lore said.

"But I just dropped Kirby's phone in the pool," Bill said. "I need a phone. I have to make an important call." He added, "There are so many fair-weather friends. Are you a fair-weather friend?"

"No, I'm not a fair-weather friend," Lore replied. "You still can't take my phone."

When Lore let him use her phone, the call was to another friend to tell him he had dropped Kirby's phone in the pool.

On the *Taipan* with his wife, Joleen, a banker, was Tom Martin, president of the Palm Beach Round Table. I had just spoken to the group, which wanted a return visit when this book comes out.

"Palm Beach loves to look at itself in the mirror," Joleen said.

After my talk, Jasmine Horowitz purchased all my books and had them signed. Toting around her bag of books, she explained, "So I don't go home empty-handed." She gave the impression, probably accurate, that Manfredo is disappointed when she doesn't buy *something*. She was on the yacht wearing haute couture.

Angela Koch, the pretty wife of the feuding brother Bill Koch, had just appeared in the Shiny Sheet's spread of the Red Cross Ball—the only woman in the photographs not wearing a heavy necklace with her low-cut dress. That was causing a stir on the yacht. Certainly she could afford the best jewelry, but some thought, why gild the lily? Besides, with everyone else wearing their biggest and best baubles, her bare décolletage stood out. As Kirby said, "You get sick of all this junk around the neck."

Helen sang Italian songs and danced the tarantella with Kirby, with the help of the pianist and accordion player. Bunnie kept singing and did an encore of "How About You?"

Jay Rossbach, jocular and urbane, and his wife, Linda, came over to chat. She is tall and striking, with her short auburn hair combed behind her ears. Rossbach, the chairman of the Palm Beach County Chapter of the Red Cross, is the stepson of Adam Gimbel, whose great-grandfather started Gimbel's department stores.

Rossbach was pleased with the approach Candy Van Alen had taken with the Red Cross Ball. She had wanted it to be a dance, not an evening of entertainment. Betty Scripps Harvey had people like Tony Bennett and Vic Damone perform. "She did a lot of things I, for one, thought were wrong, and the customers thought were wrong," Rossbach told me. "A lot of people want to go to bed early. They want to just keep dancing," not waste time watching entertainment.

Rossbach was planning to step down as chairman. Surprising everyone once again, Betty Scripps Harvey announced that she would again chair the Red Cross Ball. With her in charge, there was no need to hold a ball. Presumably, she would once again donate her own funds to help make it a success.

For all the smoke and mirrors surrounding charity events, Palm Beachers are charitable. Without the need for a party, people like Lesly Smith's mother, Mary Alice Fortin, Abe Gosman, members of the Kenan family, Nelson Peltz, Ronald Perelman, John Kluge, Max Fisher, and Alfred Taubman, among many others, give tens of millions of dollars directly to charities and educational and medical institutions. With the money, they buy immortality, their names remaining on buildings long after they are gone.

As the crew of the *Taipan* served a spectacular buffet ranging from beef tenderloin to miniature chocolate éclairs, Vicki Bagley sat in the main salon. Charming and direct, with her signature long braid of hair down her back, she began to open up to me about a subject that she said was very painful.

While Vicki is Jewish, she does not look it. That gives her a special window on Palm Beach life. Moreover, she married Smith Bagley, heir to the R. J. Reynolds Tobacco fortune. His stepmother, Anya, is a pillar of the Old Guard and has homes in Palm Beach, New York, and Paris. Being married to a WASP furthered the impression that she was a non-Jew.

After Vicki and Smith divorced, she went on to become wealthy on her own as one of Washington's most successful real-estate agents. After selling her firm, she started *Washington Life* magazine. She also owns Celebrity Service, formerly owned by Earl Blackwell, which lists celebrities' addresses and phone numbers and provides subscribers with a newsletter. Besides a home in Washington (she sold her previous home to Ben Bradlee and Sally Quinn), Vicki has a condominium on the grounds of the Ritz-Carlton in Manalapan and a home in Delray.

Nowhere has Vicki encountered more anti-Semitism than in Palm Beach. When she was still married to Smith Bagley, Vicki mentioned to a Palm Beach woman whom she had met through Anya that she was going to see Estée Lauder at her home at 126 South Ocean Boulevard.

"No, you don't want to go to that side," the woman said. "She's Jewish. We don't mix with Jews."

"Why not?" Vicki asked.

"There is an absolute line," she said. "You don't go to Estée Lauder's house."

Vicki called a girlfriend over and clued her in. Both of them egged on the woman, who made more outrageous remarks. Finally, the girlfriend said, "Vicki's Jewish."

"No, she's not," the woman said. "She's too nice."

Just recently, Vicki told me she had been with a date when one of his friends came over to their table at the Leopard Lounge. "I was just playing golf at the deli with Taubman," the man said, referring to the Jewish Palm Beach Country Club and one of its members, Al Taubman of Sotheby's.

Vicki does not hide her religion, and when anti-Semitic remarks are made, she goes on the offensive. "I bet when you're with Taubman, you kiss his shoes," Vicki said. "It's interesting how prejudiced you are behind his back, when you go to his club and you probably go to his house and brag about it."

When a woman asked Vicki to lunch at the Everglades Club, Vicki made it clear that she was Jewish. "I told her if I was putting her on the spot, I didn't want to go," Bagley said. "She was insistent that I attend regardless."

What Vicki finds ironic is that Everglades and Bath & Tennis members "honestly think all we want is to be in their clubs. Jewish people prefer to be around interesting people. The truly bigoted club members are boring. They are usually ne'er-do-wells who are angry that Jewish people now own their houses and some of their banks and corporations. They want things to go back to the way they were. I'm friends with Jewish, non-Jewish, and black people. They all have one thing in common. They're interesting."

The most common remark Vicki hears is that Jews are loud and boisterous. "As if they're not loud and boisterous themselves sometimes," she said. "The fact that West Palm Beach has fabulous hospitals and a cultural center like the Kravis Center is because of Jewish support. You don't hear prejudiced people talking about how wonderful Jews are for supporting a hospital where their kids go for emergency care."

In fact, of the five most charitable people in Palm Beach—John Kluge, Ronald Perelman, Al Taubman, Max Fisher, and Ronald Lauder—four are Jewish, according to a ranking by *Worth* magazine.

In Washington, Bagley said, "you're considered stupid if you talk the way these people talk. You are ostracized. People wouldn't stand for it, and openly wouldn't stand for it. If you are prejudiced, you are quietly prejudiced." In Palm Beach, she said, "it doesn't hurt your standing to be openly bigoted. This is where anti-Semitism is most exaggerated, the last bastion of this kind of talk."

27. ROD STEWART STRIKES OUT

"Things are in the early stages right now," Lorraine Hillman told me. "But I think I've met someone."

The man approached her at the bar at Ta-boó. He is forty-five, masculine, but has never married. He owns an offshore bank.

"He said he likes to meet nuts," Lorraine said. "That's probably why he's attracted to me."

The evening before Valentine's Day, he invited her to Café L'Europe, saying he had had to break dates with two other women. When they walked into the chic restaurant, one of the women he was supposed to go out with was sitting at the bar. They walked right out and ended up at Aquaterra—since closed—on Sunrise Avenue.

"I hate this town," the man said. "It's too damned small." He asked her, "What do I have to do to date you?" He wanted to have an "exclusive relationship" with Lorraine for as long as he was in town.

"How long will you be in town?" she asked.

"Three or four weeks," he said.

"I'll think about it," she said.

The man didn't try anything. "He was a gentleman," she said. "He's very good-looking. He makes me laugh."

To be sure, when she met him at Ta-boó, his cell phone didn't stop ringing, and most of the calls were from women. But Lorraine said, "It's worth a try. It's definitely worth a try. There's no fagginess about this guy. He's totally straight. But everyone else in town wants him. He's a player. I'm going with the cutest playboy in town."

She agreed to another date. "But he's not going to get me in the sack, I'll tell you that," she said. "I can wait. He has to be tested."

Meanwhile, two friends of hers on the island had been bitten by dogs. Nicholas, who owns radio stations in London, was visiting his aunt in Palm Beach. He ran into the ocean to escape the dog, which had bitten him on a leg.

"A woman ignored his cries for help," Lorraine said. "He went to the fire station. They thought he had been bitten by a shark. He went to Good Sam," the locals' abbreviation for Good Samaritan Hospital in West Palm Beach. "He had to go to a plastic surgeon. This plastic surgeon said, 'Are you sure you only want work on the leg?' He wanted to give him a new chin."

Lorraine was running on the beach when she saw her other friend, Jim, a landscaper, looking upset.

"What's wrong?" she asked.

"I was bitten by a poodle, a standard white poodle."

"That's funny. My friend Nicholas just got bitten by a dog," she said.

"That's not the guy who was at Good Sam? It's such a small town," he said.

Later that day, both men were comparing notes around Lorraine's pool. Patricia Dixson came by with her two white poodles.

"They were freaking out," Lorraine said.

On February 17, Lorraine attended a Rod Stewart concert in Fort Lauderdale with her friend Sharon Dresser. A blonde from Tampa, Dresser is in the same niche real-estate business as

Lorraine is. Like Lorraine, she's incredibly successful at it. So that she could easily fly over potential shopping-center sites, she became a pilot.

Sharon comes across as a glamorous party girl—until she opens her mouth: She is astute, articulate, and sensible. Even though the latter quality makes her seem out-of-place, she likes the island. At the same time, "the island stresses her out," according to Lorraine. Protective of Lorraine, Sharon asked her if she ever gets any sleep. "Not a lot, no," Lorraine replied.

Through Sharon's connections, she and Lorraine met Stewart backstage after the concert. He wound up inviting them to dinner. As it turned out, Stewart had brought along Liana Verkaden, the stunning cocktail waitress who works with Michelle Gagnon at the Chesterfield's Leopard Lounge.

Just before New Year's, Stewart, fifty-four, had separated from his wife, model Rachel Hunter. He began hanging out at the Leopard Lounge every night, trying to make it with Liana, who is twenty-five. When he first came in, Liana asked Stewart, "Aren't you married?"

"I'm divorcing," he said.

"I thought it was a temporary separation," Liana said.

"No," Stewart responded.

Born in Palm Beach, Verkaden was a cool customer, not at all impressed by celebrity. Besides, she had a boyfriend. But she agreed to have a drink with the rock singer at 251, and the next night Stewart flew her on his leased plane to Fort Lauderdale to attend the concert.

So besides Lorraine and Sharon, Liana and several other blondes went to dinner with Stewart. Lorraine began singing "When I Was Younger," one of Stewart's songs, and he joined in. "When I was younger, I wish I knew what I know now," they sang together.

"Have you got your affairs in order?" Hillman asked Stewart.

Pretending to know what she meant, Stewart replied, "Yeah, I've got my affairs in order. Do you?"

"She kept saying that all night," Liana remarked.

Lorraine thought Stewart was depressed over losing his wife.

Stewart left with Liana, and at 2:00 A.M. they returned to his $7.2 million house on South Ocean Boulevard ("the cheapest on the block," he said), where Liana had left her car. She drove off without going inside.

"He was very nice," Liana said. "He's very energetic, but I wouldn't go out with someone that old."

The *National Enquirer* got wind of the story and began trying to photograph Liana coming out of the Chesterfield at 3:10 A.M., after her shift. "Rod Stewart Strikes Out," the headline over the story said. Liana thought it was all silly. When Stewart called to invite her over for a swim, she declined.

On February 19 Helen Boehm chaired the American Cancer Society's annual ball in the Venetian Ballroom at the Breakers.

Kirby escorted her. "I'm on assignment," he told me.

She was wearing an off-the-shoulder claret satin gown with a necklace of diamonds and large pearls the color and sheen of beluga. Kirby followed a solicitous six inches behind her right shoulder.

In the ballroom, Kirby pointed to the twin floor-to-ceiling cutouts, based on the statue of David, on either side of the stage. Unlike the original by Michelangelo, the cardboard copies had no genitalia.

"Typical Palm Beach," Kirby said.

Flanked by the incongruous Davids, the Neal Smith orchestra, perhaps tired out by the Red Cross Ball, sat sleepily while a slow-moving auction took place—a piece of Boehm porcelain, a trip, a white designer gown—along with the usual back slaps and kudos for the organizers and donors. But what the Cancer Ball lacked in pomp and dignity compared with the Red Cross Ball, it made up for with its livelier, younger crowd. This was the ball for celebrities, like NBC's Matt Lauer, and for the nouveau riche set.

But someone was missing—one of the "Everglades Swamp Blondes," as Heather Wyser-Pratte called Lorraine. It was a name they had come up with when a group of women ventured into the Everglades together one weekend, then got stuck for a few hours when their airboat beached. Heather said, "Funny how you want things you can't have. We're sitting here a little bored at this ball, and Lorraine would like nothing more than to be here. But she doesn't have anyone to go with."

Later, Lorraine, sounding like Cinderella, confirmed it: "I would have loved to have gone to the ball. I didn't have a date."

The tall centerpieces were globular red roses edged in white and blue, with white trellises among the greenery. For dinner, after the rosemary-and-fontina polenta with wild mushrooms, came pale medallions of veal. Allen Manning, who brought Heather, was talking fondly of a bichon frise named Reggie he "used to own." When Allen started going out with Heather, Reggie went to her house and stayed. "First she stole my heart, then she stole my dog," Allen said.

Now the veal, pulverized and barely palatable, was going cold and uneaten. Allen decided to take a piece to Reggie; other diners offered theirs. Heather recalled how her mother once requested a doggie bag at a charity ball that she headed. A minor social disaster ensued when, one by one, other women at the ball also had to have doggie bags.

"She only got away with it because she was head of it," Heather said.

Asked for a doggie bag, a Breakers waitress said they no longer give them, as a diner once took food out and left it in the car and then successfully sued the hotel for causing food poisoning. However, after she was reassured about the existence of a dog, a piece of plastic wrap appeared.

In front of Allen, Heather said teasingly that he is always proposing to her with wine and wondered when he would start again tonight. She requested the orchestra play a selection from *The Student Prince*, a love song. "It shows you how stuck I was on my father," she said. "He died thirty years ago. It was his favorite song." Now she requests it for Allen. Wearing an antique diamond floral necklace and huge drop pearl earrings on square diamond studs, Heather explained, "My grandmother died, my mother died, I got all these jewels, and now I have to wear them."

Jokingly, Heather said that she and two other women would like to take up a collection to buy Pam pearls. When Pam isn't wearing significant jewelry and Heather and her friends have on their ornate necklaces, "the contrast is too great," Heather said. "We say: What must she think of *us*?"

It sounded suspiciously like something Lorraine had been saying to Pam: "You need some pearls—Micky. Get Micky," referring to Mikimoto, which supplies cultured pearls from the top 3 percent of Japan's harvest, not to mention the large, rare South Sea pearls from Tahiti and Australia.

If Palm Beachers decide to adopt you, they try to make you over in their own image, Pam concluded. Your being different makes them self-conscious, uncomfortable. How people dress is of extreme importance. You have to be giving off the same signals.

The talk was of new wealth in town. Netscape cofounder James H. Clark, whose company was just acquired by America Online, had paid $11 million for a forty-thousand-square-foot home at 1500 South Ocean Boulevard. The home had been built in 1930 for Peter Widener, son of the founder of Hialeah Park racetrack. The most recent owner was the late Janet Annenberg Hooker. Her brother, Walter Annenberg, founded Triangle Publishing.

"I know many dozens of people in Palm Beach who should be on the Forbes four hundred list but who are not," H. Loy Anderson, Jr., president of Palm Beach National Bank & Trust, told me. "They are people who don't want to be known for their wealth and want to lead a quiet life. They don't want to run around in Rolls-Royces. They drive cars that you might consider dilapidated."

People like Mike McIntosh, an A&P heir, and Caroline Penney, widow of the founder of J. C. Penney stores, do not show up in the Shiny Sheet. Nor, as a rule, do foreigners. Just as the wealthiest people from each city in the country tend to gravitate to Palm Beach, so do the wealthiest and most influential people from each industrialized country. Thus, in the case of Canada, former Canadian prime minister Brian Mulroney has a home in Palm Beach, as do Paul Desmarais, Conrad Black, Charles R. Bronfman, and George Cohon. Desmarais is majority stockholder of Power Corporation of Canada, a holding company that controls Great-West Life Assurance Company, one of Canada's largest insurance companies; Investors Group, the country's largest mutual fund management company; and *La Presse*, Montreal's French-language daily. While not a golfer, Desmarais is one of the few gentile members of the Palm Beach Country Club. He also belongs to the Everglades Club.

Conrad Black, Canada's dominant newspaper publisher, owns dailies that account for a quarter of Canadian newspaper circulation. He also owns the Chicago *Sun-Times* and the *London Daily Telegraph*, making a total worldwide circulation of more than 4 million, surpassed only by Rupert Murdoch's papers and by the Gannett chain. Bronfman is cochairman of Seagram, the liquor and entertainment company. And Cohon is senior chairman of McDonald's Restaurants of Canada and McDonald's in Russia.

While the press occasionally notes Mulroney's presence in Palm Beach, the fact that he owns a home on the island is never reported. The other moguls—among Canada's wealthiest and most powerful citizens—also manage to avoid local publicity.

If the extent of the wealth is often submerged, so is the unhappiness. People brought up without the need to struggle bypass life's learning processes. Many are incapable even of keeping track of phone numbers or returning phone calls, much less becoming successful at normal pursuits. Existing on inherited funds, their sole decision each day is where they should go for lunch and dinner. To create a sense of accomplishment, they turn to excluding others from their society. Inherently weak, they are susceptible to the constant pressure to drink. Many become alcoholics.

"I've never seen so many people that have so much and are so miserably unhappy," Palm Beach decorator Michael Rosenow, who was at the ball, told me. "Money, boredom, and time make them unhappy. I would say ninety percent are unhappy."

As the band played on, people went from table to table, exchanging kisses. The rich kiss more than anyone else. The air kiss, the double-air kiss, the two-cheek kiss, the two-cheek kiss with lip pressure, the kiss on the lips, the narrowly avoided kiss on the lips—all are unspoken measures of status, appeal, and even affection. To avoid confusion, the popular, European-style, two-cheek kiss travels from right to left.

Landing is optional.

28. LIVING IN A CRAZY TOWN

The night after the Cancer Ball, Jay Leno entertained at Mar-a-Lago. After greeting special guests in the tearoom, Leno and Trump proceeded to the tent, where the Planetones from Brooklyn sang doo-wop as they had done when they starred in *American Hot Wax* twenty years ago. Donald sat in the front, flanked on his left by Melania Knauss and on his right by his daughter Ivanka.

"Next week we have Celine Dion," Trump said onstage. "This is not the Bath & Tennis Club." Then he introduced the comedian: "Here's the funniest guy around, a real success story, Mr. Jay Leno."

The audience laughed nonstop for over an hour, all except a young trust-fund baby who sat near Chris Evert and barely cracked a smile. Evert, Tracy Austin, and other tennis stars were to play the next day at Trump's charity tournament on Mar-a-Lago's clay courts.

Two rows behind Trump, Lorraine Hillman and Sharon Dresser sat with Pam and me. After the show, there was the usual pool party, with "YMCA" by the Village People blasting into the night. I introduced Lorraine, looking spectacular in pink, to Trump.

"She says she can't find a guy in Palm Beach," I said.

"I can't find a straight guy," Lorraine said.

"I'm a straight guy," Donald said.

Trump was on a jag of punctuating his sentences with "fucking."

"I like all this fucking," Lorraine said, laughing.

Donald went off with Melania. Later, putting on his Miss USA hat, Trump told me Lorraine was "sexy." Soon after that, the town council approved Donald's request to build a pool and cabanas along the beach at Mar-a-Lago. It turned down his request to lift the five-hundred-member cap. And the council made it clear it would not approve a pavilion anywhere near the size Trump wanted. He then withdrew the plan.

The day after the Leno performance, as Chris Evert played her doubles match, Donald was walking around stiffly outside the clubhouse. He had just played, and his tennis whites were streaked with clay, his legs abraded with patches of brown. Sleek in tight white pants, Melania followed him with a towel filled with ice. "Do you want more ice?" she asked.

He may have fallen in his doubles match, but he had won. His tennis shoes were completely brown. But he wore them like trophies.

"There's a difference between getting hurt and being hurt," Donald said, sounding like the high school football player he once was.

The tournament raised $1.2 million for CaP CURE, founded by Michael Milken to promote research on prostate cancer. Besides Milken and Donald, moguls Larry Tisch and Carl Lindner played.

In Mar-a-Lago's cloister, Ivanka helped herself to turkey at the buffet. Tall, pretty, and very young, Ivanka is blessed with her father's pout. She was wearing flared gray sweatpants with a tank top and big gray running shoes.

Bob and Arlette Gordon, of black book fame, were waiting for omelettes. As *commandeur* of Confrerie de la Chaine des Rôtisseurs, a gourmet club, Bob had just orchestrated an eating orgy at the Breakers. The black-tie event began with Piper Heidsieck and Bourgogne Blanc with eleven hot and cold hors d'oeuvres, including beluga, osetra, and sevruga caviar; beef, tuna, and salmon carpaccio; and vol-au-vents (puff pastry) with pheasant and venison ragouts.

Then at eight o'clock, dinner in the Mediterranean Room. It began with a lobster timbale topped with osetra caviar, accompanied by a 1994 Château Margaux Pavillon Blanc, a white Bordeaux. Next came Armagnac-marinated foie gras layered between brioche slices, then sautéed in butter and baked, topped with pan-seared foie gras. This was served with a Chardonnay, Corton Charlemagne Diamond Jubilee, Remoissent, 1996. On to the herb-crusted halibut, oven-roasted loin of rabbit with truffle-flavored grits cake, and rack of lamb Dijonnaise. This was accompanied by Echezeaux Louis Latour, 1993, a Pinot Noir. Next, crumbled Roquefort folded into a mousse of whipped cream and whipped egg white, placed on top of a walnut pastry crisp served with a port-wine–poached fig and dried pear chips. Finally, dessert of chocolate sponge cake with hazelnut cream, covered with chocolate. Laurent-Perrier rosé grand champagne from Grand Crus vineyards followed.

At the Mar-a-Lago buffet, Lorraine said she had attended Rotary the previous Tuesday.

"Someone said it's becoming chic to go 'round the world," Lorraine said. Taking "'round the world" to be a sexual reference, "Heather Wyser-Pratte began laughing," Lorraine said.

On the way to the shrimp-cocktail buffet station, I introduced Lorraine to Ray Perelman, the father of the billionaire.

"She says she can't find a guy in Palm Beach," I told Ray.

"You should try someone who's over eighty," said Perelman, who is eighty-two.

Lorraine had given me the impression that she had broken up with the man who didn't have his affairs in order. But while she had stopped sleeping with him, she continued to cling to the hope that things would work out. He continued to pursue her as well, sending her a half dozen pink roses on Valentine's Day. When he heard that one night Lorraine had had a benign date with a television producer, he became jealous, knocking on her door in the middle of the night. Lorraine said she made him sleep on the couch.

"That's gay, isn't it?" Lorraine said of the roses. "I said, 'Why did you send me six pink roses?' At least send me a dozen or one. Six pink ones doesn't make any sense."

Then she ran into him at a party.

"I heard you've been going around town saying that I'm gay," he said.

"No, I haven't said you were gay," she said. "I said you were effeminate."

"I'm sensitive," he said. "I've never been with a man in my life."

Lorraine thought his reaction interesting. If he were straight, would he even say he's never been with a man? Wouldn't he consider the thought too objectionable to articulate, even if in the negative? she asked me.

If he is not gay, he certainly is anal-retentive, she said. "I was cutting the cucumbers for salad at my place," she recalled. "I was cutting the cucumbers in half."

"Could you cut them in quarters?" he asked.

"What?" Lorraine said. "I actually like cucumbers whole, myself."

Lorraine was learning more about the man, that he had spent Valentine's Day drinking champagne with a man who is married, that his former girlfriends thought he was gay. The last straw was when he inadvertently made a homosexual remark relating to himself—one she finds too nauseating to repeat.

Lorraine doesn't believe in bisexuality. She is convinced the term is used by homosexuals to hide their true orientation. She decided he was gay after all. Lorraine likes gay people, but she felt deceived, used, and helpless. In Palm Beach, wives and girl-friends are instruments of men's competitiveness. The man had been going with Lorraine to show he was straight, she decided. She had been his trophy.

Enraged, she told him to meet her in front of Green's Pharmacy.

"I don't want to see you for six months, if ever," she said.

The man called her a "tramp" and a "bad lover." The experience made her doubt her own sexuality.

"The love I spilled on that person wasn't real," she told me. "The affair was an illusion."

The next night at Galaxy Grill, three men asked Lorraine out. The first was the owner of the offshore bank. By then, Lorraine had decided he was too risky. "He is in that fishy business, offshore banking. And he's too short for me," she said. "Next was a Frenchman who comes in from New York. He asked me out. Then a golf pro asked me out. But they're all around forty-five and never married," she said. "When you get older—and you grow up really fast here—you look at these people, and they're not eligible. They've been perfecting their act for forty-five years. There are a lot of floozies and fruits and nuts. There are also a lot of beautiful men and women here. But the ones who are straight are taken. I live in a crazy town. People try to contaminate me with their bizarreness."

As the weekend approached, people began asking one another: "Are you going to polo?" They are always so disappointed at not being able to persuade someone to drive half an hour through West Palm Beach to Wellington to sit in the stands of the Palm Beach Polo and Country Club with them for a few chukkers.

The appeal is simple: another opportunity to see and be seen. Taking it a step further, a metaphor comes to mind: Palm Beach as high school. They have their proms, and polo is the weekly football game. After the first ten minutes, no one watches.

If a player gets hurt, a flurry of interest. At halftime, in lieu of a marching band, the polo crowd gets up and walks across the field, stamping down the divots kicked up by hooves and mallets. Women in high heels create more holes.

Lorraine and Sharon Dresser sat among the designer suits and outrageously big hats in the stands as Helen Boehm presided in the center of the Very VIP center box. Helen was standing, frowning with concern at the field where someone had just fallen from his horse. She had just orchestrated a Red Cross luncheon at the club—nine hundred people honoring Elizabeth Dole. The day before that, at a luncheon at Nancy Walsh's, she raised $40,000 for Dole's presidential run.

In contrast to everyone else at polo, actor George Hamilton, very tan, black hair with studied hints of white at the temples, was actually engrossed in watching the match. Meanwhile, the other VIPs in the box around him laughed, talked, people-watched, ate tea sandwiches, drank champagne, and in the case of one woman, sat in her husband's lap and gave him a proprietary smooch, choreographed for anyone watching.

A few weeks later, tragedy would befall Bren Simon, one of the VIPs, when her twenty-five-year-old son, Max—originally Joshua—would die of cardiac arrest in the Netherlands. With his brother, her husband, Mel, is cochairman of Simon Property Group, which develops and operates shopping malls and is the largest publicly traded real-estate company in North America. Mel also is co-owner of the Ritz-Carlton in Manalapan. Because of their son's death, Mel and Bren, who are based in Indianapolis, would cancel a fund-raising luncheon for President Clinton in their thirty-five-thousand-square-foot oceanfront Manalapan home. The home was designed for Harold K. Vanderbilt by Maurice Fatio. Palm Beach's second-best known architect, Fatio designed 137 homes on the island between 1925 and 1943. Besides the fifty-two-room main house, the mansion has two guest houses, a tennis court, pool, formal garden, and dock.

Over at the polo clubhouse, Franklyn bought everyone champagne and quickly polished off the limited stock of the good stuff. It was hard to make out the game from this vantage point, but he had lent his box to someone.

"What's all this about pearls? Is it a WASP thing?" Pam asked Lorraine, going back to their discussion about the need for Pam to wear pearls.

"Am I a WASP?" Lorraine asked. "I think it's a Jewish thing."

Betsy Fry, Franklyn's girlfriend, said, "It's a Jackie Kennedy thing."

Asked his opinion, Franklyn gave the final word: "You remember—if you have a black dress and pearls, you can go anywhere."

Later that night, over dinner at Café L'Europe, Helen Boehm said that when she owned a polo team and they played, "nobody talked." She was wearing a large cloisonné-and-diamond pin depicting a polo player on a horse.

Kirby proudly showed the other diners at the table the homemade collar stays in his white dress shirt. He had cut an expired American Express Platinum card in strips to create the stays.

"The Platinum card is almost white, to go with the shirt," he explained.

Kirby had been entertaining offers to rent his house for the entire year. He thought one offer too low. "When I told Kay Rybovich about the offer for my house, she said, 'I don't want anybody to take advantage of you.' I thought, 'I think I've had enough of Bill,'" meaning Kirby knew he had allowed Bill to take advantage of him. Kirby still had not fixed the dents Bill put in his BMW.

Now Kirby said he had received an offer he found difficult to refuse—$150,000 for the year. "Leasing that house for a year will bring finality to a whole chapter. It means I won't be seeing Bill. I want to do it in a kind way."

But where will you stay? I asked.

"I'll stay with Helen. Or with Jill Curcio. Either way or both."

The Cancer Ball raised $370,000, Helen said proudly. Of that total, 78 percent went to American Cancer Society programs.

In contrast to the Cancer Ball's prompt and cheery reporting of its figures, Larry Koslick, executive director of the Palm Beach Chapter of the American Red Cross, would not respond to my request for figures on how much the Young Friends and International Red Cross Ball raised, until I complained to national headquarters in Washington. Then Koslick claimed the results were not yet fully known, yet the chapter had filed the figures with the Palm Beach clerk's office two weeks earlier. When that was pointed out, Koslick said he was unaware that such figures had to be filed with the town—even though he had signed the town's form the previous year, affirming that the figures were correct. Koslick said that even if he gave out the net results, he would not provide a breakdown of expenses.

"Why do you want to know?" Koslick asked me. "You seem suspicious."

Unlike everyone from Barton Gubelmann and Celia Farris to Donald Trump and Mayor Ilyinsky, Koslick declined to be interviewed on tape.

A look at the figures shows there is reason to be mysterious. According to the filings with the clerk, if Betty Scripps Harvey had not contributed $750,000 the previous year, because the expenses of the Red Cross fund-raising events were so high, the events would have produced a net loss of $120,000. In the more recent year, the Red Cross spent $70,000 for Bruce Sutka's party decorations and recorded music and $30,000 for travel expenses of ambassadors. In the end, 70 percent of the receipts for the Red Cross Ball were left over after expenses, while only 39 percent of the income from the Young Friends went for Red Cross programs. For both events, an average of only 62 percent of the money was left for donations—substantially below the Cancer Ball's level of 78 percent. The previous year, when Harvey contributed $750,000, only 48 percent of the money was left over for Red Cross programs.

But these figures are before the chapter's overhead for organizing the events is taken into account—not to mention substantial donations of supplies. The chapter has a special-events section that takes care of sending out invitations and arranging and promoting primarily these two events. Koslick said he doesn't know how much of the chapter's salaries and other expenses are attributable to the events, but he believes the costs—whatever they are—would not wipe out the profit.

Jay Rossbach, the chapter chairman, had a different take. "If we [fully] knew what each event cost us, we might not have the event," he told me. "You have to think of it a different way. You have to let people know about the Red Cross and that we're try-ing to support distress problems. The only way is to have some visibility." If other contributions unrelated to the events are counted, "We more than break even," Rossbach said.

While that is true, if the $359,000 spent by the Red Cross on filet mignon and flowers were spent instead on advertising or paid solicitation, the chapter would likely raise far more money for disaster relief.

But then the island's megamillionaires wouldn't have as much fun.

29. INCIDENT AT THE POINCIANA CLUB

All over the island, the season was taking its toll. Tempers were flaring. Ambulances were being called to parties. People were collapsing on dance floors. Such are the perils of living in Palm Beach.

Carol Haryman threw a surprise birthday party for her husband, Gerard, at the Poinciana Club at Cocoanut Row and Royal Poinciana Way. Gerard, fifty-four, is a debonair Parisian who came to Palm Beach eleven years ago. In Europe he was a developer of residential and commercial properties. He owns Phoenix International Industries, a telecommunications holding company based in West Palm Beach.

More than a hundred people came to the party, which featured a four-course dinner and a three-piece band. Besides a prince and princess from Germany, the party drew the new rich who tend to be members of the dining club.

Franklyn de Marco took Lorraine to the party but left almost immediately when Nancy Sharigan and her husband, Bob Simmons, showed up. Franklyn and Bob not only avoid being at Ta-boó at the same time, they try not to go to the same parties. This time, the system for keeping them apart had broken down.

At eleven-thirty a sexy woman with long blond hair and green eyes strolled into the party. Measuring 36-23-35, she was wearing a black trenchcoat and a black hat. She carried a briefcase. As she revealed a gold costume beneath her coat, the theme song to *Goldfinger* began playing. A friend of the Harymans—one of two who had hired the woman—introduced her as Fifi, Gerard's long-lost cousin from France. Carol Haryman was as surprised as everyone else.

Fifi may have been from France, but her real name was Danielle Brunet. A model and actress, she had just played the sister of designer Gianni Versace in *The Versace Murder*, a movie featured at the Cannes Film Festival. A photo of her had appeared in *Newsweek* next to one of Versace's sister, Donatella. Danielle's artistic name was Dania Deville.

Soon Danielle began taking off her clothes. The guests thought she would stop with her skimpy gold underwear. They gasped as she removed that as well. All she was wearing was gold lipstick. At thirty-nine, she had the body of a twenty-year-old.

As Danielle danced to the music, some of the men began crowding around her. One of them was the husband of Vilda B. de Porro. From Spain by way of Cuba, De Porro opened her own antique furniture and art store in 1979 on Worth Avenue a few doors west of Ta-boó. Her dining room tables go for as much as $60,000, and her chandeliers fetch up to $50,000. Her clients include Donald Trump and Marla Maples, both of whom are friends. For all her connections, Vilda is down-to-earth—an uncommon quality in Palm Beach.

As Vilda's husband got close to Danielle, Vilda told her to get away. According to Danielle and another witness, Vilda kicked her in the leg.

"She was jealous or something," Danielle told me. "She said, 'Don't come near my husband.' This was a very classy place. I didn't think something like this can happen over there [in Palm Beach]. It's unbelievable."

Danielle stopped her act and put on her clothes in a hallway outside the ladies room. She left the club with her boyfriend,

Dotan Baer, and they drove off. She was crying, and two Palm Beach Police officers in their patrol car noticed the commotion. They pulled alongside Baer's car and asked what was wrong. Baer told them his girlfriend had been kicked. They got out of their cars, and she showed the officers what the police report called a "small red mark" on her left calf. The police photographed it.

When the officers tried to interview witnesses, everyone at the party claimed they had not seen anything. Everyone, that is, except Gerald Shugar, according to the police report. Shugar, who publishes medical journals, was one of the friends who had split the $300 fee charged by Captain Telegram for supplying *une femme en or*—a woman in gold.

Shugar told me Maurice seemed particularly taken with Danielle. "Maurice ended up with the girl dancing around him," he said. "I saw Vilda charge like a bull out of a stockade and kick the girl, really kick her."

Shugar was "horrified." After he accompanied Danielle to the hall where she put on her clothes, he confronted Vilda. "You kicked the wrong person," he said, meaning she should have kicked her husband.

According to Shugar, Vilda did not respond. But a few minutes later, Danielle walked in with the police. "Someone told me Vilda had been tipped off that the police were coming," Shugar said. "That's when she [Vilda] ran out the back door. Obviously, Danielle had been assaulted." Since Danielle did not know the name of her alleged assailant, Shugar was the one who identified her as Vilda.

Vilda conceded that her husband was impressed by Danielle. "Unless you were homosexual, you would enjoy a naked woman," she said. "Everybody who was a man there, I guess, was enjoying looking." But she said the women at the party were offended by the "erotic" display. Someone with "no taste" hired the woman.

"We ladies of status and quality and morality should not be exposed to this situation," she huffed. "When someone strips down to nothing, I'm not going to stand for that," Vilda said. "So I got up and said, 'Listen, lady, that's enough,' and she was gone. That's it. I didn't touch this woman or anything like that. I'm a two-hundred-and-twenty-five-pound woman. Was she knocked down on the floor? Such a small stripper, if I had touched her, she would have been down on the floor, and she wasn't."

The police told Danielle she could pursue the matter with the state attorney. Because of the mark, Danielle said she had to reschedule a shoot for a bathing-suit commercial the next day. "I'll press charges," she told me. "You cannot accept something like that."

Repercussions continued for weeks. Carol Haryman was angry at the two friends for hiring the stripper. The multimillionaires who had been at the party debated whether kicking the woman was understandable or unthinkable. Danielle hired a lawyer to pursue criminal and civil charges.

When they heard what had happened, the Old Guard was scandalized.

The rich get annual checkups at the Mayo Clinic, but it's not enough. Every season brings its losses. One night, a forty-year-old woman walked up to Kevin at Ta-boó. She asked if he had seen an eighty-nine-year-old man around. Fifteen minutes later, she came back, smiling.

"I found him," she said, and Kevin seated them. Two hours later, the woman was back at Kevin's desk. Holley, the tall twenty-year-old blond hostess, was holding her arm. The woman was crying, frantic.

"I've got to use the phone," she said. "I think he's dead."

"Come with me," Kevin said, leading her by the arm to the rear office.

After dinner, they had walked half a block, and he had collapsed. Paramedics were working on him on Worth Avenue.

"I'm from L.A.," the woman said. "Just here for a visit. I just met him tonight. He's my husband's grandfather."

She wanted to call her husband. When she couldn't reach him, she and Kevin walked back to the reception desk.

"He's dead," Holley said. "They can't revive him."

"I had never met him," the woman said. "Now he's dead."

Holley took her arm. They walked through the crowded restaurant. The disco was blaring, everyone dancing. Down Worth Avenue to the right, Kevin could see the flashing lights. Paramedics were bent over a figure. They walked toward the scene as the paramedics placed him on a stretcher.

"Holley, stay with her," Kevin said. Wide-eyed, she nodded.

"Thank you," the woman said to Kevin.

Parking was becoming easier to find on Worth Avenue. Reservations were not always needed for dinner at Ta-boó. The locals were reclaiming their island, even finding time to enjoy the sunsets. Ironically, the most beautiful feature of the island is totally free. And what does everyone do when the season is over?

"Celebrate!" Heather Wyser-Pratte said.

Already, the Shiny Sheet was running events for next season in the social calendar, the previous season a blur. Plans were being made to return to homes in Cannes, Newport, London, New York, or Paris. Full-time residents were thinking about trips to Saint-Tropez or Capri. No need to book early to take advantage of discounted rates. When they are ready to go, they buy first-class tickets or instruct their yacht or plane captains to head there.

Those who came to town hoping to make it to the A-list and were disappointed were putting their homes up for sale. The rest were amazed at how many parties they were still attending in late April.

The date for next year's International Red Cross Ball was already running in the Shiny Sheet, but Barton vowed never to go to another ball. "Balls don't need me," she told me. After throwing her last party of the season, she returned to her Newport home on a chartered Lear jet, taking her "menagerie"— her dog, her cat, and her maid.

After spending five months in jail, Bill was released. Having reclaimed his house, Kirby had him over but would not let him stay overnight. A week and a half after Bill got out, Bill claimed he had not yet had time to look for a job. Instead of attending Alcoholics Anonymous meetings, as his probation officer had urged, he told me he had read a book about the subject.

But a few weeks later, Bill got a job fueling planes at North County Airport, a west Palm Beach facility used by private aircraft. Under the supervision of a probation officer, he began seeing a psychiatrist. While Kirby kept in touch with him, it appeared he was keeping Bill at arm's length. Kirby credited Helen Boehm and me with making him see the light.

"People really have to help themselves," Kirby said.

Kevin took a vacation on the Mexican island of Cozumel. Lorraine still couldn't find a guy in Palm Beach. Seeking a change, she spent a few months in Beverly Hills, even having her Mercedes convertible shipped to her. But she soon returned to Palm Beach. And I found myself spoiled, convinced I could never find another book subject as strange and enchanting as this island.

"You remember that you were at particular parties, vaguely," Kirby told me one hushed night. "You don't have to be paranoid that you missed anything. You don't want to be suddenly out of the loop, suddenly irrelevant, not part of the family. So you're drawn to return, and the next season, you pick up where you left off."

Thanks to air conditioning, the season gets longer and longer.

"I think if the season were shorter like it used to be, it would be perfect," Kirby said. "It started at New Year's and ended on Easter. You could really cope with the three months. Now it goes from December to the end of April."

Air conditioning and everyone's struggle with their own mortality. The season gives those who can afford it the luxury of thinking they have control over the one thing they can't control. Every party, every invitation is an affirmation not only of their own desirability but of their invincibility. If the proms continue, so does their youth.

Yet in the end, their efforts are futile, their bodies shipped to where they came from, lest they remind the islanders of their own destiny. Or, in the case of Gianna Lahainer's husband, stored for forty days in a funeral home in West Palm Beach.

For those who have everything, "You can't take it with you" is a very scary concept. They have spent their whole lives amassing and accumulating, worshipping objects and things, collecting homes, furniture, art, clothes, jewelry, boats, and cars. For what? When they die, their kids often don't even come down to close up the house. Everything gets auctioned off, including, sadly, the parents' portraits and the family photo albums.

"Every month, I give away or sell to a restaurant or a club three or four life-size portraits of parents that their children don't want," interior decorator Michael Rosenow told me. "I find it strange when you don't want your parents' portraits or photo albums. They say, 'Take everything and send the check.' In some cases, I keep the portraits on the off chance they'll change their minds. They never take them back. Palm Beach is different."

Yet for those who remain for the next season, living on Fantasy Island has its compensations.

"If you have to go, you might as well do it in style," Heather Wyser-Pratte said.

ACKNOWLEDGMENTS

Fittingly, as recounted in the first chapter, the idea for this book materialized after my wife, Pam, and I consumed a bottle of Chardonnay at Testa's, one of Palm Beach's best restaurants. When I said, "Wouldn't it be great to do a book on Palm Beach?" she said, "That's the only book I would collaborate with you on."

Pam's response turned idle chatter into a serious concept, but her contribution had only just begun. Pam accompanied me on most of my ten subsequent trips to Palm Beach, and to Nantucket and Newport, where Palm Beachers play during the summer. Together we attended black-tie functions, charity balls, and private parties on a yacht and in sumptuous homes and clubs. One weekend we flew back and forth to Palm Beach with Donald Trump on his Boeing 727-100, staying at his Mar-a-Lago Club. It was a hard job, but someone had to do it.

Besides helping to soften my image—some called her my ambassador—Pam took notes and wrote gemlike vignettes and narratives that appear throughout the book. The best writing in the book is hers. She then came up with the title for the book. Finally, she pre-edited the manuscript. Pam is the love of my life, my trusted advisor, and my best friend. I could not be luckier.

My agent, Robert Gottlieb, executive vice president of the William Morris Agency, with his associate Matt Bialer, helped shape the idea for the book, sharpening the focus. Robert, who heads the agency's literary department, continued to contribute his wisdom and enthusiasm throughout.

My editor, Paul D. McCarthy, senior editor of HarperCollins, applied his brilliance and dynamism to every phase of the book's publication. In a triumph of editing, he came up with the idea of describing in the first person how I came to Palm Beach and how I did the book. This is my sixth book with Paul. An author could not imagine a better editor.

I could not have succeeded at writing books without the support and love of my two talented children, Rachel and Greg Kessler. My equally talented stepson, Mike Whitehead, is part of that team. I am grateful to my mother, Minuetta Kessler, for her example.

My friend Dan Clements offered insightful suggestions, as did my sister Jean Brenner. My friend and fellow author Edward Klein introduced me to Donald Trump.

Palm Beachers who went out of their way to help included Vicki Bagley, Helen Boehm, Franklyn de Marco, Jr., Barton Gubelmann, Lorraine Hillman, Jasmine and Manfredo Horowitz, Kirby Kooluris, Allen F. Manning, Kevin O'Dea, Cynthia Stone Ray, Kay Rybovich, Judy Schrafft, Dennis E. Spear, Mickey Spillane, Donald Trump, and Heather Wyser-Pratte.

Those who were interviewed or helped included:

Sherman Adler, Braddock Alexander, Bill Allston, Ann Anderson, H. Loy Anderson, Jr., Arthur N. Avella, M.D., Dotan Baer, Vicki Bagley, Vincent Bailey, James Hunt Barker, Cathy Barrett, Dr. Larry Bell, Mimi Beman, Pamela Bergmann, Carmen Bissell, Dr. William Bissell, Wes Blackmun, Julio Blanco, Michael A. Blank, Antony Boada, Helen F. Boehm, Bill Bohrer, Joel C. Bokhart, Catherine Bradley.

Clare Britton, Danielle Brunet, Tanya Brooks, Bertram S. Brown, M.D., F. Ted Brown, Jr., Richard L. Brown, Donald Bruce, Jean Bruckert, Elizabeth Bryant, Vincenzo Bucci, Rachel Butler,

Bufford H. Cain, Don Camp, Dennis Campbell, Joe Cannizzaro, Pat Capalbo, Lucien Capehart, James Carmo, Beatrice de Holguin Fairbanks Cayser, Kevin Chaffee, Dean Chagan, Adair Chew, Jason Cimino, Julia Clark, Helen S. Cluett, Alain Cohen.

Frank Coniglio, Gerry Connick, Doris Coppeletti, Ralph Cowan, Jacqueline Cowell, Richard C. Cowell, Jill Curcio, Pat Danielski, Bob Davidoff, Willie DeGray, Franklyn P. de Marco, Jr., Gloria DeMoura, Luiz DeMoura, M.D., George Dempsey, Vilda B. de Porro, Wrendia Devary, Cosmo DiSchino, Patricia Dixson, Gregg Dodge, Shannon Donnelly, Mike Donovan, Sharon Dresser, Dame Alma DuPuy.

Polly A. Earl, Robert Eaton, Robert T. Eigelberger, Elaine Sargent Elman, Lee M. Elman, Tommye Elrod, Joseph D. Farish, Jr., Celia L. Farris, Jim Fazio, Hope Fiene, Loretta Fine, Rodney B. Fink, Norma I. Foerderer, David Forward, Maryann Forward, Louis Fourie, Betsy Fry, Michelle Gagnon, Anna Carmelina Garguilo, Gigi Goelet, David J. Goodstal, Jane Grace, Anne-Marie Graff.

Laurence Graff, Linda Greenwood, Anthony S. Griffin, Special Agent Michael D. Grogan, Barton Gubelmann, John Gurl, Burton Handelsman, Jane Hardy, Carol Haryman, Gerard Haryman, Gillian Haughtaling, George Heaton, Allen Heise, Lorraine Hillman, Conrad Hilton, Jr., Alvan Hirshberg, Earl Hollis, Gloria Hollis, Toni Hollis, Jasmine Horowitz, Manfredo Horowitz, Randy Hribkow, Mimi Humphrey.

Nicole Humphries, Mayor Paul R. Ilyinsky, Linda Irwin, Rise "Ginger" Jackson, Tom Jacomo, Huldah C. Jeffe, Richard O. Jenkins, Barbara Pearson Johnson, Rolf Kasten, Barbara R. Katz, Mort Kaye, Anne Kazel, Arthur "Skip" Kelter, Arnelle Kendall, Mary Kendall, Alan Kessler, Sue Kessler, Cynthia Kinkela, Barry Kinsella, Janet Kinsella, Edward Klein, the late Judge James R. Knott.

Kirby Kooluris, Larry Koslick, Natalie Krolczyk, Gianna S. Lahainer, Karen Lane, Alfred Lanusú, Dino Laudati, Alan Lebow, Denise S. Lee, Adrienne Lefkowitz, Robert P. Leidy, Bernd Lembcke, Jean-Pierre Leverrier, May Bell Lin, Gary Link,

Albert M. Littleton, Franklin J. Logalbo, Guido Lombardi, Detective Sergeant Sanford P. Lopater, Doris Magowan, Maurice Malacarne, Allen F. Manning, Allin Mansfield, Lynn Manulis, Marc Mariacher.

Cheryl Marshman, Homer H. Marshman, Jr., Joleen Martin, Thomas Martin, Colleen Matthews, Denise McCann, Maggie McCloskey, Mildred "Brownie" McLean, Paul McKenzie, Betty Metcalf, David Miller, Kathy Miller, Paul L. Miller, Herme deWyman Miro, Robert M. Montgomery, Jr., Prince Simon Mihailesco Nasturel Monyo, Roy Moyer, Nancy Myers, Wyckoff Myers.

Sheriff Robert W. Neumann, Jesse D. Newman, Bernard Nicole, Kevin O'Dea, Gwen Odom, Laura Oregero, Chesbrough "Chessy" Patcevitch, Susanne Steinem Patch, Lady Patricia "Trisha" Pelham, Raymond G. Perelman, Ruth Perelman, Helena Perry, John Perry, Suzie Phipps, Henri Polinski, Sally Polinski, Mary A. Pollitt, Jane Poston, Michael J. Pucillo, James A. Ponce, Susan Potter, Roxanne Pulitzer, Franny Purnell.

Gary Quattlebaum, Cathy Rampell, Palmer Rampell, Paul Rampell, Richard Rampell, Pat Randolph, Anna Raphael, Cynthia Stone Ray, Joyce Reingold, Mark Rechnitzer, Phyllis Reed, Assistant Chief Michael S. Reiter, Sue Ricker, Dr. H. J. Roberts, Special Agent H. Reid Robertson, Peter Rock, Philip J. Romano, Cindy Rosa, Brooks Rose, Leslie Rose, Marjorie Rose, Dr. Marvin M. Rosenberg, Michael Rosenow, Robert Routhier.

Raymond W. Royce, Kay Rybovich, Special Agent Alan Sadowski, Angelia Savage, Jill Schaeffer, Judy Schrafft, Ronald Y. Schram, Anthony P. Senecal, Robert A. Shaheen, Kiki Shapero, Nancy Sharigan, Alice Shaw, Natalie Sherman, Marc Shiner, Peter Silla, Robert L. Simmons, George C. Slaton, Donna Smith, town council president Lesly Smith, Lore Smith, Neal Smith, Tony Smith, Dennis E. Spear, Sir Bobby Spencer, Mickey Spillane, Reginald J. Stambaugh, M.D.

Bunnie Stevens, the late George Stinchfield, Gerald Shugar, Herbert Bayard Swope, Jr., Dorothy A. Sullivan, Reidun Torrie Sullivan, Bruce Sutka, Vera Swift, Jean Tailer, Richard Tilford,

James J. Torrie, Ingrid Tremain, Donald Trump, Wilbert Turner, Peter Vallas, Charles Van Rensselaer, Jean M. VanWaveren, Anna Veksler, Liana Verkaden, Richard M. Viscasillas, Gunilla von Post, Nancy Walsh, Ann Webb, Baxter Webb, Chip Welfeld, Jade Wellmer, Richard Whitaker, William Bryan White, Hermine Wiener.

Robert D. Williams, M.D., D. Imogene Willis, Henry L. Wills, Howard Willson, Mollie Wilmot, Maureen Woodward, Orator Woodward, Heather Wyser-Pratte, Bruce Zabriski, and Ann Zweig.

INDEX

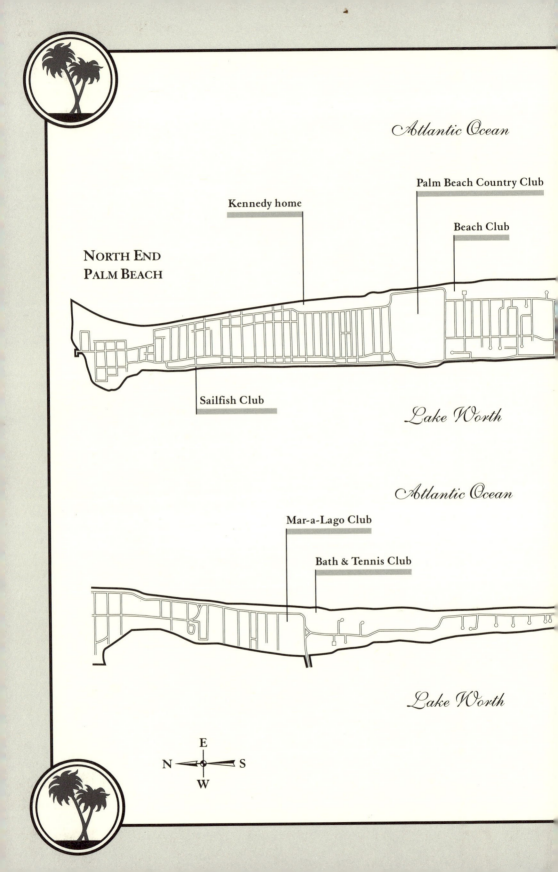

Atlantic Ocean

Palm Beach Country Club

Kennedy home

Beach Club

NORTH END
PALM BEACH

Sailfish Club

Lake Worth

Atlantic Ocean

Mar-a-Lago Club

Bath & Tennis Club

Lake Worth

E
N — S
W